Becoming Refugee American

THE ASIAN AMERICAN EXPERIENCE

Series Editors
Eiichiro Azuma
Jigna Desai
Martin F. Manalansan IV
Lisa Sun-Hee Park
David K. Yoo

Roger Daniels, Founding Series Editor

A list of books in the series appears at the end of this book.

Becoming Refugee American

The Politics of Rescue in Little Saigon

Phuong Tran Nguyen

Urbana, Chicago, and Springfield

© 2017 by the Board of Trustees
of the University of Illinois
All rights reserved
1 2 3 4 5 C P 5 4 3 2 1
∞ This book is printed on acid-free paper.

Library of Congress Control Number: 2017952798
ISBN 978-0-252-04135-8 (hardcover)
ISBN 978-0-252-08288-7 (paperback)
ISBN 978-0-252-09995-3 (e-book)

To Mom and Dad

Contents

Acknowledgments ix

Introduction: A Nation of Refugees 1

1. Accidental Allies: America's Crusade and the Origins of Refugee Nationalism 17

2. From Grief to Gratitude: Reaffirming the Past by Rewriting It 33

3. "Farewell, Saigon, I Promise I Will Return": Social Work and the Meaning of Exile 53

4. The Anticommunist Việt-Cộng: Freedom Fighters and the New Politics of Rescue 77

5. Assimilationists and the Postwar: Model Minority Politics in Little Saigon 97

6. Divided Loyalties: America's Moral Obligation in the Post–Cold War Era 120

Conclusion: Finding Roots in Exile 139

Notes 147

Bibliography 183

Index 207

Acknowledgments

The genesis of this book is professional in nature, but its completion is mostly personal. At the end of my third year of graduate school at the University of Southern California, Jane Iwamura had the foresight to suggest that I conduct research in Little Saigon—"the belly of the beast," as she called it. For my mentors it seemed a natural fit, but I had yet to find a suitable entry point into this emerging field of Asian American studies. Karin Aguilar–San Juan generously gave me a copy of her paper for the 2000 American Studies Association conference in Detroit, but studying anticommunist protest did not excite me. The following year at the Association for Asian American Studies conference in Toronto, the always-supportive Linda Võ told me about a special Vietnamese American studies edition of *Amerasia Journal* she was editing, but alas, I had nothing to contribute.

After all, I had just recently committed myself to learning the historian's trade, so I spent the first two years of grad school figuring out the difference between one discipline and the next. In this regard, I am indebted to the instruction I received from talented scholars such as Arlene Davila, Lisa Duggan, Phil Harper, Toby Miller, Tricia Rose, Andrew Ross, and George Yudice. Friday seminars with Vijay Prashad never failed to deliver laughter and inspiration. Manthia Diawara's core seminar on Black Culture and Politics and the Africana Studies Center in general provided one of the most welcoming and intellectually stimulating spaces at New York University. I will never forget the day Manthia treated the whole class to a meal at the Torch Club right before Thanksgiving. Just across the hallway I could find Jack Tchen, a man capable of distilling the intricacies of academia into sentences of unrivaled clarity.

Here I first met Gary Okihiro at the Communities of Interest symposium and discovered another community east of California. Being the devoted teacher he is, Gary graciously volunteered his time, his food, and his Columbia University office space to lead graduate seminars in Asian American studies. During the spring of 2002, four NYU graduate students took the subway to Broadway and 116th for another class with Gary.

The fact that my undergraduate professors—including such leading minds as Yen Le Espiritu, George Lipsitz, Lisa Lowe, Jane Rhodes, and Leland Saito—bothered to answer my emails proves that faculty can indeed balance teaching with scholarship. Neil Gotanda, the closest thing I had to family in New York, deserves much love for allowing me to audit his Asian American jurisprudence course at Columbia Law School.

Although countless people told me that I would learn more from fellow graduate students than from professors, I did not believe it until I enrolled in the Program in American Studies and Ethnicity at the University of Southern California. One of my first seminars introduced me to four of the most amazing friends anyone could ask for, and all of them, like me, were first-generation college students. Their contributions to my academic career are too numerous to list, but here are a few. Claudia Martínez impressed me with her knowledge of European history and gift for listening. Gustavo Licón possessed the uncanny ability to lead an intellectual discussion one minute and crack a hilarious joke the next. Alexander Aviña demonstrated a work ethic second to none and constantly challenged me to raise my game another notch. More than anyone else in this group, Jerry González embodied the spirit of community and connectedness. Through his example, I realized that none of us could succeed without each other's support and friendship.

Speaking of support and friendship, I would not have gotten this far without an adviser as patient and dedicated as Lon Kurashige. Though possessed of a razor-sharp intellect, he has no need to show off. As one colleague told me, Lon epitomizes unpretentiousness. In the fall of 2005, Lon convinced me that a social history of Little Saigon needed to be written and that I should write it. He exhibited more confidence in me than I deserved while simultaneously keeping my ego in check. As meticulous a reader as any, he has edited many more drafts than I care to admit and never allowed me to make unsubstantiated claims. During the past seven years, Lon knew that pushing one more draft out of me—when I did not want to write any more—was the key to more efficient writing and more friendly prose. The minicommunity that Lon created by organizing basketball games at the Lyon Center proved E. P. Thompson's point that social cohesion goes hand in hand with political cohesion.

I have discovered an exciting new community of people doing Southeast Asian American studies. Thuy Vo Dang showed how to fuse ethnic studies and Vietnamese American popular culture. Her annual Tết get-togethers introduced me to some of the brightest and most generous young minds in Southern California. Mariam Beevi Lam happily walked me through the promises and pitfalls of doing work in this field and convinced me that there was an audience for refugee studies. And Mark Padoongpatt, a fellow USC grad student in American studies, possessed no shortage of valuable insight on the intersection of area and ethnic studies.

In the Department of American Studies and Ethnicity, I found a nurturing and collaborate environment for generating interdisciplinary research. I think I spent more time in the American Studies Center my first year than I did at my apartment. Sandra Hopwood, Kitty Lai, Sonia Rodriguez, and the rest of the staff deserve a hearty thank you for putting up with my constant presence. Jujuana Preston never broke a sweat sending letters of reference on my behalf. Even in the age of email, cell phones, Skype, and Facebook, nothing beats an old-fashioned physically grounded space for creating a sense of community and exchanging ideas.

After space comes people, and ASE has no shortage of quality peeps. During my first visit I met such tremendously down-to-earth faculty as Jane Iwamura, Laura Pulido, Roberto Lint Sagarena, and Janelle Wong. Basketball on Fridays were much more fun when Ricardo Ramírez brought his tenacious defense and patented hook shot onto the Lyon Center courts. Off the court, he taught me to visualize where I want to be five years from now and work backward from there. My committee members mastered the art of delivering tough criticism in the most gentle and dignifying manner. Any knowledge I have of theory in general and economics in particular likely bears the imprint of Ruthie Gilmore, who was also one of the first to insist that I acquire the skills to access Vietnamese-language sources. Long before winning a Pulitzer Prize, Việt Thanh Nguyễn exuded positive energy and possessed a laser-sharp focus. He knew the theoretical and political trajectory of any argument before I had finished explaining about it. William Deverell generously offered to serve as the outside member on my committee and pointed out valuable sources on anticommunism in Southern California. And George Sánchez, the heart and soul of American Studies, saw the value of refugee nationalism early on and encouraged me to see its relevance to Cubans and other groups as well. His seminar on Los Angeles ranks as one of my favorites. I promise not to wear tank tops when it is my turn to teach.

My interest in the historical method picked up speed when I discovered the treasure trove of primary sources in Southern California. In the fall of 2005,

I paid my first visit to the Southeast Asian Archives at the University of California at Irvine. Its librarian, the now retired Anne Frank, treated a complete stranger like a familiar face and drafted more than a couple important letters of recommendation on my behalf. Inside a humble twelve-by-eighteen-foot space were enough books, periodicals, multimedia materials, and ephemera for a dissertation many times larger than this one. One of the archives' advisers, Jeffrey Brody, a professor of communications at Cal State–Fullerton, kindly met with me and shared the vast knowledge of Little Saigon he acquired during his days as a beat writer for the *Orange County Register*. Stephanie George, the archivist at Fullerton's Center for Public and Oral History, put up with my presence for an entire week and hooked me up with interviews and books relevant to my project. Cornell University had one of the best collections of Vietnamese American periodicals around. Derek Chang and María Cristina García offered to meet with me on short notice and lend sage advice. Oiyan Poon referred me to a friend in possession of valuable documents related to the flag resolutions in Little Saigon. The Vietnam Library in Garden Grove, an archive I discovered by accident, housed some of the earliest issues of the refugee press and donated to me an impressive stack of extra periodicals. Thanks to the virtual archive otherwise known as the interlibrary loan system, I obtained refugee camp newsletters, organizational literature, and rare books without having to travel all over the world.

I found the greatest pleasure mining the memories of the refugee generation. Songwriter Lê Quang Anh opened the door to a flood of interviews. His friend Nam Lộc Nguyễn connected me with an amazing array of contacts, including Việt Dzũng, Trịnh Hội, Nhật Ngân, Lê Văn, Hồ Xuân Mai, and Ngô Thụy Miên. I met Yvonne Hùynh on the first day of Vietnamese class at Goldenwest College, and she not only became my research assistant but introduced me to Pastor Nguyễn Xuân Bảo, Tony Lâm, Loretta Sánchez, and Nguyễn Cao Kỳ. The rest of the interview subjects have asked to remain anonymous, but I nevertheless owe them a humongous debt of gratitude for opening up their lives to me.

Bắc Hoài Trần and his talented staff at the Southeast Asian Studies Summer Institute at the University of Wisconsin at Madison promised fluency to anyone who put in the work, and they kept their word. My classmates—most notably Hải-Đăng Phản, Graham Hiệp Hallman, Chau Quach, and Carolyn Ly—along with the friendly people of Madison made me feel at home in the Midwest.

I received generous funding while at USC, including an Irvine Foundation Fellowship package, a John Randolph and Dora Haynes Foundation dissertation writing fellowship, and a USC Final Year Dissertation Year Fellowship.

The brave and loyal USC colleagues who put their red pens to these chapters deserve recognition. My partners in the Los Angeles Studies Dissertation Reading Group—Michan Connor, Jerry González, Sean Greene, Daniel HoSang, and Hillary Jenks—performed like alchemists, helping turn my desiccated prose into something worth reading. If there is anything resembling quality interdisciplinary work in these chapters, some of the credit goes to them. Cam Vu and Viet Le took time out of their furiously busy schedules to critique the chapters and to socialize me into Southern California's growing network of Vietnamese American scholars.

At Northwestern University, I was lucky enough to join a talented and generous community of scholars. Ji-Yeon Yuh welcomed me to the Asian American Studies Program and mentored me extensively on the academic universe. The program's assistant director, Jinah Kim, proved a constant source of positivity and inspiration. Shalini Shankar offered fantastic guidance about ethnic studies east of California. Nitasha Sharma read early drafts of my manuscript. Carolyn Chen frequently checked on my progress and demonstrated some of the best teaching skills I've seen. In Latino Studies, I met wonderful faculty members including Frances Aparicio, Jaime Domínguez, and Micaela Díaz-Sánchez. In African American Studies, I cannot forget the connections I made with junior faculty such as Kinohi Nishikawa and Lisa Calvente along with the great career advice I received from the current department chair, Celeste Watkins-Hayes. In the History Department, I was fortunate to meet a fantastic group that included Michael Allen, Kathleen Belew, and Geraldo Cadava. Though I consider myself a Trojan, I do bleed a little purple, too.

At Ithaca College, I was proud to work with colleagues who live and breathe—and perhaps even bleed—Ethnic Studies. Thanks to colleagues Sean Eversley Bradwell, Changhee Chun, Sue-Je Gage, Paula Ioanide, Christine Kitano, Jessica Lozano, and Stephen Sweet. Special recognition goes to Asma Barlas for having faith in me when she hired me, Belisa González for mentoring me, and Gustavo Licón for being the brother I never knew I had. Because of them and the wonderful students and staff, I felt very much at home on the East Coast. The companion Asian American Studies Program at Cornell was a wonderful resource run by the amazing team of Derek Chang and Vladimir Micic. Cornell also has an outstanding Southeast Asian Studies Program with young minds such as Hồng Bùi, Sean Fear, Nguyệt Tống, Mai Vân Trần, Alex Thái Võ, Hoàng Vũ, and Madeline Yến Vũ, who I have no doubt will make a difference in this world in their own special ways. My Ithaca family consisted of unbelievably kind and dynamic human beings: Rafael Aponte, Jed Ashton, Sandra Bruno, Nandi Cohen, Chrissy Lau, Veronica Martinez, Mike Matsuda, and Jennifer Stoever. Though I have since moved west to California State University, Monterey Bay, my Ithaca family will always remain close to my heart.

This book would not exist in its current form without the spectacular efforts of the University of Illinois Press. Vijay Shah, the acquisitions editor there in 2010, believed immensely in this project and its place in the rebooted series in Asian American Studies edited by Eiichiro Azuma, Jigna Desai, Martin F. Manalansan IV, Lisa Sun-Hee Park, and David K. Yoo. Vijay was a valuable advocate for this book. His successor, Dawn Durante, is a paragon of professionalism and patience. I am incredibly grateful for their help. Every press should have editors of this caliber.

In many ways, this project has been a lifetime in the making and bears the influence of my family. All their adult lives, my father, Danh Xuân Nguyễn, and mother, Bảo Thị Trần, worked low-paying manual-labor jobs in hopes that my brothers and I would enjoy opportunities they never had. My parents occupied spaces in Vietnamese and American society so far removed from the Ivory Tower that they only recently learned the Vietnamese word for *doctorate*, *tiến sĩ*. My mother named me Phương (Direction) because I symbolized their hopes for the future. They named their second child Đông (East)—a person who is, pound for pound, the best basketball player I have ever seen. My youngest brother, Nam (South), exhibited a modesty and minimalism for which I have always aimed but have yet to achieve. And I cannot forget Woody, the beloved Boston terrier mutt we credit with bringing our family closer together when he entered our lives in early 1998. The day Woody passed away, June 5, 2009, was less than a month after my graduation from USC and brought us all together in collective and profound sadness. Woody was the only family member unable to vote for Barack Obama, but he has the distinction of being the sole witness when I popped the question to the love of my life.

That woman, Betty Châu Nguyễn, defies categorization. Born in a refugee camp, raised in Canada, and influenced by a multitude of cultures, she nevertheless has a phenomenal appreciation for her Vietnamese heritage. She processed every new idea before I started writing and willingly perused through draft after draft of my dissertation. A talented singer and dance teacher, she interpreted Vietnamese popular culture in ways an academic never thinks to do. Only someone as patient and understanding as Betty could put up with me, and for that I am externally grateful.

Becoming Refugee American

Introduction

A Nation of Refugees

> Exile is compelling to think about but terrible to experience. It is the unhealable rift forced between a human being and a native place, between the self and its true home: its essential sadness can never be surmounted.
>
> —Edward Said, *Reflections on Exile and Other Essays*

Throughout history, refugees have formed communities in new lands while holding onto memories of exile and harboring aspirations for reclaiming their lost nations. Refugees have often been lumped into the same category as immigrants even though fleeing from war, violence, or persecution left little possibility for return. Only since World War II has the fate of refugees become a humanitarian concern for the United States, as forced migration has increasingly become linked to U.S. foreign policy. This national guilt reached a climax shortly after the Vietnam War, when liberals and conservatives cited a moral obligation to rescue 130,000 wartime allies, along with America's humanitarian image, both of which imperial hubris had nearly rendered obsolete. Rory Kennedy's 2014 documentary, *Last Days of Saigon*, is the latest retelling of a rescue operation that restored America's identity as global savior. This compelling and uplifting narrative also restores imperial relations, whereby the rescued remain forever indebted to their American benefactors. Such narratives hold powerful sway over society, offering a satisfying closure to a painful period. We, in turn, rarely question these narratives, rarely wonder aloud about what other kinds of feelings, aside from melancholy and nostalgia, occupied the refugees' collective consciousness. We know far more about the causes of their exodus and the national guilt of the receiving country than how the uprooted collectively made sense of their experience after arriving in the United States.[1]

Enmeshed in this nexus of American guilt and refugee gratitude is a process I call "refugee nationalism," and this book studies its origins, development, and persistence within Southern California's Little Saigon, by far the largest and most influential of the overseas Vietnamese communities.[2] We see refugee nationalism every day in ethnic enclaves and cultural performances that evoke nostalgia for the good old days. Though exiled from their homeland, residents of Little Saigon keep alive the symbols of the old regime, never doubting for a moment their claim to statehood. Refugee nationalism came into clear focus in 1999, when thousands of anticommunist demonstrators, both young and old, gathered for weeks outside a Southern California strip mall to protest a shop owner's display of the current Vietnamese flag and a portrait of communist leader Hồ Chí Minh. One scholar described these nationalist passions at the earliest refugee camps as the allegedly tragic "illusions of a refugee."[3] Despite their preference for cultural assimilation, mainstreamers grudgingly tolerate these long-shot fantasies because refugees, by definition, lack the option to repatriate. The persistence of a refugee mentality has also confounded those who expected assimilation into Asian America. As historian Ronald Takaki has famously lamented, "Many Vietnamese see themselves as sojourners, hopeful they can return to their country someday."[4]

This perspective fails to appreciate the fact that refugee nationalism has flourished in conjunction with becoming American. We already know that the refugee experience, born of involuntary migration in search of a safe haven, tends to nurture a cultural identity distinct from that of immigrants. In the context of U.S. history, refugee nationalism has represented not so much a refusal to assimilate but rather a particular mode of becoming American—becoming Refugee American. Forced migration defined most refugee departures, but their experience in America hinged on a particular politics of rescue in both discourse and policy. The fact that an astounding 90 percent of all refugees admitted to the United States during the Cold War hailed from communist republics left little doubt among refugees and Americans alike about how high their particular victimization ranked, thus shaping expectations as to what a guilt-ridden nation still owed them.[5] After all, America's foreign policy failures bore partial responsibility for risking the lives of so many Cold War allies. For Vietnamese Americans, the charity they generally received after arriving and the elevated threat level accorded to communism gave them extra incentive to identify as refugees, whether as a shield against racism or as a strategy to influence foreign policy, long after their resettlement. Yet for too long, refugee nationalism has gone misdiagnosed.

Expanding our framework beyond the familiar rescue narrative reveals that refugees have nurtured an intimate—if not contentious—relationship with their adopted homeland, often for years prior to their migration. During the Cold War, America made subtle promises of last-line defense if its Eastern allies provided front-line opposition to communist expansion. When that last line of defense never arrived in places such as Hungary, Cuba, and Vietnam, America's quest for atonement became the unofficial basis of refugee admissions, even though it was never written into policy. This politics of rescue gave anticommunist refugees a potentially strong moral claim to admission and belonging. It was the least a guilt-ridden nation could do to protect its allies and its reputation as global savior.[6] It was also a favor rarely extended to refugees of other sorts.

If resettled refugees were accused of being overly anticommunist, as was the case with earlier waves from Hungary and Cuba, that attitude was at least consistent with America's well-documented goal of embarrassing the Soviet Union by making synonymous the words *refugee* and *anticommunist*. It was consistent with the belligerent anticommunist stance that America had encouraged, albeit at great risk to the local population. And it represented a way for stigmatized foreigners to stake a higher claim to America and distinguish themselves from the enemy. The implied message was simple: only an ideology as monstrous as communism would compel so many millions to risk their lives fleeing their ancestral lands to escape its reach. Given that state of affairs, America, often their ally prior to exile, was obligated to give them shelter. Refugee Americans represented both sides of national identity: an enduring symbol of America's humanitarian character and a reminder of a mighty nation's past foreign policy failures that made asylum necessary. Indeed, this theme of atonement is rooted in the history of America's response to the Holocaust. When an international delegation met in France to propose a collective framework for resolving the Jewish refugee crisis of the late 1930s, only the tiny Dominican Republic stepped forward to accept a significant number of refugees, thus consigning Hitler's Jews to death and America to another embarrassing legacy of hypocrisy that would take generations to correct.

A Very Brief History of Refugee Nationalism

Since 1951, the United Nations has defined refugees as people who must live outside their country because of a profound fear of persecution based on ethnicity, race, religion, or politics. Displaced by war, famine, and/or natural disaster, refugees are ultimately wanderers in search of a government that will respect and protect their human rights. Because recognition of refugee status precludes the possibility of deportation (known as *refoulement* in policy circles) every sovereign nation has an incentive to define the category as narrowly as possible. Refugees have existed throughout history, but there was little understanding of the term until nation-states became the norm in the twentieth century. With the assumed need to create a homogeneous citizenry came the mass migrations and deaths of people who did not fit that norm.

Historical resistance to refugee admissions also reflected fears of diplomatic fallout from accusing neighbors and trading partners of genocidal practices. During World War II, Franklin Roosevelt's men seemed more concerned about complying with existing immigration laws than saving innocent lives when they admitted fewer than one thousand Jews from Europe. By the time the United States had begun formalizing refugee programs in the late 1940s to provide a home for a tiny fraction of the Eastern Europeans whose countries were now communist territories, Senator Pat McCarran and other ultraconservative xenophobes worried that America was opening its doors to Soviet spies posing as refugees. The 1965 Immigration Act's repudiation of nativist agendas nevertheless created a set of preference categories that defined refugees as those fleeing communism or the Middle East. Not until the 1980s did refugees become an official part of the admissions quotas, meaning that they were no longer admitted on an ad hoc, case-by-case basis, a change that made the process much fairer on paper but also harder to execute.

The fact that refugees admitted to American shores often originated from communist countries obviated the need for diplomatic discretion. Beginning in 1949, the United States maintained no embassies in any communist republic outside of the Soviet Union. Popular discourse tended to dehumanize communists as bloodthirsty atheists, making refugees the lone source of morality and civilization in an otherwise nihilistic abyss. The extreme characterization of communism as the greatest threat to Western civilization thus made it difficult to argue against admitting those fleeing it, especially when complicity with the United States had earned them their fugitive status.

Refugee admissions has never won the support of a majority of Americans, but the passage of time softened the nation's resistance to exiles to some extent. In 1938, an overwhelming 68 percent of Americans, obviously swayed by anti-Semitism, opposed the entry of German and Austrian refugees. Less than twenty years later, thanks in part to an aggressive public relations campaign, only 34 percent opposed the entry of Hungarian refugees, though that number topped 50 percent for Vietnamese and Cubans after 1975.[7] The majority's opposition to their arrival and their admission outside the jurisdiction of immigration quotas, along with the structural conditions of their reception, heightened pressure on refugees to be on their best behavior. Living with sponsor families they did not know and eligible for government aid not available to the rest of the population also created economic incentives to identify as refugees, particularly for non-Europeans such as Cubans and Vietnamese. Without the protective bubble provided by refugee status, members of those groups would no doubt have been subjected to the virulent racism faced by most Latinos and Asians. Their refugee status established a moral belonging in the United States that trumped any legal grounds, especially in the eyes of those who supported their entry. Since 1975, U.S. refugee communities have been joined by people from Africa, South Asia, and the Middle East, and their arrival has provoked varying degrees of opposition and inclusiveness.[8]

Prior to the passage of the Refugee Act of 1980, most admissions were onetime events that signaled the beginning and end of America's moral obligation to any one class of displaced persons. In the case of Cuba and then Vietnam, the U.S. government responded to sustained waves of out-migration over many decades by authorizing new resettlement programs, crafting new admissions preferences for each new wave of exiles, and recruiting new cohorts of sponsoring families. These admissions preferences often meant that applicants were virtually guaranteed official refugee status, resulting in five distinct waves of Vietnamese refugee migration to U.S. shores.[9] The Indochina Migration and Refugee Assistance Act of 1975 legalized the entry of 130,000 exiles of war, most of them government officials, relatives of U.S. citizens, or skilled professionals evacuated en masse within the span of a few days. This first wave of Vietnamese migrants were transported by the U.S. military to stations in Guam, Wake Island, and the Philippines. From there, they would be housed at four mainland bases—Camp Pendleton in California, Fort Chaffee in Arkansas, Eglin Air Force Base in Florida, and Fort Indiantown Gap in Pennsylvania—until the voluntary agencies, most of them Christian-based, matched them with sponsor families. Most Americans assumed that the first wave of 130,000 would be the last, and indeed, only 17,000 Indochinese arrived over the next two years. But in 1979, another large wave of 80,700 migrants were admitted to U.S. shores. These "boat people" fled Vietnam by the hundreds of thousands in hopes that Malaysia, Indonesia, or another neighboring country would grant them political asylum. Stirred by profound guilt and international pressure, the United States opened its doors, resulting in a massive influx of 166,700 in 1980 and 123,250 in 1981.[10] By this time, the U.S. Vietnamese population had reached 230,000, and new legislation as well a multilateral agreement, the Orderly Departure Program, sought to legalize migration directly from Vietnam to the United States for those with ties to the West. This third wave arrived steadily throughout the 1980s, with about 40,000 coming each year and asylum approval rates at or near 100 percent.[11] After passage of the

Amerasian Homecoming Act of 1987, a fourth wave (not discussed in detail in this book) began: 23,000 mixed-race Vietnamese and nearly 70,000 of their family members. By 1990, the Vietnamese American population had topped 500,000, and the final wave of refugee migration began, as hundreds of thousands of political prisoners and their families were granted access to a life in America. Members of the fifth wave are known colloquially as the people of the Humanitarian Operation program (HO people). According to U.S. Census estimates, the United States had a Vietnamese population of nearly 2,000,000 by 2017.[12] Each wave of migration was cast as a small gesture of atonement for failing to prevent the spread of communism, and with atonement came refugee nationalism, an exile identity confident in its legitimacy because of support from the West despite lacking a state of its own. The fact that the United States classified these people as special admissions outside of regular immigration quotas suggested that the cause they had fought for had merit, even if the refugees were publicly encouraged to not think about it.

In the dystopian political novel, *Nineteen Eighty-Four*, George Orwell pointed out that "[He] who controls the past controls the present; [he] who controls the present controls the future."[13] Without a government of their own, refugees have always faced an uphill battle to legitimize their version of the national past and thus their claims to ethnic authenticity. The crucible of the Cold War and the resulting mutual embargo on goods and information created a unique opportunity for refugee history—at least the anticommunist variety—to go largely unquestioned in the capitalist world. Unburdened by diplomatic constraints, Refugee Americans and their allies wrote history from a perspective that was incomplete at best and was institutionalized propaganda at worst. Ukrainians, the single-largest beneficiary of the 1948 Displaced Persons Act, befriended Columbia University history professor Clarence Manning, who published nine books on their pre-Soviet society. In 1964, approximately one hundred thousand people gathered in Washington, D.C., as former president Dwight Eisenhower helped unveil a statue of Ukrainian poet laureate and independence activist Taras Shevchenko, whose likeness was eclipsed in the homeland by statues of Lenin.[14]

Likewise, the history of Hungarian refugee nationalism illustrated the power of collective action in the absence of diplomatic constraints. In 1963, a group of eight Hungarians petitioned the Denver City Council to dedicate a public park to the memory of those who perished in the face of the 1956 Soviet aggression. Hungarian Freedom Park became a reality in 1966, and a refugee memorial occupied the grounds in 1971. Before the end of the Cold War, at least sixteen memorials dedicated to the failed Hungarian Revolution had sprung up in prominent cities, including Los Angeles, Boston, Miami, New York, San Francisco, New Orleans, and Cleveland. These public memorials, while designed to institutionalize refugee collective memory, also tap into American exceptionalism by suggesting that such a long sojourn in the United States makes exiles, already the lone hope to restore freedom and democracy to their country, even more qualified to do so. In this uncomplicated narrative where American values trump native ones, both refugees and the United States get to stand on the right side of history.

Nationalism, Collective Memory, and American Exceptionalism

The creation of such a collective memory was far from inevitable. The fall of Saigon represented a historical nadir for the losing coalition, leaving little apparent value in identifying as either South Vietnamese or American. Standing on the wrong side of history, the losers of the Vietnam War suffered from what theorists of nationalism refer to as a crisis of collective memory.[15] According to historian Peter Novick, "A collective memory, at least a significant collective memory, is understood to express some eternal or essential truth about the group, in this case a nation. A memory, once established, comes to define that eternal truth, and along with it, an eternal identity, for the members of the group."[16] In this light, it is easier to see why, after all these years, Vietnam and the United States still obsess over the outcome of the Vietnam War. For the winning side, the war is known simply known as the Revolution, the culmination of a centuries-long independence movement that overcame the imperial designs of China, France, and the United States. For the losing side, the war marked an all-time low and the accompanying fear that group identity would forever be associated with recent history.

The first war America lost lay to waste the twin myths of U.S. military and moral supremacy.[17] The unauthorized release of the Pentagon Papers revealed that, among other things, the bombings continued, if only to postpone an inevitable and embarrassing defeat. Appalled by what they perceived as an endless war of imperialism, a new generation of American youth vigorously opposed the U.S. government's presence in Southeast Asia while shunning their brothers in uniform when they returned. As one dismayed veteran concluded, "There were really two wars in that era: the first was a military war fought in Vietnam where 57,000 Americans died and . . . the second was a political war waged here at home."[18] In fact, the war on the home front was first waged by various administrations, which began by denying any interest in Southeast Asia, followed up with fabrications justifying military action, and ultimately claimed that withdrawal would do more harm to the region than the U.S. military had already inflicted. Declaring itself a force for world democracy, the United States was in reality becoming more and more a threat to world peace—not the most desirable quality for a superpower wanting to differentiate itself from the Soviet Union.

And with the dissolution of the South Vietnamese state, whose twenty-one-year lifespan was plagued by chronic instability and rampant corruption, how could its former citizens still claim to be the legitimate heirs to the centuries-long independence movement? Their nationalism having literally reached an all-time low, they could rightfully anticipate perpetual vilification as colonial puppets by scholars in Hanoi and the West. But their dilemma was twofold: tens of thousands were expected to shower with refugee gratitude the same country that had sanctioned the assassination of their controversial but strong-willed first president, had treated its South Vietnamese allies with paternal disdain, and had abandoned the fight against the Việt-Cộng without even consulting with these allies. With memories like these, refugees had no incentive to proudly identify with the United States.

The losers of the Vietnam War quickly learned to affirm the past by rewriting it. Sociologist Maurice Halbwachs, who introduced the concept of collective memory in 1925, anticipated this move when he asserted that present conditions play a vital role in reconstructing the past.[19] Rather than reflect too long on defeat, the *New York Times* and other U.S. media shifted the narrative to stories of redemption when they declared the "rescue" of 130,000 Southeast Asian allies "one of the few shreds of glory that the United States has been able to retrieve from the closing days—or years—of the Vietnam war."[20] Even the ultraconservative *Orange County Register* argued, "We have to accommodate [the refugees], absolutely must," despite their anticipated burden on a sluggish job market. "We'll think about those practical matters later," the editors continued. "Right now we must think of the moral imperative."[21] Moral imperatives had already opened America's doors to three thousand orphans, many of whom had been fathered by U.S. servicemen.[22]

Scholars have often cited a May 1975 Gallup poll indicating that 54 percent of the American public opposed the admission of much larger numbers of older Indochinese refugees but have neglected to acknowledge how much that number had fallen since 1938. Indeed, lingering national guilt over the Holocaust had led Franklin Roosevelt and his successors to admit refugees in a category separate and exempt from any immigration quotas. In short, the nation had become much more open and humbled, willing to receive hundreds of thousands of displaced persons, albeit from mostly communist nations, and to provide the conditions for refugees-in-name to proudly identify as such.

The importance of American collective guilt cannot be overstated, if only because refugees, lacking a nation-state of their own, have always depended on the goodwill of host countries to institutionalize their collective identity.[23] Goodwill was always a priority for refugees, given the danger of being confused with the communists and tyrants from whom they fled. A popular route toward avoiding that confusion was to construct a refugee identity that highlighted the narratives of rescue and emphasized the attributes that overlapped with the larger host culture. Their anticommunism, however out of place it appeared in post-McCarthy America, helped refugees elude the ire of ultraconservatives and those Americans who had lost family members overseas. Rescue made these foreigners appear a little less foreign and a little more assimilable. American guilt provided the push needed to move refugees past the shame of being homeless, hopeless, and hungry and of waiting for rescue by the same people who had hung them out to dry. In short, refugee identity, while partly a tribute to old ways, served as a survival mechanism in new places.

Good Refugees and Bad Refugees

Many scholars have implied if not stated directly a distinction between "good refugees," who accepted either cultural assimilation or racial formation as the dominant—and perhaps inevitable—mode of becoming American, and "bad refugees," who in reactionary fashion clung unapologetically to the past. The exploits of Florida's Cuban exile community were already well known by the time the Vietnamese arrived, and scholars naturally assumed that Vietnamese émigrés would have similar problems transitioning from refugees into immigrants. In 1995, twenty years after the fall of Saigon, Vietnam War expert Stanley Karnow questioned the mental health of those clinging stubbornly to their refugee mind-set. "Unable to acclimate to what they regard as exile," he wrote, "many older ones cluster in the Little Saigons of Southern California or Northern Virginia, and dream of somehow returning to Vietnam."[24] To be fair, many scholars and activists in the ethnic studies tradition have also misunderstood the refugee condition. Challenging the idea that becoming American constituted a singular, universal trajectory based on the experiences of European immigrants, historian Ronald Takaki has argued that Asian immigrants remained outside of the mainstream because a racist society viewed them as "strangers from a different shore." But rather than giving up on the United States and contemplating repatriation, the majority of them *became* Asian American.[25] Takaki and his peers fully expected future generations of Vietnamese Americans to break away from Old World politics and adapt to U.S. society in the same way as earlier Asian Americans. To avoid potentially divisive squabbles over communist leader Hồ Chí Minh, ethnic studies has incorporated Southeast Asians by sidestepping the Vietnam War and instead cultivating a shared opposition to racism, poverty, and discrimination. Recent work in the field of critical refugee studies by scholars such as Yen Le Espiritu and Mimi Thi Nguyen provide excellent critiques of American imperialism but still want to focus on the role of American malfeasance in the social construction of refugee identity.[26]

But by analyzing these groups as minorities solely in the domestic realm, ethnic studies unintentionally blinds itself to how Refugee Americans are minorities in multiple locations.[27] This lesson comes courtesy of María Cristina García, one of the first historians of refugee communities from a transnationalist perspective. In her history of Cuban refugees in Miami, García explains, "The political culture of the exile community in south Florida evolved in response to events in both Cuba and the United States."[28] Like the Cuban émigrés, the former South Vietnamese tried to influence the course and writing of history, often blurring the line between exile and ethnic politics. Racism threatened their life chances in the United States, while communism threatened the life chances of family and friends in Vietnam. Sociologist and refugee scholar Peter Rose argues that "relatively few [immigrants] would be classified as minorities in their own countries. *Most migrants became 'minorities'—and 'ethnics'—after they arrive here.*"[29] Minority status in one's country of origin partly qualifies one as a refugee, but within what historian Matthew Frye Jacobson termed the "diasporic imagination," refugee nationalism potentially exists as a normative majority identity because the Cold War ensured that Vietnamese American refugees would hardly come into contact with procommunist coethnics.[30] Citing longstanding customs discouraging migration, refugees posited communism as the Vietnamese diaspora's raison d'être, or as one famous refugee song put it, "Only for freedom do I live in exile."[31] And only in the West—and especially in a country as scarred by the Vietnam War as the United States was—would they find a host society so invested in validating their version of Vietnamese identity, culture, and history. Or, to put it more directly, so willing to fight the postwar. And that fight to win the postwar was waged most visibly in the enclaves of Southern California.

Little Saigon in Orange County, California, is the largest and best-known enclave within the Vietnamese diaspora. Once the semirural home of whites and Latinos, the cities of Westminster, Garden Grove, Fountain Valley, and Santa Ana had not enjoyed the kind of upscale suburban development taking place in the coastal communities and thus had less incentive to oppose the Indochinese influx. By the early 1980s, those not relocating from east of California were at least making self-described pilgrimages to the unofficial overseas Vietnamese capital, which had a population of well over two hundred thousand. While many locations were invested in winning the postwar, the Little Saigon area of Orange County had a critical mass of refugees, including artists and intellectuals, along with white locals whose eagerness to atone for the sins of the Vietnam War resulted in a tolerance toward refugees that, while far from ideal, was friendlier than Asian Americans had historically received. Treated like family by their compassionate and conservative church-affiliated sponsors, the early Vietnamese refugees knew another side of Southern California—and conservative America—that prior studies have not taken into account. The stories of generous sponsors handing over keys to house and car nearly free of charge overshadowed the horror stories of exploited refugees. During the early 1980s, when one racial panic after another followed the Vietnamese in Orange County, relatively moderate Republican politicians defended their unpopular Vietnamese constituents. Under the circumstances, Vietnamese Americans gravitated toward the hyperpatriotic Republican Party. Of course, membership in the staunchly anticommunist GOP appealed to their new identity as exiled U.S. allies fighting the postwar, whether via armed struggle or as model minorities.

The Development of Refugee Nationalism in Little Saigon

This book focuses on how Vietnamese Americans tested the limits of American guilt, creating spaces and opportunities for themselves through a refugee cultural identity. In addition to consulting English-language newspapers, personal records, government documents, and memoirs, I used Vietnamese-language sources in an effort to provide a more complete account of how the South Vietnamese became Refugee Americans. I conducted personal interviews; consulted the refugee press, memoirs, and personal narratives; and translated popular songs into English. This study balances top-down changes and bottom-up dynamics, the internal politics of Little Saigon and the relationship between Vietnamese Americans and their local community.

The book focuses on Vietnamese in America, but the story of refugee nationalism begins with America's Cold War adventures in East Asia. Chapter 1 places the Vietnam War in the context of a larger U.S. effort to secure an

Asian anticommunist coalition in the aftermath of China's turn to communism and the Korean War. Formerly insignificant Indochina, like Taiwan and South Korea before it, became for reasons both pragmatic and idealistic an important site of struggle for the United States, and the Indochinese people naturally believed that in light of the perceived threat posed by communism, American intervention implied a special relationship that could never be severed.

Chapter 2 begins with the fall of Saigon and explains how the losers of the Vietnam War affirmed the past by rewriting it. Conservative and liberal guilt coalesced around the notion that admitting Vietnamese refugees could atone for the tragedy of the war. While refugee camp newspapers presented America as a friendly society, a bubble of charity created the perception that the United States was a guilt-ridden society with the resources to help Vietnamese émigrés get back on their feet.

Chapter 3 investigates how the emergence of a semiautonomous Vietnamese community and the arrival of a second wave of refugees from Vietnam inspired the formation of a community noticeably more proud of its refugee roots. By moving to California, far away from their protective sponsors, refugees now had to depend on an ethnic political economy and a strong welfare state to keep them economically afloat. But these conditions enabled people to resurrect their pre-1975 careers, resulting in a critical mass of musicians, journalists, activists, and intellectuals whose "social work" cast refugees as heroic eyewitnesses to the horrors of communism. They realized that only in this light could the former South Vietnamese be placed so easily on the right side of history.

Chapter 4 looks at how Little Saigon became home to an anticommunist insurgency in the 1980s. The rise of a militaristic refugee nationalism was rooted partly in Reagan-era policies favoring anticommunist guerrilla "freedom fighters" such as those in Nicaragua and Afghanistan as well as in the desire of working-class Vietnamese to be viewed as equal partners in the Cold War and to command the basic respect and admiration they had often been denied during the Vietnam War. Out of this context emerged fascist organizations willing to kill their Vietnamese critics. In other words, the refugee community created its own anticommunist version of the Việt-Cộng, equally shadowy and repressive.

Chapter 5 highlights how assimilationists stepped into leadership positions in Little Saigon. With their bilingual abilities and awareness of racism's reach, the assimilationists deemed themselves most qualified to help ease tensions between refugees and Orange County's Anglo community. As long as white politicians pitied the Vietnamese, the assimilationists could afford to promote the stereotype of perfect refugees.

Figure 1. In 2003, Westminster unveiled a twenty-thousand-dollar concrete gateway sign welcoming visitors to its most famous attraction. Photo by author.

Chapter 6 explains the intensification of refugee nationalism during the post–Cold War era, when Little Saigon's demographics enabled the community to lean on local politicians even after its clout waned at the national level. Fearing that globalization would transform Little Saigon into Little Ho Chi Minh City, local activists used their local influence to institutionalize their collective memory via memorials, new legislation, and the educational system.

Becoming Refugee American

Since 1975, most people have assumed that Vietnamese American exile identity (what I call refugee nationalism) would not afflict future generations living in the United States. Sympathetic observers such as Gail Paradise Kelly and Stanley Karnow wanted refugees to forget the pain of exile so they could move on with their lives. Others like Takaki and Espiritu felt that Vietnamese Americans, whose debt of gratitude to the United States had long ago been paid in full, did themselves a disservice by playing along with the politics of rescue. What they did not realize was that refugee nationalism represented an attractive mode of becoming American for those who had little power. The ability of working-class people with limited English skills to extract concessions from a guilt-ridden public proved effective enough that campaigns for civil rights seemed unnecessary in the face of appeals to sympathy. Despite entering the United States in the aftermath of the Asian American movement, the Vietnamese have been extremely slow to adopt the model of civil rights protest.

So much of the Vietnamese entry and advancement in American society was based on moral belonging that they found it easy to think of themselves as a special people whose unique suffering at the hands of communist oppression and American indifference entitled them to special treatment, thus blinding them to the suffering of other minority groups. In addition, conservatives have taken the lion's share of credit for helping Vietnamese Americans, passing along selfish notions whereby refugees are expected to pay back instead of pay forward. This fascist quid pro quo meant forgetting about America's past failures in Vietnam and present failures everywhere else. Vietnamese émigrés' exposure to an unusual bubble of charity in which America's deficiencies could be corrected without recourse to political struggle only reinforced the myth of a self-correcting American moral compass and indifference to people of color. The language barrier facing the older generation of Vietnamese Americans hindered attempts to form alliances outside that conservative bubble of charity. For a group without access to the culture industry or even sophisticated rhetoric, refugee nationalism and anticommunism represented the most accessible strategies for avoiding the wrath of ultraconservatives and those Americans who had lost loved ones to the Việt-Cộng. Not until the end of the Cold War did a critical mass of Vietnamese Americans—born in the United States, fluent in English, more liberal in their politics, and unburdened by memories of war and communism—build political alliances outside of the conservative bubble of charity. Ironically, members of this younger generation also face a language barrier, one that prevents them from fully understanding why their elders followed such a rigid script of eternal gratitude toward America or why they kept so much of their history from the Anglophone world. This book provides an entry point to understanding this divide.

A Note on the Vietnamese Language

The Vietnamese language is a tonal language in which vowels possess multiple specific tones, as indicated by diacritical marks. While certain names (for example, *Saigon, Hanoi, Vietnam,* and *Ho Chi Minh*) are readily understood by English- and Vietnamese-language speakers regardless of tonal accuracy, a Vietnamese-language speaker would not understand most Anglicized pronunciations. In addition, this book is likely to be read by people fluent in the Vietnamese language. I feel that reintroducing diacritical marks judiciously will not detract from the reading experience and will provide Vietnamese-language speakers or learners the means to pronounce words properly. If the original source material lacked diacritical marks or if the word is well-established in the Anglophone world, I generally omit diacritics; otherwise, they are included. Unless indicated, all English translations are provided by the author.

1 Accidental Allies

America's Crusade and the Origins of Refugee Nationalism

The free peoples of the world look to us for support in maintaining their freedoms.
—President Harry S. Truman, 1948

If I left [the war in Vietnam] and let the Communists take over South Vietnam, then I would be seen as a coward and my nation would be seen as an appeaser, and we would both find it impossible to accomplish anything for anybody anywhere on the entire globe.
—President Lyndon B. Johnson, 1964

Modern-day discussions of the Vietnam War often conclude that as a war of choice, it was fought for reasons other than national security and that it ultimately did not justify the sacrifice in American blood, treasure, and prestige. The human costs of that war—fifty-eight thousand Americans and millions of Vietnamese killed—provide a painful, uncontroversial lesson in American imperialism gone wild. Intervention was billed as necessary, given the domino theory's prediction of a dystopian and monolithic communist-dominated landscape, an outcome that never came to fruition. In fact, Asia specialist Robert Kaplan argues that communist Vietnam poses more of a threat to neighboring communist China than it does to capitalist America.[1] According to modern-day discussions, pragmatism finally prevailed in 1972, when American rapprochement with communist China foreshadowed the end of its misguided commitment to capitalist Vietnam. Finally, framing the Vietnam War as a war of choice often treats it as an aberration, magically decoupling it from the rest of America's Cold War foreign policy in Asia, a strategic rewriting of the past that ignores the pragmatic importance of Vietnam—at least up until the 1970s—as part of a larger Asian-American Cold War front. In other words, the Vietnam War, though far different in outcome from the rest of America's foreign policy in East Asia, must be understood as an extension of that policy. This chapter investigates how a combination of ideology and pragmatism led the United States to intervene in a country so small only to lose so much as well as how anticommunist alliances with Taiwan, Korea, and Vietnam bordered on the kind of special relationship whose unconditional bond must never be broken. The self-righteous dimension of the Cold War shaped the origins of refugee nationalism, whose idea of belonging in America has been based more on moral than legal, grounds.[2]

The Cold War as a whole has always had a moral dimension courtesy of Presidents Harry S. Truman and Lyndon B. Johnson and other zealous politicians who all too often depicted it as an epic struggle between good and evil. Speaking to the nation on March 12, 1947, while seeking to aid Greece and Turkey in the face of communist encroachment, Truman left little doubt that in the interest of preventing the further spread of totalitarianism, the United States had a moral responsibility to reduce "misery and want" across the entire globe. The speech played well in Seoul, where America's handpicked hard-line anticommunist leader, Syngman Rhee, wrote a personal letter thanking the president for his "courageous stand against communism" and reminding him not to forget his friends on the Korean peninsula.[3] Prior to the Korean War, Rhee's desire for a special relationship involved asking for "a specific assurance the United States would come to the defense of the Republic of Korea in the event of an armed attack against it." Even though Washington considered such a move "out of the question" at the time, Rhee, Nationalist Chinese leader Chiang Kai-shek, and Philippine president Elpidio Quirino collectively proposed the formation of a "Far East Security Pact" with the United States.[4] Their wish came true after the Korean War broke out in 1950 and the United States had been pushed to the brink of nuclear warfare. Failure in the region was no longer seen as an option. Massive nation building and defense mobilization in East Asia, measured in dollars and manpower, made it obvious that, as historian Gregg Brazinsky has pointed out, "the United States would suffer a tremendous loss of prestige if it abandoned its commitment there."[5] As a result, such seemingly inconsequential nations as Taiwan, Korea, and Vietnam acquired strategic significance in the context of the Cold War. Their ambitious contingency plan involved transforming recently liberated, formerly feudal colonies still toiling in the agricultural mode of production into industrialized liberal states. The speed and fury with which foreign policy experts assembled a workable coalition of anticommunist Asian republics to prevent any further spread of communism constituted what historian James Irving Matray has termed "the reluctant crusade," and Vietnam became a part of that crusade.[6]

Given America's long history of anti-Asian racism, the prospect of nation building in faraway Korea, Taiwan, and Vietnam also required an ambitious adjustment in American racial attitudes toward Asia and Asians. Stereotypes of the East as alien, exotic, and heathen would no longer suffice if the United States wanted to sustain public—that is, congressional—support and credibility for an undertaking of such massive scale. At the time, overcoming stereotypes simply meant convincing Americans that Asians were indeed an assimilable race, a people willing and able to function in a Western-style civilization, thus justifying the mission there. Postwar legal reforms eliminated racial bars to marriage, citizenship, and homeownership. Some of this shift was also reflected in post–World War II Hollywood films such as *Sayonara* and *Japanese War Bride*, which approved of interracial marriages between former enemies, albeit on the colonizer's terms. American public opinion aside, there was also the equally daunting task of convincing the people of Asia that a U.S. presence in the region would benefit the Asian people. It thus helped that the China Lobby, the coalition most ardently committed to propping up America's accidental allies, could handle both tasks. As intellectuals, businessmen, and politicians whose authority in matters of the Far East stemmed largely from Christian missionary work, they equated involvement in Asia with a moral crusade to be won at all costs on behalf of allies our Founding Fathers would envy. As trusted friends of Free Asia's new leaders, they could portray themselves as responding to the needs of America's accidental allies rather than imposing an imperialist blueprint.

The men of the China Lobby and the leaders of Free Asia had previously crossed paths in spirit. The former were the spiritual heirs to an earlier generation of missionaries who were, ironically, among the few defenders of Chinese and Japanese immigrants in America, while the latter were among the small cohort of native elite who benefited from Western imperialism. Decades of colonialism propelled Western schools to the top of the social hierarchy, ensuring that nearly every intellectual, doctor, or person of prominence was also indoctrinated in Christianity and the superiority of the West. These elite, among them Yung Wing and Hu Shih, were also among the first Asians to enroll in Ivy League universities. It is therefore not too surprising that modern leaders such as China's Sun Yat-sen, Korea's Rhee, and Vietnam's Ngô Đình Diệm were all Christians who rose to prominence through the colonial infrastructure.

Western education unified both parties in the superiority of whiteness, capitalism, democracy, and Christianity, which the United States had rebranded as modernization theory, the neocolonialist proposition that all economies moved through five linear stages of development, with traditional societies at the bottom and mass consumer societies such as the United States at the top.[7] Their mutual faith in the top-down model of racial uplift—the great man theory of history—nevertheless put them in the company of famous antiracist W. E. B. Du Bois, who accepted it as "the history of human progress."[8] The China Lobby consequently cared very little that the native Christian elite—the rare beneficiaries of colonial rule—shared almost nothing in common with the vast majority of their race. In fact, exposure to Western-educated and Christianized people more attuned to American anticommunism only reinforced the China Lobby's false impression that the vast majority of Asians would naturally internalize the Western worldview and act on those interests. If history could be reduced to emulating great nations and great men, Cold War nation building made perfect sense.

Prior to World War II, no one imagined that a Free Asia would be dominated by nations other than China and Japan. But the Cold War made major players out of minor nations such as Korea, Taiwan, and Vietnam, which became America's accidental allies. This seismic shift engendered official gratitude toward the United States and feelings of racial superiority among the chosen few lucky enough to enjoy a modern standard of living. If a 2013 South Korean Ministry of Patriots and Veterans Affairs poster thanking the United States for "60 Years of Commitment, 60 Years of Friendship" is any indication, America's accidental allies were very much invested in constructing a "special relationship," an everlasting bond in which South Koreans (at least officially) were "forever indebted" to an America seen as nothing less than welcome savior and pivotal guide along the path to modernity.[9]

Underlying expressions of gratitude were the subtext of Cold War tensions that would have plunged South Korea into the communist orbit if not for the steadfast support of the United States since 1950. But more than merely giving thanks, South Korea's economic success and Christian leanings—with Christians outnumbering Buddhists by 6 percentage points—affirms the past by rewriting the Korean War as a good war that resulted in one of the most successful nation-building stories of the latter twentieth century. Vietnam wanted to be the next nation on that list, and any discussion of the Vietnam War and the path of the refugees from Saigon must take this larger historical context into account. This interplay of competing models of American imperialism—realists working on Plan B and idealists who saw it as Plan A—led America's accidental allies to begin believing that they were not merely allies of convenience but rather allies of destiny, beneficiaries of a moral crusade. Only in this light can we begin to fully understand the basis of Vietnamese refugee nationalism.

Realism and Idealism

Between 1945 and 1950, foreign policy realism had an unmistakably racialized component as Washington insiders favored rebuilding Europe. If those countries wanted to reclaim their former colonies, so be it. No individual at the time better summarized this realist school with regard to Asia than diplomat George Kennan. Known to most historians as the intellectual father of the Cold War, Kennan believed that containing the Soviet threat should involve East Asia as little as possible. Writing on February 28, 1948, he saw little benefit in a Pacific presence beyond alliances with Japan and the Philippines.[10] The former, a puppet government controlled by Douglas MacArthur, would serve as the region's economic nucleus, while the latter, a U.S. colony from 1899 to 1946, would serve as a military stronghold. Channeling the kind of Orientalism that has become part of the center-left discourse against intervention, Kennan argued that "our political philosophy and our patterns for living have very little applicability to masses of people in Asia. They may be all right for us, with our highly developed political traditions running back into the centuries and with our peculiarly favorable geographic position; but they are simply not practical or helpful, today, for most of the people in Asia."[11]

Kennan anticipated that the problem of scarcity would engulf the "greatest of the Asiatic peoples—the Chinese and the Indians"—in a process so "long and violent" that communist revolution might be "unavoidable." Well aware that most Asians would resent the United States controlling 50 percent of the world's wealth, Kennan believed that a minimalist, hands-off approach to Asia was the best option available: better to be seen as imperialists from afar than from up close. To his credit, Kennan took into consideration the plight of the Third World majority, only to conclude that winning their hearts and minds was a losing proposition. The February 1948 memo, the Truman Doctrine of 1947, the Displaced Persons Act of 1948, and the Marshall Plan of 1948–52 reflected a Cold War agenda focused almost exclusively on European security and prosperity. In fact, the United States did not oppose France's post-1945 campaign to regain its former colonies in Southeast Asia as long as those efforts did not impinge on the new U.S. empire, which had seen its military presence expand from fourteen foreign installations in 1940 to more than thirty thousand by the end of World War II—what historian Chalmers Johnson has termed an "Empire of Bases."[12]

Kennan may not have felt a need to ally with China, but the men of the China Lobby knew that Eastern markets constituted the new frontier of American empire. These men included Republican Congressman Walter Judd and Senator William Knowland, military men such as Generals

Douglas MacArthur and Claire Chennault, and Alfred Kohlberg, *Time-Life* publisher Henry Robinson Luce, and other businessmen. Born in China in 1888 to missionary parents, Luce was raised around Chinese ever grateful to be taught by Americans. As historian Robert E. Herzstein has noted, Luce "used his vastly successful journalism as a kind of secular pulpit from which he preached the virtues of American engagement in Asia."[13] His ambitious 1941 essay on the "American Century" justified imperialism on the claim that the United States could not have a free market unless such markets existed elsewhere in the world.[14]

The China Lobby and its allies liked to think of themselves as friends of Asia, but they simply represented the softer, more idealistic side of imperialism. Historian David Barrows channeled the racist colonial mind-set, writing, "The white, or European, race is, above all others, the great historical race; but the yellow race, represented by the Chinese, has also a historical life and development, beginning many centuries before the birth of Christ."[15] Western militarism—from Britain's conquest of China in the 1800s to America's later dominance in Japan, Hawaii, and the Philippines—had blunted Asia's threat to white supremacy, while missionaries installed an educational system ensuring that only converts to Western norms and ideology moved up the economic ladder. It was a familiar racist system: minorities could prosper as long as they knew their place.

If China could be transformed into a modern capitalist republic, members of the China Lobby, led in part by Luce, saw Chiang Kai-shek as the heir apparent to Sun Yat-sen. Born in 1887, Chiang was a young charismatic military officer whose marriage to Sun's sister-in-law offered an inside track to power but whose conversion to Christianity moved a *Time* magazine reader to declare that America needs more "men of faith, men of character" like the generalissimo.[16] Never one to shy away from hyperbole, Luce described Chiang as a man who would be remembered for "centuries and centuries."[17] Luce especially adored Madame Chiang Kai-shek. The articulate Wellesley-educated First Lady of China spent much of 1943 on a goodwill tour of the United States organized by Luce in hopes of swinging public opinion toward a Sino-American special relationship. Given the extent of exclusion laws barring most Asians from immigrating and becoming U.S. citizens, Luce's model minorities acquired a level of honorary whiteness well beyond the normal reach of "aliens ineligible for citizenship." Between 1927 and 1955, the Chiangs graced the cover of *Time* no fewer than eleven times, including a 1937 cover honoring them as "Man and Wife of the Year."[18] The longest published testimonial, from a reader in Ohio, praised them "for reuniting the largest and most ancient country in the world in the face of common danger; for learning perforce to unleash bombs from nowhere, mines from nowhere, planes from nowhere in a land where every gesture is a tradition; for advancing national progress and a New Life in spite of centuries of worship and changelessness."[19]

The end of World War II and the accompanying decline of European empires marked America's opportunity to become the hegemonic Western power in the Far East, as Luce and company had hoped. But trouble quickly emerged in China, where postwar partitions had shut the Communists out of power, prompting Mao Tse-tung's forces to fight back. Not content to let pro-Nationalist propaganda do all the work, the China Lobby did its part to silence Chiang's critics. Washington's hope that Nationalists and Communists could form a coalition government prompted *Life* magazine to publish a 1948 article attacking the Truman administration's alleged "pro-Communist" position.[20] When Chiang's situation worsened, the China Lobby went after journalists and bureaucrats who reported the bad news, especially after a *New York Times* headline declared that "U.S. Puts Sole Blame on Chiang Regime for Collapse."[21] While news of Chiang's incompetence and corruption certainly shifted American public opinion against intervention to some degree, Luce and company remained convinced American public opinion was the primary prerequisite for maintaining American empire. They did not care that the *New York Times* had little to no influence over Chinese public opinion, which—out of a combination of love and fear—had swung in favor of the Communists. On October 1, 1949, Mao Tse-tung emerged victorious in the civil war, while the Nationalist government fled to the nearby island of Taiwan. All that Washington could do at the point was cut off diplomatic ties with Mao and pressure the United Nations to recognize Taiwan as the only legitimate government of the Chinese people.

Accidental Allies

Though they had lost Free China, Luce and company still believed that the Free China model could be transplanted to the rest of Asia. When North Korea invaded South Korea on June 25, 1950, U.S. officials saw the action solely as a Soviet-orchestrated offensive and decided that they could no longer assume a peripheral role in East Asia. Truman admitted in private, "Korea is the Greece of the Far East. If we are tough enough now, if we stand up to them like we did in Greece three years ago, they won't take any next steps."[22] He thought that if communist expansion "was allowed to go unchallenged it would mean a third world war, just as similar incidents had brought on a second world war."[23] The absence of the Soviet delegation from the United Nations allowed the Security Council to unanimously approve the use of military force against the North Korean Army, which by June 28, 1950, had occupied Seoul. Only with the help of U.S. combat forces was South Korea able to defend itself, and the war came to an unofficial end in 1953 with the two Koreas still divided at the thirty-eighth parallel. Truman also sent the U.S. Navy's Seventh Fleet to protect Taiwan, which would have been particularly vulnerable to invasion if North Korea had assumed full control of the peninsula. All of a sudden, Taiwan became what Gen. Douglas MacArthur called "an integral part" of the "western strategic frontier."[24] The truce that ended the Korean War coincided with Josef Stalin's death in 1953, but the United States was still moving full speed ahead with nation building. In 1953, the United States and South Korea signed a mutual defense treaty that guaranteed Korea's military security "indefinitely." When the United States did the same with Taiwan in 1954, the security of East Asia arguably had blurred the line between idealism and realism.[25]

With military assistance assured, U.S. officials hoped that Taiwan could dedicate resources to developing its economy. According to historian John Garver, "U.S. leaders invested considerable resources in making that model successful, in the expectation that the Free China model would play a significant role in the struggle against Communism throughout the developing world."[26] Economic aid went beyond charitable as a consequence of the importance accorded to winning the Cold War. From 1950 to 1965, Taiwan received an annual average of one hundred million dollars in nonmilitary aid from the United States, more per capita than any other receiving nation at the time and all of it grant money until 1955. During those years, U.S. aid accounted for 6.4 percent of Taiwan's GDP and 34 percent of the gross investment in the country's economy and subsidized 40 percent of the country's imports.[27] Without American aid, according to a U.S. government study, Taiwan would have needed another thirty years to reach the standard of living it had achieved by 1964.[28]

Washington's newfound insistence on defending its accidental allies at any cost forced the United States to put up with autocrats. In Taiwan, Chiang took advantage of this reservoir of funds by allowing the military to account for 15 percent of GDP and 85 percent of the national budget in hopes that he could one day orchestrate an offensive to reclaim mainland China.[29] Luce did his best to imbue Rhee, General MacArthur's handpicked choice to lead South Korea after World War II, with messianic qualities, putting the Ivy League–educated and Christianized Rhee on the October 16, 1950, cover of *Time* magazine and describing him as a dedicated patriot who "for 55 years ... has been running for the job of 'father of his country.'"[30] With the Korean

War in full swing, such a flattering portrait depicted Rhee, who received 92 percent of the vote in 1948, as a man of the people, enabling his supporters in the China Lobby to win the hearts and minds of the American public. In reality, Rhee alienated nearly everyone around him and held onto power for twelve years only by declaring martial law, arresting his opponents, and rigging elections.

Because of South Korea's unique geopolitical position, it could and did try to squeeze as much aid money out of the United States as possible. Like Taiwan, the government of South Korea preferred money with no strings attached. During the 1950s, Seoul could afford to engage in deficit spending to fund domestic projects, hoping that U.S. aid would cover the difference.[31] Between 1950 and 1965, the U.S. Congress provided South Korea with approximately $2.8 billion in economic aid, an astounding average of $186 million per year, almost all of it in grant money.[32] What M. Shalid Alam called "the most massive aid flow to any Third World country" made sense given America's new crusade in Asia.[33] Learning from the mistakes made in China, land reform was instrumental to economic development, and the creation of a rural middle class staved off the threat of a communist-led populist uprising in Korea as well as in Taiwan.[34]

In the midst of decolonization movements throughout Asia and Africa, South Korean intellectuals strived to bridge the gap between modernization theory and self-determination, proposing instead the concept of a hybrid modernity that, as one professor wrote in 1965, "does not represent simply Americanization" but rather constitutes a path "peculiar to Korea."[35] Framing South Korea's path to capitalism as an indigenous phenomenon had the practical benefit of fending off suspicions of foreign rule. Given the country's potential for growth, this line of thinking also benefited the propaganda machine, with scholars arguing that seemingly foreign concepts such as democracy and capitalism were actually an inevitable outgrowth of Korean tradition and other scholars arguing the same regarding authoritarianism to avoid incurring Seoul's wrath.[36] As historian Gregg Brazinsky has noted, scholars' desire to outline an uniquely Asian modernity reached a high point at a 1965 conference at Korea University that was organized by the Ford Foundation and Asia Foundation and featured scholars from the United States, South Korea, Japan, India, Hong Kong, and other noncommunist nations.[37] George E. Taylor of the Ford Foundation was impressed that "Asians were talking to Asians, even Koreans to Japanese, about their own problems." And because South Korean modernization remained anticommunist, as Brazinsky notes, "its general outlook meshed with the goals of American social engineering."[38] Belief in modernization theory meant that scholars generally embraced the

United States not so much as a negative foreign influence but as a friend assisting Korea on its supposedly natural and indigenous journey toward liberal capitalism. According to scholar Chung-in Moon, during this period, pro-American ideology (*chinmi*) "began to dominate the national psyche" and South Koreans eschewed antiimperialist slogans such as "Yankee, Go Home!"[39]

The introduction to a 1982 publication celebrating the one hundredth anniversary of Korean-American relations that was signed by the presidents of both South Korea and the United States echoed the recurring theme of gratitude for an unbreakable special relationship: "Since the Korean War, at no time has any American administration, Republican or Democrat, ever deviated from a policy of strong commitment. With the help of American military and economic aid, South Korea emerged from the rubble of war to a proud, industrialized nation."[40]

The Rise and Fall of South Vietnam

On April 7, 1954, President Dwight Eisenhower gave his famous domino theory speech, suggesting that America's Asian alliance, while successful thus far, remained a fragile work in progress, capable of unraveling completely if Southeast Asia succumbed to communism. Once the Geneva Accords established a nominally democratic Vietnamese state headquartered in Saigon, the United States had the political cover it needed to expand its post–Korean War crusade. Former air force commander Nguyễn Cao Kỳ's assessment that America's preferred solution was to simply "make everyone in South Vietnam happy, give everyone all the good things of life, and nobody would become a Communist" reflected a unvarnished faith in the template established in Taiwan and Korea.[41] It also provided a further example of what historian Seth Jacobs has described as "messianic liberalism," in which American opinion leaders and policymakers invested heavily in Asian leaders cast as heroic personalities more valued for their Christian beliefs than any commitment to democratic principles.[42] In the case of South Vietnam, America's choice was Ngô Đình Diệm, an exiled nationalist fluent in Latin, French, and classical Chinese who longed for a Vietnamese republic independent of Soviet communism and French colonialism. American media treatments of the "George Washington of Vietnam" during the late 1950s also adhered to the great man theory of history. *Life* magazine prepared a story on Diệm with the headline, "The Tough Miracle Man of Vietnam." The editors proclaimed that "every son, daughter and even distant admirer of the American Revolution should be overjoyed and learn to shout, if not to pronounce, 'Hurrah for Ngo Dinh Diem.'"[43] The same messianic branding was applied to the inaugural leaders of Free China, Free Korea, and Free Vietnam to cast them as the equals of history's great white men—"Hannibal, Caesar, Napoleon, Wellington, Lincoln."[44] The *New York Times* lauded Diệm's "five year miracle" in South Vietnam. *Foreign Affairs* boldly claimed that "history may yet judge Diem as one of the great figures of twentieth century Asia."[45] At the very least, as historian Robert Herzstein asserts, "the entire China lobby had indeed taken the president of Vietnam under its wing."[46] In Jacobs's analysis, Washington's top foreign policy minds naively "believed a puppet Catholic was preferable to any non-Christian Vietnamese with indigenous support."[47]

All these plaudits came on the heels of what seemed like a miracle indeed. Externally mapped in 1954 and slated to be subject to reunification with North Vietnam following the 1956 elections, the new anticommunist republic was little more than a diverse collection of religious, political, economic, and geographic interest groups when the handpicked Ngô Đình Diệm assumed power in 1955. He had inherited a refugee influx after more than a million northerners defected to South Vietnam to escape communist-led purges that also claimed the lives of those formerly loyal to Hồ Chí Minh.[48] His cancellation of the 1956 elections impressed Washington and seemingly brought together the South's many factions into an imagined community. Because their education, Catholic backgrounds, and anticommunist credentials earned many in the 1954 refugee cohort disproportionately high influence in Saigon's political and cultural sphere, northern refugee culture spread quickly under the guise of South Vietnamese nationalism. Among those refugee themes was the idea that only an ideology as monstrous as communism would compel so many to flee their ancestral land, a concept immortalized in popular films, including *Chúng Tôi Muốn Sống* (1956).

But aside from anticommunism, the mood in the Republic of Vietnam in the 1950s reflected the hope that a perpetual site of conquest could transform itself into one of Asia's young giants. For the next twenty years, the U.S.-backed southern regime exhibited enough trappings of modernity to instill national pride among a people accustomed to lower-tier status.[49] Following the example of Japan and Korea, South Vietnam entered the automobile business with the introduction of Đà Lạt Motors and even developed a small but sustainable movie industry. The grandchildren of farmers flew planes and practiced medicine, while others studied overseas in Japan, France, and the United States. If the contributions of what W. E. B. Du Bois called the Talented Tenth could lift up the entire race, then South Vietnam's expanding educated class potentially foreshadowed a bright future. It was a long shot, but citizens anticipated another Korea and Taiwan success story in the making.

But that hope rarely extended beyond the Saigon elite, a fairly homogeneous bunch of 1954 northern exiles who lacked either the desire or the authorization to share power with Vietnam's other religious and political factions. Like his fellow Free Asia counterparts, Diệm preached democratic virtues while maintaining autocratic rule. Civil unrest inevitably ensued, and a popular uprising convinced the Saigon military and the U.S. Central Intelligence Agency that President Ngô Đình Diệm had to go. Following his November 1963 assassination, the people of South Vietnam endured years of uninterrupted political instability and mediocre leadership. More than $150 billion in economic and military aid produced rampant corruption and repression at the top, an economy overly dependent on American dollars, and a grinding civil war with the Soviet-backed northern regime that would have lasted far fewer than ten thousand days if not for the intervention of American troops. The campaign to win hearts and minds yielded mixed results, as indicated by public opinion surveys showing that a majority of South Vietnamese had no opinion of American intervention, while a significant minority viewed it as imperialistic.[50] Even Nguyễn Cao Kỳ and other elites saw Americans as doing little to discourage the perception that they, not Saigon, were running the country. "Americans selected or influenced the selection of our politicians and leaders, even at the village level, and had a natural tendency to pick the most compliant rather than the most gifted. American culture—its films, television, and advertising—swamped our own. Conscious of their dollar-bought superiority, the Americans patronized us at all levels. GIs thoughtlessly but hurtfully referred to [South] Vietnamese as Dinks and Gooks, Slants and Slopes. (Charlie, Chuck, and Claude were reserved for the Viet Cong.)"[51] The bourgeois cosmopolitanism taking shape in the cities left urbanites disconnected from the rest of the country yet still looked down upon by their American allies. Hồ Chí Minh's people used that imagery to their advantage, painting their southern neighbors as imperial puppets lacking an indigenous core. Magnificently disciplined, the communists rarely deviated from their script, insisting there was no civil war, only an anti-American, antiimperial conflict led by Hồ Chí Minh. They denied the Saigon regime any hint of legitimacy. Even on April 30, 1975, the day Saigon surrendered, North Vietnamese colonel Bùi Tín maintained, "Between Vietnamese there are no victors and no vanquished. Only the Americans have been beaten."[52]

A great many Western writers have debated the wisdom of U.S. involvement in Vietnam, and several anthologies have captured portraits of American guilt, but almost none have delved into the ominous sense of betrayal felt in South Vietnam after U.S. forces withdrew in 1973.[53] Regardless of how they felt about American intervention, locals knew that the war, depicted around the world as white people failing to win despite bombing the hell out of yellow people, would tilt overwhelmingly in favor of the communists when American troops and funding evaporated. But given the endless stream of Western propaganda declaring communism the greatest threat to humankind, a withdrawal of U.S. troops seemed sacrilegious and morally unconscionable. But that is precisely what happened when Richard Nixon assumed the presidency in 1969. His "Secret Plan" to end the war relied on a military withdrawal marketed as Vietnamization alongside a more flexible posture toward communist nations. Nixon's 1967 article in *Foreign Affairs* foreshadowed that shift by stating, "America cannot afford to leave China forever outside the family of nations."[54] In his first inaugural address two years later, Nixon affirmed that "after a period of confrontation, we are entering an era of negotiation."[55] As promised, his administration moved aggressively to normalize relations with the People's Republic of China. Within a few years, South Vietnam lost its strategic importance, and any veneer of a special relationship began to fade.

The United States did not acquit itself well as the war came to a close in 1975. In early April, the Voice of America (VOA) radio service, based on orders from senior officials in Washington, ceased broadcasting bad news from the battlefront to avoid "contribut[ing] to apprehensions amongst Vietnamese and Americans."[56] Americans had spent years detailing the horrors of communism only to keep their allies in the dark when doomsday neared. The VOA news blackout made little sense considering that no other news organization, including the BBC, was required to observe it. To say, as a former VOA employee did, that "it was not, to put it mildly, one of our better days," constituted quite an understatement.[57] Instead of a well-coordinated effort that could have saved more lives and kept families together, America's foot-dragging resulted in an ad hoc, haphazard mess in which 75 percent of the designated evacuees in Operation Frequent Wind left by U.S. transport on April 29 and 30 alone.[58] Military transports left Saigon's Tân Sơn Nhất Airport under the cover of darkness, allowing the U.S. and South Vietnamese governments to avoid extensive and embarrassing press coverage of the evacuation. An American correspondent noted how the crowds at the U.S. embassy "literally tried to storm the gates each time one was so much as cracked." From the embassy rooftop, overstuffed helicopters whisked away the last few thousand Vietnamese to safety as frantic crowds below drowned in a sea of despair. Inside the embassy, one diplomat described the grisly scene in terms usually reserved for crimes against humanity: "I hope the Lord spares me from ever seeing anything like this again. It is heartbreaking. It is seeing people naked—without any dignity left."[59] Whether just or not, these U.S. actions remind us how much disillusionment among the South Vietnamese refugee gratitude would have to silence in the name of rescue.

North Vietnamese tanks rumbled uncontested into Saigon on Wednesday, April 30, 1975, two years after the last American combat troops had withdrawn. Photos capture South Vietnamese people swarming through the streets, welcoming their "liberators" from the north. But who in a city of three million would have dared to resist? Hundreds of thousands of people had spent the past few days frantically scrambling to hustle their way onto the short list of Vietnamese to be evacuated by the United States. Recalled one person who was there, "We saw soldiers running for their lives, tearing off their uniforms, and begging for civilian clothes from anybody nearby. Without a military, we were helpless. It took only one unarmed North Vietnamese soldier to round up 500 of us college students. That is power."[60] In the midst of the final invasion and fearing for their lives, southerners had no choice but to feign allegiance to the new regime. Many in the international community naturally assumed that genuine Vietnamese national independence had finally arrived.[61]

Discussions of Vietnamese Americans often draw comparisons to Cuban exiles, and at first glance, the two groups have much in common: both fled communism, and, like most travelers throughout history, the earliest emigrants were among their nation's most privileged. Their entry into the United States was based far more on moral than legal obligations. But on closer evaluation, the first wave of Vietnamese refugees came in with far fewer advantages than the Cubans who fled their homeland after Fidel Castro ousted the Batista regime in 1959.[62] Gradually deteriorating U.S. relations with the Castro regime bought enough time for more than two hundred thousand Cubans to exit through legal and semilegal channels.[63] As a result, Cuban émigrés from 1959 to 1962 set new standards for selective exile migration. The white-collar workers who made up 22.9 percent of Cuba's population constituted an astonishing 68.1 percent of its pre-1963 exiles. In comparison, white-collar workers constituted 41.7 percent of the earliest Vietnamese refugees and 49.8 percent of the overall U.S. workforce in 1970.[64] Cuban lawyers and doctors could restart their careers after enrolling in government-subsidized refresher courses. And just as important, more than 90 percent of the early Cuban refugees could potentially pass on a white racial identity to their children—an asset the Vietnamese refugees lacked. In short, Cuban families were more likely than their Vietnamese counterparts to flee together, settle together, and mobilize a critical mass in Miami.

In contrast, the rushed nature of the Saigon evacuation meant the loss of so much economic capital that the older hierarchies could not be transplanted onto American soil. Family members struggled enough to stay together amid the chaos, and more than one-third of evacuees complained about the lack of food.[65] U.S. cargo ships conducting last-minute scouring of the South Vietnamese coast for evacuees wound up rescuing so many boat people—up to ten thousand per ship—that starvation, filth, and sickness became inevitable. The refugees who left Vietnam on C-130 cargo planes "were told to sit side by side on the floor like prisoners."[66] Individuals accustomed to multistory villas in Saigon might have "only mattresses, pieces of cardboard or blankets only" in refugee camps.[67] Just like the worthless South Vietnamese currency stashed in their pockets, all their military medals, college degrees, and artistic gifts were certain to lose their exchange value in the American job market.[68]

In a matter of hours, people went from being America's allies against communism to wretched, penniless, powerless, and nameless survivors. On the verge of losing their political selfhood to become little more than instinctual biological existence, the South Vietnamese refugees embodied Giorgio Agamben's concept of "naked life."[69] Until America's rescue mission delivered more, there would be few signs of refugee gratitude. What had begun as an apparent special relationship with the United States ended with a pragmatic resolution that left one partner stripped of honor and the other stripped of hope.

In 1975, those Vietnamese fortunate enough to make it out were more consumed by grief than gratitude. Among those evacuated was Phạm Duy, a popular folk musician who had made a fortune by composing and performing more than five hundred songs, including "Vietnam, Vietnam," the country's unofficial anthem. On April 28, 1975, Phạm Duy, his wife, and their two daughters were aboard a B-52 headed for the Philippines; his four sons and his fortune had been left behind.[70] Not surprisingly, no one on the plane was happy—everyone had said their good-bye to kin and country. Former restaurateur Nguyen Van Quon waited too long to put his house and business up for sale and left Saigon empty-handed: "I lost everything. Even three of my daughters who stayed behind to take a later plane"—which never showed up.[71] "Considering the size of the Soviet empire at the time," said one Saigon evacuee, "we assumed we would never see Vietnam again."[72]

Attempts to extract Vietnamese people from Saigon were initially wrapped in legalistic language. A war-weary American public was assured that Operation Babylift would spare the mixed-race children of American citizens from the ravages of communism. They were told that Operation Frequent Wind would bring to America those 130,000 individuals employed by the U.S. government or related to American citizens. But as the North Vietnamese Army drew near, moralistic concerns prevailed. For example, Richard Armitage, a former naval intelligence officer, was put in charge of destroying South Vietnamese military assets before the fall of Saigon but discovered that a flotilla of twenty-six ships was carrying as many as thirty-five thousand undocumented Indochinese.[73] Without consulting his superiors, he routed all ships to the Philippines, where the passengers eventually received asylum and entry into the United States. Armitage, a Republican, was not a member of the China Lobby, but his paternalism indicated that only a few degrees separated them. Years later, Armitage, still guilt-ridden, compared America's withdrawal from Vietnam to "getting a woman pregnant and then leaving town. It is not a beautiful or good image either but I thought that we acted like an irresponsible father."[74] America had started the Cold War in 1947 by promising, as a moral necessity, to keep its allies safe from communism. For the world's top superpower, nothing could match the embarrassment of losing to a less imposing but more determined foe despite dropping more bombs than in all previous wars combined. As the Vietnam War and the short-lived Saigon regime came to an end, refugee admission was framed as a way to uphold that promise of protection, albeit for a far smaller number of accidental allies.

2 From Grief to Gratitude

Reaffirming the Past by Rewriting It

> Nevertheless, as soon as we were saved—and most of us had to be saved several times—we started our new lives and tried to follow as closely as possible all the good advice our saviors passed on to us. We were told to forget; and we forgot quicker than anybody ever could imagine.
> —Hannah Arendt, "We Refugees" (1943)

From the moment they landed on American soil in 1975, the former South Vietnamese were expected to forget the past and assimilate as quickly as possible. That was the price of arrival under terms that a majority of the American public opposed. To placate the masses and ensure quicker assimilation, Operation New Life would disperse the 130,000 refugees from the four mainland camps—Camp Pendleton in California, Fort Chaffee in Arkansas, Eglin Air Force Base in Florida, and Fort Indiantown Gap in Pennsylvania—to every corner of the States.[1] Although this cohort of refugees featured many skilled and well-to-do Saigon families, politicians wanted no Vietnamese version of Miami's Little Havana. That would have spoiled the illusion that America had permanently extricated itself from Vietnam. Diaspora made for good politics but was a cruel punishment for these newly uprooted. They were denied a basic comfort known to most immigrants, that of an ethnic community in an otherwise strange land, but if they were good refugees, they would express nothing less than eternal gratitude for this most alienating of arrangements. From the perspective of camp administrators, Phạm Duy and family embodied these good refugees. Unlike some of his compatriots, who refused to leave the ethnic enclaves they had created in the refugee camps, the Woody Guthrie of Vietnam, though nearly penniless and already in his mid-fifties, eagerly departed when a suitable sponsor was found in less than two weeks' time. "The further from home the better," he wrote in his memoirs, hoping the solitude of Florida's panhandle would help bury the pain of losing his country and his four sons, who remained trapped there.[2] For those tens of thousands of Vietnamese refugees who lacked social and economic capital, a future punctuated by loneliness offered little to be grateful for.[3] They would have to learn how to become good, grateful refugees, to become Refugee American.

This chapter details the first steps on grieving refugees' path to gratitude. It also tells the story of America's perceived transformation from imperialist aggressor to humanitarian champion. The losers of the Vietnam War came to grips with a troubled past by rewriting it, this time via a postwar narrative of rescue and redemption, and by taking advantage of selective memory to forge a new collective memory. In so doing, both Americans and former South Vietnamese hoped to restore the Cold War narrative of Western savior and Eastern model minority that ten years of failed foreign policy had badly tarnished. Never before had the United States welcomed so warmly a large impromptu influx of Asian migrants. Their belonging in this country, like their claim to American protection in prior years, was framed as a matter of moral obligation rather than legal rights. Guilt-ridden resettlement authorities exposed refugees to a protective bubble of American charity and goodwill. This, combined with stories of American honor and compassion, sought to project a benevolent American essence. The chance to redeem the nation's soul galvanized a sizable coalition of liberals, who regretted going to war, and conservatives, who regretted giving up, to portray the postwar humanitarian efforts of the United States—as opposed to the war itself—as the act most representative of America's character.[4] Given their desperate situation and their overwhelmingly positive impressions of America, the new arrivals came to occupy the role of the good refugee, grateful and proud that such a noble and steadfast nation stood by their side during such hard times.

The politics of rescue highlights the role of gratitude as a form of social control.[5] The focus on rescue itself amounted to a narrative sleight of hand that provided an uplifting conclusion to the events of 1975. Temporarily liberated from an identity as a fallen empire, the United States could treat the war and postwar as unrelated events, with the failed Vietnam conflict reimagined and reclassified as an aberration in an otherwise just and robust American Cold War mission. That mission entailed saving the world from communism, a goal that the United States had furthered by rescuing 130,000 Southeast Asians in the spring of 1975. Good refugees, reminded constantly of their indebtedness to the United States, felt relentless pressure to repay their benefactors by committing to a life of acculturation and eternal praise. Perfection was the price of rescue. The politics of rescue eventually allowed the losers of the war to situate themselves on the right side of history but unfortunately left the refugees with little space in which to critique U.S. imperialism and racism.

Good Refugees and Bad Refugees

Any success the resettlement process recorded occurred despite the fact that, as a regional director of Catholic Charities admitted years later, "in 1975, none of us knew what we were doing."[6] There was nothing easy or inevitable about coaxing gratitude out of a diverse cohort in which middle-class status did not guarantee good refugee standing. The U.S. State Department's original list of 130,000 evacuees consisted most prominently of political and military leaders, members of the industrial elite, contract employees, and relatives of U.S. citizens. One writer described South Vietnam as a society "alienated from the roots of its own civilization by decades of dependence on the Americans," a judgment reflecting racial and class biases as to who counted as truly Vietnamese, truly a refugee, and truly worthy of rescue.[7] The first wave of refugees was considered "educated" even though only 16.7 percent of the adults had college degrees and more than 60 percent of the entire cohort spoke no English whatsoever.[8] In short, a cohort often labeled as elites in the Vietnamese context had nearly the same ratio of white-collar, blue-collar, service, and farm laborers as the American population as a whole.[9]

High government officials received unflattering coverage in the American press, where profiles in greed made it clear that Americans were better off not knowing what kind of allies justified $150 billion and fifty-eight thousand casualties. For example, former millionaires from a now defunct country "were still addressing each other as 'Mrs. Lieutenant General' or 'Mrs. Vice Chairman.'" One reporter in the camps noticed a pretty thirty-something Vietnamese woman wearing enough diamond jewelry "to cause a Tiffany clerk to swoon."[10] General Trang Sĩ Tấn, a clean-shaven man of atypical plumpness, was rarely seen without "his hair well-groomed and clothes immaculately pressed."[11] And South Vietnam's former prime minister, Nguyễn Cao Kỳ, a forty-something fighter pilot with a trademark Clark Gable moustache, boarded a U.S. Navy ship less than a week after announcing over Saigon radio that only "cowards" would flee with the Americans, while "those who love South Vietnam" would "stay and fight."[12] One former officer admitted that in the refugee camp, he was "living better than I ever did at home," at least materially, in a trailer complete with air-conditioning, a refrigerator, and a telephone.[13] Despite promises of equal treatment for all the refugees, the U.S. government expedited the processing of Saigon's millionaires and housed them in separate quarters, enabling them to avoid the wrath of their less privileged brethren. "If the top people show their faces here, there will really be trouble," exclaimed one member of the rank and file back in Guam. "The people here are very angry. They say it is because the generals were corrupt that we lost the war."[14] Based on these statements and assumptions, good refugee status had as much to do with attitude as it did with education. Bad refugees included the poor and indigent as well as some more privileged émigrés who shamelessly persisted in old habits the host society deemed unseemly among grateful refugees. From early on, the politics of rescue not only situated the losers of the war on the right side of history but also required the right kind of losers.

Resettlement for the elite often meant being reunited with relatives, old friends, or even their wartime employers.[15] Bilingual doctors, the ultimate good refugees, were in high demand, particular from small rural towns that needed physicians.[16] Most if not all of the sixty-six hundred refugees who left Camp Pendleton after the first week of May were physicians.[17] Those remaining in the mainland camps generally possessed far less human, social, and economic capital and were thus more attached to the ethnic community found in the camps. Their relative youth—more than 80 percent were under the age of thirty-five—made them good refugees as far as the labor market was concerned but bad refugees if they decided to have large families.[18]

Many of those who arrived in the United States had not been included on the select list of 130,000 people to be evacuated. For example, estimates showed that Catholics accounted for as much as 40 percent of the first wave of refugees, partly because thousands of rural fishing families had abandoned their homes at the last minute and had sailed out to sea with their large families. For example, 109-year-old Trần Thị Nam and fourteen of her family members left by motorboat from Phủ Quốc Island before being picked up by an American vessel.[19] During the spring of 1975, American ships transported as many as fifty thousand boat people to safety.[20] Despite the large size of Vietnamese families, approximately one-third of the first-wave arrivals were by themselves, demonstrating that many scheduled rendezvous never occurred.[21] Rather than deporting any undocumented individuals, President Gerald Ford, citing a "moral obligation to help these refugees who fled from the Communist takeover in Vietnam," granted parole to virtually all Indochinese in U.S. custody until the 130,000 figure was reached.[22] The ability to simply admit an entire class of people was typical of refugee admissions prior to the passage of the 1980 Refugee Act, but until enough sponsors stepped forward, the refugees would remain in military custody at one of four mainland bases. Yen Le Espiritu refers to this pathway to resettlement as "militarized refuge," but the politics of rescue encompassed both a militarized and Christianized component.[23]

Obstacles to Success

The politics of rescue had to overcome two additional obstacles: the dreadful conditions of camp life in the Pacific Islands and the bigger problem of American opposition to the new Vietnamese influx. The lack of any comprehensive legislation governing the admission of refugees meant that the first wave of Vietnamese refugees would follow the same militarized path Jewish and Hungarian refugees traveled decades earlier, allowing the Vietnamese to witness firsthand the reach of U.S. empire from Thailand and the Philippines to Wake Island, Guam, and Hawaii. Ironically, the branch of government most responsible for the decline in American prestige would be the first one tasked with restoring its humanitarian image.

One journalist somberly referred to the camps in the South Pacific military bases as "Ellis Island West . . . where refugees pay their dues, as if they had not paid enough already."[24] During May 1975, around 4,000 new refugees arrived daily on Guam, and by June, the head count had topped 40,000, or nearly half of the small island's civilian population of 105,000.[25] Thousands of refugees were diverted to nearby Wake Island. Nevertheless, a backlog of refugees remained in Thailand, the Philippines, and elsewhere. Lack of food was a major problem.[26] One refugee remembered going hungry after dropping her plate at the mess hall: "When I asked for another one, not only did I not get it, I was almost beaten. That was the most degrading thing for Vietnamese people."[27] One man who had spent nearly two hours waiting in a chow line that extended for nearly a quarter of a mile, exclaimed, "Son-of-a-bitch! If I had known that it would be like this I would not have gotten out of the country. It is just like being a beggar. What do you think when in a civilized world we are received like beggars?"[28] Morale dropped so low that the Guam camp newspaper published a front-page story promising much better living conditions in the United States.[29] But refugees spent an average of twenty-seven days on Guam before departing for the mainland bases; those on Wake Island were even less fortunate, with an average wait of forty-nine days.[30]

Unwilling to merely dump one hundred thousand foreigners onto American soil, the Ford administration set up an "Interagency Task Force" to recruit sponsors willing to make a "clear moral commitment" to "insure that refugees do not become public charges, and to help each refugee make the transition from refugee status to status as a self-sufficient member of his community."³¹ Prior to entering a Christianized sponsorship bubble, the refugees would be transferred to one of four mainland military bases. Camp Pendleton, a U.S. Marine Corps base nestled between Orange County to the north and San Diego County to the south, was the first and busiest of the mainland refugee camps. It took the marines less than a week to ready all the Quonset huts, tents, and other basic facilities in eight separate campsites to accommodate up to twenty thousand Southeast Asian refugees at any given time.

These mainland camps promised improved conditions compared to Guam and Wake Island, but what about the rest of American society? A Gallup Poll published in the May 19, 1975, issue of *Time* magazine revealed that "54% of Americans [were] opposed to admitting Vietnamese refugees to live in the United States and only 36% [were] in favor."³² The trauma of losing a long war in a faraway land combined with the worst economic crisis since the Great Depression convinced the masses that it was time to put Americans first.³³ In an ironic twist, the U.S. military, though providing only temporary accommodations, represented the first friendly face in an otherwise divided nation.

Not surprisingly, the communities surrounding the camps voiced the loudest opposition to the influx. Politicians received letters and calls from thousands of angry constituents, with some of the protests resorting to outright racist rhetoric.³⁴ In the Sunshine State, where officials at Eglin Air Force Base had erected 170 twelve-person tents to handle the new arrivals, residents of the ironically named Niceville collected signatures for an antirefugee petition. As the ultraconservative and often racist John Birch Society told the *New York Times*, "There's no telling what kind of diseases they'll be bringing with them."³⁵ One U.S. senator from Florida cited compassion fatigue in a state that had already received four hundred thousand Cuban exiles since 1959: "We feel like in Florida we did our part on refugees."³⁶ Antirefugee protesters in Arkansas held signs that read, "Only Ford Wants Them" and "Gooks Go Home." After reading about the protests, a nervous refugee on Guam asked an American reporter, "Do most Americans feel this way?"³⁷ With so much press attention devoted to antirefugee sentiment, about one-third of refugees questioned whether leaving Vietnam had been the right choice.³⁸ While the camps certainly could not be mistaken for a permanent home, refugees there at least had each other as well as Americans who seemed to care.

Even articles in the black press, while sympathetic to the plight of another nonwhite group, stuck to an "Americans first" theme.³⁹ National Urban League president Vernon Jordan critiqued the Ford administration for exercising fiscal conservatism regarding programs such as food stamps and GI benefits that helped African Americans but spending liberally—to the tune of half a billion dollars—to care for the Vietnamese refugees.[40] One University of California professor of black studies publicly chafed at the idea that African Americans must take the moral high ground on these issues only to see another wave of migrants adopt antiblack attitudes after becoming American.[41] Touching on this theme, comedian Richard Pryor imagined the army literally teaching the new arrivals "how to say 'nigger' so they can become good citizens."[42]

Proponents of the admission of Vietnamese refugees framed their arguments in moral rather than legal terms, hoping that this act of charity could give Americans a reason to be proud of their country once again. Looking past local concerns, many of these supporters invoked the theme of redemption for one's sins and implied that the world was watching in judgment. Liberals felt guilty for extending a war they knew to be unwinnable, while conservatives felt guilty for not doing more to stave off the communists. Their mutual guilt was driven by moral imperative of salvaging American exceptionalism, which was currently in critical condition.

Politicians of color, among them California's superintendent of public instruction, Wilson Riles, an African American, and Congressman Norm Mineta, a Japanese American who spent his teenage years in a World War II internment camp, felt strongly that racism fueled some of the antirefugee sentiment and made admission a civil rights issue. Mineta publicly shamed his congressional colleague, Burt Talcott of Monterey, after he complained that his mostly white district had "too many Orientals already."[43] Mexican American congressman Edward Roybal of Los Angeles put antiracist thought into action by introducing legislation to cover education costs for refugees over a three-year period.[44] The voters of Monterey did their part by replacing Talcott with civil rights ally Leon Panetta the following year.

Negative news coverage of antirefugee protests in the communities surrounding the camps shamed locals into putting on a more welcoming posture. Antirefugee protesters were nowhere in sight on May 1, 1975, when the first Vietnamese refugees arrived in Arkansas and heard a stirring rendition of the "Star Spangled Banner" by a local high school band and received a personal welcome from Governor David Pryor.[45] In Pennsylvania, Governor Milton Shapp of Pennsylvania and other state officials, representatives of the U.S. Army, about three hundred spectators, and a band playing the "Battle Hymn of the Republic" greeted the first 340 refugees sent to Fort Indiantown Gap. Local children carried signs reading, "May you have love and joy," and "Welcome to the land of immigrants."[46]

Welcoming parties greeted the new arrivals to California and Florida as well. These overt signs of American goodwill elicited an early sign of refugee gratitude from the same man who had so vehemently cursed the conditions at Guam: in Florida, by contrast, "everybody was courteous, generous, and willing to help the refugees."[47]

Camp Life

To the dismay of many officials but the delight of many inhabitants, drab military bases on the mainland became meaningful ethnic sanctuaries where some semblance of community could flourish. As one camp administrator put it, "They're secure. They're with their countrymen. They have access to shopping. They're getting their driver's licenses. They keep hiding out on you when you're trying to match them with a sponsor."[48] At the height of its capacity, Camp Pendleton provided all the basic services from recre-

Figure 2. Phuong Van Hai and Nguyen Thi Tuyet (front) and Nguyen The Hung and Nguyen Thi Kieu were among the dozens of couples who married at Camp Pendleton in 1975. Photo by Joe Kennedy, Copyright 1975, *Los Angeles Times*. Reprinted with Permission.

ation to education to religion, enabling refugees to forge some semblance of civil society. Between May and September 1975, more than eighty refugee couples exchanged wedding vows at Camp Pendleton alone.[49]

Before leaving the Florida refugee camp in early May, Phạm Duy noted the generally upbeat mood among his peers: "Many folks enjoyed their stay at Camp Eglin. I do not recall a time thousands of Vietnamese lived this close together with so much carefree indulgence. Everything from meals to medical care was provided free of charge."[50] One Pendleton refugee's summary of camp life as little more than eating, sleeping, bathing, and films reflected the abundance of free time.[51] Refugee life had taken a turn for the better, and postcamp life began to seem like a step backward.

Few outsiders realized that because most Vietnamese spoke little or no English, they could not afford to separate ethnic community from economic survival. In the camps, they had a daily newsletter published in both English and Vietnamese that kept them abreast of the news as well as helped them navigate the bureaucracy, the cultural barrier, and their emotions. The early departure of the more withdrawn, such as Phạm Duy; the homesick, who chose repatriation; and the privileged, such as Nguyễn Cao Kỳ, created a camp population of more uniform socioeconomic status. With no relatives in the United States, this segment of the first wave nurtured tight-knit bonds with kin and nonkin alike in the camps, a process similar to what sociologist Nazli Kibria has referred to as "patchwork." In her study of Vietnamese families in the Philadelphia area, Kibria noticed that few working-class households followed a conventional hierarchical nuclear or extended family structure; instead, they relied on the human capital and access to scarce resources each member brought to the household.[52] This model also applied to the improvised kin networks among the early exiles. In late July 1975, Camp Pendleton authorities discovered that "250 refugee children were living with people other than their parents."[53] Trần Quốc Sỹ, a former military officer in his late twenties who had been separated from his family, arrived at Camp Pendleton accompanied by an octogenarian he called "Ngoại" (Grandma) even though the two were not related. Unable to speak English or locate her married daughter in the United States, she had moved in with him when they were on Guam, and they kept each other company until Camp Pendleton authorities located her daughter in Mobile, Alabama. When she sought to express her gratitude, he replied, "Helping each other is what we do."[54]

But the politics of rescue complicates efforts to distinguish between authenticity and performativity. American guilt and Vietnamese gratitude encompassed both real emotions and scripted roles. Caught in a rescue narrative that had saved their lives, the former South Vietnamese felt obligated constantly to praise their American benefactors. The same held true for those who spurned rescue. Many evacuees who subsequently changed their minds and sought repatriation issued statements akin to loyalty oaths in hopes of securing a warm welcome from the Vietnamese communists. For example, Lê Minh Tân, a military man whose entire family was still in Vietnam, was part of a group that threatened a hunger strike if they were not returned to their native land.[55] When pressed about the dangers of going back, one military officer answered, "I'm afraid [of the Việt-Cộng], but I cannot live here without my children, my family."[56] "I am very confident that the new regime will consider my situation," stated a Vietnamese air force sergeant, "because I had no desire to leave my country—it was just an accident."[57] These desperate men convinced themselves that they could pass for good enough revolutionaries by distancing themselves from America. Further attempts to sound revolutionary led to a heated exchange and to two arrests when would-be repatriates at Fort Chaffee praised the communist regime in front of their compatriots in June 1975.[58] At Camp Pendleton, several Vietnamese Americans, mostly exchange students who had arrived during the war, pressed the refugees to request repatriation rather than endure further exploitation at the hands of the Americans. The earlier arrivals passed out copies of a local procommunist tabloid, *Thái Bình*, whose May 1975 issue claimed that the United States had in fact kidnapped the 130,000 to create the impression of a humanitarian crisis in postwar Vietnam.[59] After months of waiting, the *Thương Tín 1* finally set sail for Vietnam on October 16, 1975, with 1,546 repatriates on board.[60]

Under official policy, refugees could not leave the camps until an employer or family agreed to provide sponsorship, meaning not just a job but also a surrogate family to help the acculturation process. Americans took out advertisements in the camp newsletters offering employment opportunities that would enable refugees to obtain sponsorship and thus leave the camp. One Californian offered $150 per month for a single female live-in "housekeeper child companion," while an Alabaman sought a family of between eight and eleven members to help with farm and garment work.[61] Recalled one Pendleton refugee, "People were contemplating a future milking cows, picking oranges, cutting grass, or washing dishes in a restaurant."[62] Some sponsors such as chicken processors or fishing companies offered to hire hundreds of Vietnamese at a time, circumstances that appealed to large refugee families that sought to stay together.[63] However, in such cases, sponsorships amounted to little more than jobs and lacked the kind of refugee support services that had been envisioned. Moreover, some of these arrangements placed the émigrés in difficult circumstances. In October 1975, for example, twenty-four refugees were found living at an abandoned Fresno airbase, where, in conditions "not fit for anybody," they cooked and cleaned while eighty-six other Vietnamese received training as security guards.[64] Two months earlier, a large Ventura County egg ranch had hired dozens of Vietnamese refugees as strikebreakers.[65] With a December 31, 1975, deadline to close the camps, 40 percent of refugees were allowed to leave the camps without securing sponsors, and most members of the first wave Vietnamese ultimately resettled in California; Texas; Washington, D.C.; and locations near the original mainland camps.[66]

Even refugees who found sponsors who were genuinely interested in helping sometimes questioned whether fleeing Vietnam had been a wise choice. If refugees associated communism with oppression, then freedom became synonymous with depression. Sociologist Peter I. Rose has observed that loneliness is an "ever-present companion" of the uprooted.[67] After leaving camp, one isolated Vietnamese woman tallied more than one thousand dollars in long distance phone calls.[68] After resettling in Connecticut, Tran Ly Le sent a poem that appeared in the Pennsylvania camp he had left months earlier:

> Vĩnh biệt Indiantown với nỗi sầu đầy
> Ngày chia tay em đã nói rất nhẹ
> "Indiantown, đừng quên em nghe!"
> Và em đã gắng như long "Đừng khóc
> Nhưng sao nỗi xúc động dâng tràn
> Và nước mắt em buồn vẫn nhỏ lã chã.
>
> [I left Indiantown, full of sorrow.
> When my friends waved to me I softly said:
> "Indiantown, do not forget me."
> And I consoled myself not to weep,
> But why, am I so moved that my tears
> Continued to run over my cheeks.][69]

Refugee poetry printed in camp newsletters frequently touched on themes of loneliness and grief. The first published refugee poem, "My Country and Me," appeared in the Camp Eglin newsletter, written by an author "born amid cries of exiles" who found himself weeping for his lost homeland.[70] When the Camp Pendleton newspaper held a poetry competition, it received forty-nine submissions from more than a dozen authors. The winner, Nguyen Tuyet Ngan's thirty-two-line "Plight of the Refugees," merged the migrants from 1954 and 1975 into a single imagined community whose members depended on each other in the absence of intact households:

> Twenty years have passed
> Since we fled to the South
> After so many years of hard work
> We began to feel secure.
>
> We were enjoying our togetherness
> When they drove us apart
> By shelling the Tan Son Nhat air base
> And shooting at our ships on sea.
>
> How many families were split up
> Some remained behind, some got away
> From now on husbands are separated from wives
> And fathers from sons.[71]

Camp poetry connected the dots of an emerging collective memory among the refugees. They had seen their families and communities torn apart multiple times and now found themselves a racial minority in a country that had not historically been hospitable to Asians. The U.S. government had inadvertently nurtured a decent existence inside the camps, where ethnic community and economic survival went hand in hand, only to undermine the possibility of both outside the camps. Given the terror associated with relocation, the government had yet to give fearful refugees something for which to be truly grateful.

The Newsletters and Sponsor Success Stories

Because fewer than 15 percent of refugees were proficient in English, the camp newsletters often constituted the refugees' only published source of information about the world outside the camps and thus had the power to shape public opinion by recasting the United States as a humanitarian nation acting in everyone's best interests.[72] The camp newsletters could serve practical purposes such as providing news about post-1975 Saigon or helping reunite family members spread across the States. However, the newsletters' primary purpose was to encourage assimilation and gratitude by reassuring the evacuees that America would not fail the South Vietnamese this time. Nervous Vietnamese émigrés would more easily buy into a rescue narrative if constantly bombarded with positive representations of a savior nation that merited assimilation. Rather than seeking refugees' forgiveness for failing them, America imposed a moral obligation on these recipients of exceptional kindness to assimilate as swiftly and eagerly as possible—that is, to become Refugee American.

The earliest articles portrayed the American people teeming with jubilant paternalism as they welcomed the Vietnamese refugees. A letter from two private citizens assured Camp Pendleton refugees that millions of Americans "will lend a helping hand" to the "much wanted" Vietnamese.[73] Another letter from Muncie, Indiana, insisted that although the antirefugee protests were "always more newsworthy than mere acceptance," they did not reflect the more tolerant views of the "Silent Majority."[74] Despite mangling a few Vietnamese expressions, San Diego mayor Pete Wilson (later a xenophobic governor of California) extended his city's "warmest wishes and greetings" to the new arrivals, citing their "courage and strength" as "an example for all our children."[75] Such postwar views testified to the severity of America's failure during the war itself.

During the first few weeks in May 1975, the Interagency Task Force's special toll-free phone number was inundated with calls from nearly twenty thousand potential sponsors.[76] The authorities did their best to screen out "people obviously looking for cheap household help or from elderly gentlemen looking for one girl."[77] The job of resettling refugees would have to be outsourced to voluntary agencies such as the International Rescue Committee. In the end, faith-based organizations found sponsors for almost 75 percent of the refugee caseload that year.[78] As one such organization observed, "The church structure guaranteed a kind of built-in conscience which would guard against mistreatment."[79] The U.S. Catholic Conference sponsored more than fifty thousand refugees, while the American Lutheran Church exceeded its goal of sponsoring ten thousand refugees.[80] Los Angeles minister Lester Kim did his part to ensure that Asian Americans would be among those to welcome their "sisters and brothers from Southeast Asia."[81] With their ability and willingness to provide for refugee welfare by screening sponsors, finding jobs, donating clothes and housewares, and providing free English classes, church organizations reinforced the moral basis of Vietnamese belonging in America and quickly became a magnet for the new Southeast Asian arrivals regardless of their previous religious affiliations.[82]

Southern California churches' ability to absorb so many refugees allowed more families to stay intact, a harbinger of future community building.[83] According to Alice Cooper, who worked for the International Rescue Committee at Camp Pendleton, Orange County's Catholic and Episcopalian churches were particularly welcoming: "It was nothing for a church in Orange County to take twelve or thirteen families." St. Anselm's in Garden Grove reportedly "never said no" to any of the refugees. "It did not matter if there were two people in that family or twenty people in that family," said Cooper. "If you called Father Habibi and said, 'I have this family, Father, and I have to get them out of here by five o'clock tonight or there's to be serious trouble,' he would say, 'OK.'"[84] Because of generous churches and California's desirable climate, on October 31, 1975, Camp Pendleton's refugee center was one of the first to close its doors even though it had received more than 40 percent of the first-wave refugees.

Prior anticommunist refugees felt a kinship with the Indochinese and aided them in becoming Refugee American. The director of Catholic Charities in Los Angeles reported, "I even have Cuban and Hungarian families who were resettled through our office who want to assist."[85] Indeed, the Los Angeles Cuban Chamber of Commerce visited Camp Pendleton to donate clothing, toys, and medicine: "We welcome you to this country, and you can count on the Cubans, because we ran from Communists, too," said the group's spokesperson.[86] In June, a Vietnamese family of seven moved into a three-bedroom house in Chino courtesy of five Cuban families and the Catholic Welfare Bureau.[87]

Officials responsible for publishing the camp newspapers knew that the best way to allay refugee fears and encourage gratitude toward the United States was by publishing "sponsor success" stories and other testimonials from contented comrades. The publications rarely mentioned and never criticized U.S. intervention in Vietnam outside of the last-minute 1975 mass evacuation. The newsletters thus verged on propaganda.

Letters to President Ford and Governor Shapp published in the Fort Indiantown Gap newsletter conveyed some of the first signs of refugee gratitude, which might assuage American guilt: "All Americans we have contacted: Military or civilian, men or women, old or young, have been kind toward us and assisted heartily. That is why most of our suffering and worries have been soothed. They have been for us a source of consolation and have made us believe that we had been right in leaving in Vietnam all our precious things in order to seek for freedom."[88] The Camp Pendleton newsletter published a lengthy letter of appreciation to the "very open minded and warmhearted people of America" who have given the refugees "hope for a wonderful new life." U.S. military personnel projected "an image of peace and human acceptance when they play with our children with heart and smile, and we smile also," despite their loss, "because this country gives us hope again, hope for a wonderful new life, we arrive at May 75 to enjoy a second 'Mayflower period.'"⁸⁹ If the Vietnamese were exposed to countless testimonials from happy refugees, how could they possibly make further demands? Aware of the opposition to their presence, the refugees could not afford to criticize the United States lest they risk being lumped with America's communist adversaries.

The Camp Eglin newsletter ran a profile of Triêu Anh Tuấn, a former U.S. Embassy employee and landowner looking forward to working at his sponsor's construction firm. "I lost everything in Vietnam—my farm, tractor, house in Saigon—but I have my liberty," he said. "Liberty is expensive, but it is good for me. Here we can sing when we want and complain when we want. I would like to leave [the refugee camp] as soon as possible so I can work with my sponsor. I hope to buy a farm of my own some day and raise cattle and hogs."⁹⁰ Vũ Việt Dương, another new arrival at Eglin, almost lost a fight with pneumonia until American military doctors and nurses intervened, earning his immense gratitude: "I hope that my children and grandchildren will become good Americans and amongst them there will be doctors to help other people. It is my only wish."⁹¹ A former Arkansas refugee shared with the camp her wonderful resettlement experience: "We must write to you and let you know that you had done a very perfect job. We also want to build up an idea on the sponsorships in our refugee's mind, so they will not feel perplexity or be afraid of the rumors which are absolutely unfounded, that we heard when we were at Fort Chaffee before."⁹² Requests by some male refugees to show their gratitude (and earn a respectable income) by joining the U.S. armed forces received prominent coverage in the camp newsletters.⁹³ The staff of the Pennsylvania camp newsletter told émigrés that "becoming self-sufficient and established in America as soon as possible" would be the best way to repay the kindness of sponsors.⁹⁴ These published testimonials paint a picture of a United States that had done no wrong during the Vietnam War and urge refugees to assume their proper place in the rescue narrative by assimilating without haste.

Postcamp pro-America propaganda was most needed at Fort Chaffee, where 20 percent of sponsorship offers were rejected. As of October 11, 1975, 12,569 of the 48,499 refugees admitted to the Arkansas camp since May continued living on-site.⁹⁵ The remaining refugees were often rural fishing families not on the official evacuation list. They had arrived with the smallest amounts of social and economic capital and were the most likely to depend on patchwork kinship after landing in an impoverished region of the United States known for its hostility to nonwhite people. One extended family at Fort Chaffee thus claimed eighty-nine members, making resettlement as a unit nearly impossible.⁹⁶ American authorities mistakenly assumed that separating families would expedite economic adaptation and referred to this refusal to leave as "camp-itis." Camp-itis got so bad that assimilationist good refugees implored their compatriots to have faith in the American Dream, urging, "Let's not forget the future."⁹⁷ But the bad refugees had already glimpsed an appealing future in the camps, which the press had begun to call Little Saigons.

The Sponsorship Bubble

Phạm Duy described postcamp life as his journey into the "real America," but the profiles of sponsor families represented a very distinct slice of the nation.⁹⁸ In the Florida panhandle, where Phạm Duy's family of six sojourned in the three-bedroom home of retired U.S. Army pilot Jon Carle, they quickly learned that conservatives were more likely to support the Vietnam War. Their benefactor had spent a good portion of his military career piloting the personal aircraft of General William Westmoreland, commander of the U.S. forces in Vietnam from 1964 to 1968.⁹⁹ Phạm's family and other refugees learned that many sponsoring families had a personal investment in the war effort and were haunted by the guilt of having left their erstwhile allies to fend for themselves.

Ben and Ellen Matthews considered themselves "typical of the 1975 sponsors," with Ben, who ran a Maryland construction company, offering his refugee charge an entry-level job. A conservative whose tour of duty in Vietnam brought him face to face with people he considered "the most passive . . . but also the most basically *nice*," Ben took more of an interest in sponsorship than did his liberal wife, Ellen, to whom he admitted, "You *do* feel guilty leaving them stranded like that. You feel you've got to take the responsibility." They contacted their congressional representative, who put them in touch with Catholic Charities. The experience brought out Ben's liberal side, as he extended the benefit of the doubt to almost every bit of bad refugee behavior, while Ellen expressed relief when the people they sponsored realized that "in America, they themselves, not outside benefactors, would power their lives."¹⁰⁰

Profound guilt and moral obligation fueled semifeudal bonds between paternal sponsors and their adopted refugees. In Southern California, M. B. Uchida, a Vietnam War veteran of Japanese descent, sponsored a family whose patriarch found a job at a Hollywood hotel that later became the first Vietnamese American nightclub.¹⁰¹ Some families hired refugees far less qualified than their coworkers, further reinforcing the sponsor's role as a surrogate parent. With his family's housing and food costs covered by sponsors, Phạm Duy could afford a used Volkswagen.[102] His family reciprocated by referring to the Carles as their American parents. Guilt most likely explains why a Baltimore man rented out his three-bedroom apartment to a refugee family that paid only $135 per month and helped to maintain the property.[103] An American family in Valparaiso, Florida, sold their one-year-old car to their refugee family for just one dollar.[104] Guilt-ridden sponsoring families in Pennsylvania reportedly assisted refugees with paying rent and buying clothing and color televisions as well as with finding jobs and arranging transportation. The recipients of such overwhelming charity clearly understood that they would benefit from showing gratitude toward the United States. Without the guilt that weighed on America's conscience, such kind treatment would be much less forthcoming. The general sense of atonement that accompanied the admission of the Vietnamese to America created a level of intimacy between sponsor and refugee that in many cases resulted in years-long relationships.

Churches of course hoped to convert refugees to Christianity, and Vietnamese families often gratefully complied, adopting the religion of their sponsors or naming their children after saints. "Our sponsors were Lutheran and we did not want to disappoint them after all they did for us," recalled Thomas Nguyễn, who arrived as a teenager. A church in Topeka, Kansas, helped the members of Nguyễn's family find jobs and housing and alerted them to a bigger Vietnamese presence at a sister church 160 miles away in Wichita.[105] In the absence of a critical mass of refugees and economic mobility, the first signs of postcamp community among members of the first wave emerged in existing spaces such as churches, college campuses, and the streets of Chinatown.

But even many months of generous sponsorship often proved inadequate to enable Vietnamese refugees to achieve economic self-sufficiency, as would have held true for any isolated group. Mainstream America, too obsessed with the trajectory of individual assimilation, had not yet caught on to the link between ethnic community and economic survival. Despite their willingness to learn English, the refugees yearned for a community fluent in their native tongue where they could not only express themselves more fully but also benefit from gossip, advice, and counsel not accessible via the formal political economy. Refugees had already used this ethnic social capital to squeeze more resources from their sponsors. One of the better known strategies was appealing to Christian charity. As Ellen Matthews noted,

"The refugees are handled by so many religious groups, sponsored by so many churches, that they think we will be spurred into action by the merest religious reference."[106] Sponsors stressed the short-term nature of charity but neglected to acknowledge how personal favors constitute an important long-term component of any informal economy. Such connections, even when legally questionable, were essential to Vietnamese American survival, given that refugee wages were 37 percent below the national average in 1976.[107] Even when Vietnamese families had multiple wage earners, the median family income remained 32 percent below the national average in 1980, and 34 percent—three times the national average—lived below the poverty line.[108] The fact that approximately 30 percent of refugees in 1976 and nearly 35 percent the following year received public assistance (about four times the national average) resulted in sensational headlines.[109] Press coverage of potential welfare dependency reflected a tendency to portray the South Vietnamese as a perpetual drag on the American people's patience, as a paternalistic project gone awry.[110]

The urge for ethnic community would remove refugees from the protective bubble provided by their sponsors, who constituted the slice of America most sympathetic to their plight. Leaving behind sponsors could feel almost like abandoning family, a prospect that tore at Vietnamese American consciences. Without a welcoming American environment worth assimilating into, ethnic community would potentially be defined by distrust of the greater society instead of gratitude toward it. Refugees would feel less enthusiastic about assimilating if they considered English the language of their oppressors. Traditional Vietnamese culture prized the family that stayed close together, but nothing about refugee life was traditional. Like everyday Americans, émigrés yearned to carve out lives of their own despite the fact that most Americans felt no strong moral obligation toward the Vietnamese. Under these conditions, assimilation made sense as a form of protection against an otherwise hostile world.

Major newspapers compared the Vietnamese and the Cubans, painting the reputed economic success of the latter as a best-case scenario for the former.[111] But replicating that success was difficult in the absence of the structural advantages—such as the Spanish language, Catholicism, whiteness, government benefits, and the existence of a large Miami ethnic community—available to Cuban Americans. The successful but unreflective Cuban entrepreneur might insist that the Vietnamese simply needed to work hard "to be like Cubans and avoid becoming parasites," but those outside the business sector knew better than to individualize the issue.[112] A senior staffer for the Cuban Refugee Program acknowledged the benefits of ethnic community to the mental and economic well-being of Cuban Americans since the formation of Little Havana in the early 1960s, lamenting "I think there will be no 'Little Saigon' in America."[113]

Access to Chinatowns at least enabled Vietnamese refugees to enjoy familiar foods. Refugees at Camp Pendleton missed fish sauce, a condiment widely used in Asian cooking but virtually unavailable in the United States outside of urban Chinatowns; base staff often trekked into Los Angeles to procure the sauce and give the refugees a taste of home.[114] Multilingual and business-savvy Vietnamese of Chinese descent could open up markets catering to speakers of Cantonese, Vietnamese, and English. Mỹ-Bình's family, which resettled near West Point, New York, occasionally traveled the two hours to New York City and brought back fish sauce and other Asian foods.[115] Sino-Vietnamese in Chicago's Chinatown found a niche catering to Cantonese- and Vietnamese-speaking clients who came from as far as three hours away in Peoria.[116]

Orange County's twelve thousand Vietnamese frequently made the hour-long trip to Los Angeles's Chinatown, which offered not only fish sauce and other goodies but also opportunities to reunite with old friends or find fellow Vietnamese. According to future politician Tony Lâm, "We either met each other in Chinatown or we called every Vietnamese name in the phone book."[117] In this safe, pseudo-familiar space, Vietnamese Americans could immerse themselves in a community capable of appreciating the spirited nature of the lunar new year, an occasion most Americans at the time associated with the tragic Tết Offensive of 1968.

The process of turning Vietnamese émigrés into good refugees committed to assimilation thus required constructing an America worth assimilating into. Refugee gratitude emerged in response to a rescue operation capable of undoing the calamitous damage that twenty-five years of failed foreign policy had done to American exceptionalism. Casting refugee admission as a tale of redemption for America also required the active participation of refugees swayed by experience, peer pressure, and propaganda. Refugee gratitude reversed some of the signs of naked life and helped both sides overcome the shame of losing the Vietnam War. Although identification with the United States could have dire consequences for relatives back home, refugees proudly embraced their America with a level of enthusiasm many of those born in the United States lacked at the time. The process was abetted by the fact that sponsors comprised the slice of America most sympathetic to the refugees' plight and thus most willing to make material and emotional sacrifices for their benefit. This sponsorship bubble nurtured paternal bonds between sponsor and refugee, ensuring that a dispersed population would belong to some form of community. Conversely, it required accepting rescue on the protector's terms. As camp newsletters and mainstream media suggested, refugees could best repay their debt by leaving the past behind and assimilating immediately into American society. Owing their lives to American benevolence, they also had little moral or political cover to overtly criticize the United States. Conversely, Americans supportive of refugee admissions had their faith in American exceptionalism restored with little contradiction and instead could point proudly to their nation's enduring status as a beacon for the world. Rarely had the fate of foreigners been so intimately linked to American exceptionalism. Americans thought they had achieved a small postwar victory that represented a morally uplifting end to an otherwise tragic war, while the exiled Vietnamese came to see belonging in terms of moral obligations rather than legal rights. That semifeudal bond continued to define Refugee American identity in the years ahead.

3 "Farewell, Saigon, I Promise I Will Return"

Social Work and the Meaning of Exile

> It was only until 1977 that I achieved a certain degree of emotional balance and started to face my conscience with the question: Is there any meaning to this forsaking of my homeland? I answered with my first song as an exile, "Did We Fight or Did We Flee?"
> —Phạm Duy, folk musician in exile

> For us the Vietnam War is over. Like it or not, we lost that war. But while there, we sold many of its people a way of life, an attitude. And now they are the losers and we face a moral dilemma. Out there is the Statue of Liberty with its inscription, *Give me your tired, your poor, your huddled masses, yearning to breathe free*. It says nothing about Category 1, 2, 3, or Category 4.
> —Ed Bradley, CBS Reports, *The Boat People*, 1979

In the summer of 1977, Phạm Duy suddenly reversed course on his pledge to steer clear of Vietnamese people in the United States. Embodying good refugees committed to assimilation, the fifty-six-year-old folk musician and his family had spent the past two years in Fort Walton Beach, Florida, saving enough income from nostalgic concerts and guitar instruction books to afford a used car and a small place of their own. But only a few months after buying the house, this family of four, like thousands of their coethnics, migrated to southern California, where the largest overseas Vietnamese community was taking shape.[1] Phạm Duy, whose career as the voice of a nation had come to an end with the fall of Saigon, had discovered a new transnational audience eager to learn the meaning of exilic ethnicity beyond just gratitude to the United States. Eager for reinvention, he joined a literal movement of former South Vietnamese that redefined refugees—once little more than the losers of the war—as the new heroes of the postwar. Though trained as a musician, Phạm Duy became a social worker of sorts, as did others who longed to make meaning out of exile. In less than five years, good refugees were no longer just assimilationists in America. They were exiles of a lost nation, casting themselves on the right side of Vietnamese history.

Not too long after the United States had finished resettling more than one hundred thousand Indochinese refugees, more than four hundred thousand others poured out of communist Southeast Asia and sought asylum in neighboring noncommunist countries. Known as the boat people, the members of this wave of refugees were far less urbanized, educated, and Christian than those who left in 1975.[2] Some were ethnic Chinese, a group treated as outsiders once their adopted nation went to war with their ancestral home. Some hailed from Cambodia and Laos rather than from Vietnam. For the most part, these were precisely the people the communists had promised to liberate, but those who survived the dangerous journey by sea reported widespread human rights abuses in Vietnam. The plight of Saigon's upper crust suddenly appeared much more representative of the fate of the Vietnamese people as a whole.

Vietnam's post-1975 history has always been a contentious one, with pro- and anticommunist camps distrusting each other's sources and stories. The first wave of Vietnamese refugees brought to American shores, especially those who worked for the Saigon and U.S. government, had reason to fear communist reprisals, but their testimony, lacking much in firsthand knowledge, bordered on hearsay and hyperbole. The subsequent exodus of hundreds of thousands of other people without the aid of American warships told a different story. Because they had lived under communism and had firsthand experience with censorship, new economic zones, and reeducation camps, their stories conveyed a complexity and realism missing from both pro- and anticommunist propaganda. That so many braved the South China Sea, despite the fact that they were nearly as likely to die as to escape, spoke volumes about the society they could no longer tolerate.

This chapter examines how refugee history, so often lost within official histories that depict émigrés as either disaffected losers of a civil war or grateful recipients of some nation's kindness, experiences that rare moment when—to paraphrase Nhi Lieu—the exile becomes the authentic.[3] For all their gratitude and hard work, the first wave of refugees, with their worldwide reputation as out-of-touch elites collaborating with imperialist America, garnered little sympathy beyond U.S. shores. They pondered the meaning of exile, mildly confident that loneliness in America was preferable to persecution in Vietnam yet unable to escape their identity as abject failures now suffering from survivors' guilt. The enormity of the subsequent boat people crisis cast survival in a new light. Stories of oppression and escape that seemed singularly harrowing in other contexts proved quite typical for the Vietnamese. Vilification of the communists provided vindication for fellow escapees, enabling once-disgraced exiles closely allied to the once-disgraced United States suddenly to claim ethnic authenticity with little hint of irony. Mainstream media coverage of the boat people crisis turned even opponents of U.S. military aggression into critics of the Hanoi regime.

Efforts to internationalize the rescue of the boat people had to address both humanitarian and political considerations. Refugee status could not reverse the outcome of the war, but worldwide concern for the boat people could prompt many in the Western world to critically reassess the revolutionary intentions of its victors. The United States parlayed the crisis into an opportunity to use soft power to undo much of the damage to its moral credibility that hard power had wrought, mainly by offering asylum to more than ten thousand boat people per month. The postwar refugees themselves enjoyed far greater social standing as exiled victims of an oppressive regime than they ever had during the war itself.

This transformation of refugees from losers to heroes was most visible in Southern California, where even before the emergence of Little Saigon early communities nurtured the formation and development of an exile collective identity through what I consider social work.[4] Instead of providing traditional social services such as formal counseling and access to basic economic resources, these social workers operated in fields such as the refugee press and popular music. The refugee press interpellated readers as concerned citizens continuing the fight against communism by other means, while songs put refugees' social history to music from a variety of perspectives, including those of refugees in America and of loved ones in Vietnam. Việt Dzũng and other musicians rose to fame by writing ballads about the boat people, earning the admiration of the diaspora and the full wrath of the communists. This music reflected the defiant tone of the boat people exodus, enabling Vietnamese finally to speak freely about life under communism, a process of vindication through vilification.[5] In refugee lore, the boat people came to approximate latter-day Holocaust survivors, offering compelling testimony that brought the world to tears and to action.[6] Given that refugee popular culture made its way back home via the Voice of America and BBC radio, future boat people learned to identify as refugees in the cultural sense before their journey at sea made them refugees in the legal sense.[7] Even in America, exiles were imagined as the most authentic ethnics because the fissures generated by the Cold War in general and the Vietnam War in particular ensured that, for twenty years, Little Saigon's inhabitants would be characterized as anticommunist refugees. As refugees, the former South Vietnamese achieved a level of credibility and moral authority that was never available to them during the war and found themselves held in a position of high regard that the global community did not accord them either before or since.

Early Civil Society

Unlike immigrant transnational communities, refugees could not rely on their country of origin in navigating strange new lands. Just like the mainland camps themselves, the first signs of an ethnic community took shape in preexisting spaces such as churches, college campuses, and the streets of Chinatown. In these spaces, refugees encountered individuals far more charitable and welcoming than the American population as a whole. Even outside the orbit of their sponsors, the politics of rescue kept Vietnamese Americans within an insulated bubble of hospitality. Conditioned to express nothing but gratitude for every American intervention, from war to resettlement to a place of their own, refugees living outside that charitable bubble kept their disappointment to themselves. Consequently, Little Saigon's formation was wrapped in a discourse and history of American goodwill.

Vietnamese Catholics had a relatively easy time getting along in preexisting spaces. The legacy of Western imperialism ensured that Christians would be recognized early on as good refugees worthy of rescue. Orange County's Vietnamese Catholic community included three thousand parishioners, and approximately two hundred of them attended their first postcamp Vietnamese mass in October 1975 at the auxiliary hall of St. Boniface Church in Anaheim. From the onset, diocese officials organized mixers for the refugees, who "cherished every opportunity to see each other."[8] Carpooling from as far as Norwalk and El Monte, often with the help of diocese volunteers, the Vietnamese soon convinced Monsignor John C. Keenan to grant them the nine o'clock time slot every Sunday morning at St. Catherine's Military School. Only one priest, Father Vũ Tuấn Tú, initially served the Vietnamese community, but by the end of 1977, in the wake of secondary migration from colder parts of the United States, the Diocese of Orange had three Vietnamese priests leading prayer at five different parishes.[9] Attendance at Sunday Mass St. Barbara's in Santa Ana routinely exceeded the church's twelve-hundred-seat capacity despite the 6:30 a.m. start time. The concentration of Vietnamese Catholic services in Orange County provided space to worship God and build community and consequently drew refugees, especially the elderly and poor, to the region.[10]

Public colleges also proved essential to early community formation. Unlike the mainstream population, the Vietnamese American college population consisted of adults in their twenties and thirties, and their socioeconomic status led them almost exclusively to local public schools. Gayle Morrison, a counselor at Santa Ana College in the 1970s, took a particular interest in the new influx of Southeast Asian students, serving as their liaison to the outside world. Although she had no background in Vietnamese, Morrison cofounded the New Horizons program and advised the Vietnamese Student Association. With her assistance, the association staged one of the first refugee Tết lunar new year festivals at Santa Ana College on February 7, 1978.[11] Aware that her students could not get far without financial assistance, she petitioned the federal government to grant fee waivers so that hundreds of Vietnamese community college students in Southern California could take the Test of English as a Foreign Language exam and then transfer to four-year colleges.[12] New Horizons also published a list of forty-five subsidized child-care centers in Orange County to assist Vietnamese parents in obtaining a college education.[13]

Though campuses were generally welcoming spaces, South Vietnamese perspectives were often marginalized or demonized in the classroom. A homesick Northern Virginia Community College student "went to a movie showing once [in 1976], hoping to see how life was going in Vietnam, but the film was heavy with [Vietnamese communist] propaganda and was very boring."[14] Vietnamese students enrolled in a Vietnam War class at the University of California at Berkeley felt betrayed by the professor's willingness to judge the South Vietnamese so harshly while refusing to criticize North Vietnam.[15] But rather than defend Saigon officials, campus organizations staged political protests, letting it be known that the triumph of communism did not reflect the popular will.[16] For three weeks in 1977, dozens gathered at California State University at Fullerton, where the activists voiced opposition to the screening of films such as *Vietnam in the Year of the Cat*, a documentary about the "liberation" of South Vietnam. On one occasion, twenty-four protesters had to be handcuffed. The man responsible for bringing in these films, Professor Edward Cooperman, added fuel to the fire by describing the protesters as ex-Saigon military, a scathing euphemism for right-wing anticommunist extremists who deserved to lose the war.[17] Refusing to remain silent, the protesters sought "to make it clear to the American people that the Vietnamese refugees fled their native land for political reasons, not economic reasons as the Communists falsely claimed."[18] For their evidence, they relied on newspaper reports, letters from home, and, most important for a people who think of their culture as poetic, the newly composed songs of the diaspora.

Vietnamese Music

Permanently cut off from their country of origin, the Vietnamese refugees initially treated music like any other cherished fragment of nostalgia, such as photographs or family heirlooms. Refugee sponsors such as Ellen Matthews, for all their generosity and compassion, struggled to comprehend the totality of refugee needs. Thinking of survival only in economic terms, Matthews wondered why the family she sponsored had left Saigon with only clothing, music, and a photo album: "They cannot have seen their situation as I do, to bring records instead of survival items," she later wrote.[19] Matthews did not realize that most first-wave refugees had less than forty-eight hours to gather their belongings and head out to the airport.[20] Under those circumstances, human nature often leads people to think first about irreplaceable sentimental items rather than such practical items as cash. Celebrated folksinger Phạm Duy, for example, grabbed only twenty U.S. dollars but stuffed an entire suitcase with music albums, photographs, and other keepsakes.[21] By the time the Vietnamese reached the mainland refugee camps, cassette tapes of pre-1975 favorites had become a cottage industry. Recalled musician Việt Dzũng, a teenager at the time, "The only business that was thriving in the camp was making copies of tapes for five dollars apiece, which was a lot of money at the time. You could make a fortune overnight because everyone was asking you to do it, up to the point the tape was so worn out, where it did not sound original anymore, but people still wanted it—all kinds of music at that time . . . whatever they could get their hands on."[22]

The two major genres of popular music in pre-1975 Saigon were wartime narratives about love and family, particularly the promises soldiers make to return home, and the antiwar songs of Trịnh Công Sơn.[23] References to the Saigon regime and deference to the military found their way into many songs, but the distinguishing characteristic of most South Vietnamese popular music was its unmistakably sentimental aesthetic, which bordered on the melancholic.[24] Among the most famous of those songs was 1969's "Xuân Này Con Không Về" [I Will Not Be Home for New Year's], a song composed on behalf of troops forced to remain on duty for the Tết lunar new year to prevent a repeat of 1968's infamous Tết Offensive. The song's theme of empty seats at holiday gatherings, along with its incredibly mournful vocal delivery, resonated with exiles:

> Nếu con không về chắc mẹ buồn lắm,
> Mái tranh nghèo không người sửa sang
> Khu vườn thiếu hoa vàng mừng xuân
>
> [If I do not return, mom will be in tears
> Who will fix the roof, neglected for years
> Who will tend to the blossoms this coming spring]

When Saigon fell to the North Vietnamese, the communists banned all South Vietnamese propaganda along with symbols of bourgeois decadence such as beauty pageants, modern dresses, and love songs.[25] The communists also did their part to emasculate South Vietnamese music, giving it the subtly effeminate label *nhạc vàng* (literally "yellow music") along with the blatantly effeminate label *ủy mị* (weak, effeminate, sentimental). This move naturalized the outcome of the Vietnam War as a triumph of native masculinity, exemplified in revolutionary songs such as "Liberating the South," with its strident prowar lyrics and crunching rhythms.

> Giải phóng miền Nam chúng ta cùng quyết tiến bước.
> Diệt đế quốc Mỹ, phá tan bè lũ bán nước.
>
> [We march onward to liberate the South
> Eliminate the American imperialists, destroy the traitorous hordes.][26]

No one knew the excesses of postrevolutionary society better than the hundreds of thousands of military men and intellectuals imprisoned in the post-1975 camps in remote Vietnamese jungles. After long days of forced manual labor, these South Vietnamese political prisoners endured nightly indoctrination sessions designed to "reeducate" them in the history of Vietnam from the communist perspective. If they did not die from starvation, disease, or landmines, these "students" could return home when they had demonstrated their allegiance to communist doctrine.[27] When high school teacher Nguyễn Ngọc Ngạn asked his jailers why love songs were deemed antirevolutionary, he was told, "We communists respect love. But it has to be the right kind of love—real love. We respect the love of the Party, the love of Hồ Chí Minh, the love of the Revolution. These are the proper and acceptable objects of love. The emotion of which you speak [between people] is the basest and most selfish corruption of love: a vile, shallow indulgence of the bourgeoisie."[28] At the time, most of these details were unknown to the outside world.

Getting in Touch

The communist victory in 1975 put an end to America's diplomatic ties with South Vietnam, imposing what refugees described as a nearly impenetrable Bamboo Curtain between them and their home country. Personal letters provided the most meaningful as well as most frustrating mode of communication because updates arrived so infrequently. Unable to send direct mail through the U.S. Postal Service, refugees had to discover alternative means of correspondence. Mỹ-Bình, a young mother of three with family members in Vietnam—including her husband, who spent nearly two decades in a reeducation camp—sent letters to her uncle in France, who forwarded the mail to Vietnam using an alias to avoid further endangering family members. An entire year passed before Mỹ-Bình finally heard back from her mother in Saigon.[29] Phạm Duy's overall mood took a turn for the better in November 1975, when he finally heard from his sons five months after writing to them.[30] Nevertheless, nearly all letters from Vietnam featured bad news—lost jobs, incarceration, death—and pleas for money or medicine. Phạm Duy sent remittances to his children through a college student all the way in Long Beach, California, whose father back in Vietnam converted the money into gold that would pay for multiple attempts by Phạm's sons to be smuggled out the country by boat.[31]

Regardless of their anticommunism and their precarious finances, refugees almost universally sent remittances.[32] In 1978, the U.S. government legalized remittances of up to twelve hundred dollars per person to Vietnam and two thousand dollars to Cuba.[33] Almost overnight, an entire industry sprang to life. In Southern California, businesses such as Laser Express, Vinamedic, Vietimex, Overseas Vina Air Service, and T&D Express International sent money, food, and medicine to Vietnam through Canada, France, and other countries. T&D charged the lowest rate, $2.17 per pound, which exceeded the federal minimum hourly wage at the time, $2.10. To buy drugs for family in Vietnam, some low-income refugees in California abused their Medi-Cal health care benefits.[34] Most refugees worked multiple jobs so that they could help relatives in Vietnam: "I only planned on working one year and going back to school," said a young social worker, Nam Lộc Nguyễn. "But at the time I started hearing from my family, so I had to work two jobs. All I wanted was to have money to send."[35]

Hollywood Nights

Nam Lộc Nguyễn, a thirty-year-old from Saigon, fled Vietnam on one of the final transports out of the country but soon discovered that none of his relatives had made it out. Though dejected, he made himself useful inside and outside the camps. His knowledge of English enabled him to translate songs into Vietnamese, earning Nam Lộc, a musician from a Buddhist background, a position with Catholic Charities in Los Angeles. By the end of 1975, approximately twenty thousand Vietnamese refugees had resettled in Southern California. Although 60 percent had made their way to Orange County because of its proximity to Camp Pendleton, its abundance of altruistic Christian sponsors, and the availability of affordable housing (Garden Grove's Villa Park complex housed seven hundred refugees, for example), no centralized Vietnamese ethnic enclave existed outside the camps.[36] Although thinking about the past rekindled traumas of war and exile, most émigrés did not have the luxury of forgetting about Vietnam, and these emergent community formations helped to alleviate their heartache by attaching more positive connotations to their present condition. As Nam Lộc explained, "Every weekend, people from Orange County drove to Chinatown or Hollywood. That was their treat . . . after a hardworking week, go to Chinatown, go to Hollywood. There was a Vietnamese nightclub and Vietnamese restaurants on Hollywood Boulevard."[37] Consequently, the first video concert series released by Vietnamese Americans in the late 1980s was *Hollywood Nights*.[38] Hollywood Boulevard thus became a nighttime destination for Southern California's first-wave Vietnamese.

Through a combination of luck and goodwill, Vietnamese Americans transformed Hollywood's aging Roosevelt Hotel into what a frequent guest called "the most significant cultural hangout for Vietnamese from late 1975 to 1976."[39] Busboy Hồ Xuân Mai became the Roosevelt's pianist, while fellow Camp Pendleton alumni formed the New Life band. Most weekends, the Cinegrill lounge became a Saigon-style nightclub specializing in the upbeat tunes popular among urban youth.[40] In November 1975, Nam Lộc, now a regular at the Roosevelt, brought the audience to tears with an original composition, "Farewell, Saigon," a title that simultaneously referenced the spatial distance between the refugees and Vietnam and the social distance between the émigrés and the place the communists had renamed Hồ Chí Minh City.⁴¹ Nam Lộc had penned the song during one of his many sleepless nights in his Inglewood apartment. Like Phạm Duy, he knew the pain of exile but refused to stay silent.

> Sài gòn ơi, tôi xin hứa rằng tôi trở về
> Người tình ơi, anh xin giữ trọn mãi lời thề
> Dù thời gian, có là một thoáng đam mê
> Phố phường vạn ánh sao đêm
> Nhưng tôi vẫn không Bảo giờ quên.
>
> [Oh Saigon, I will be back, I promise
> My lover, I will keep my word always
> Although here love begins at night
> The city lights are bright
> But you still are on my mind.]⁴²

The final stanza acknowledged the ambivalence present in the refugee condition. With little idea if they would ever again see the loved ones left behind in Vietnam, many refugees agonized about whether leaving their country had been the right choice. Even band members could not hold back their emotions. As Nam Lộc performed the song, pianist Hồ Xuân Mai reflected on his last day in Saigon: "I wanted to let more of my people on that military plane, but the Americans refused to let anyone get out once we were boarded."⁴³ Surprised by the show of tears, Nam Lộc thought to himself, "Wait a minute. This isn't just my story, my feeling, but everyone's."⁴⁴

No one was better qualified than Nam Lộc to write the first refugee ballad. As a traditional social worker at Catholic Charities, he had access to hundreds of stories about nostalgia, alienation, estrangement, and melancholy; as a musician, he could engage in social work by translating postcamp affect into poetry for his people. "Farewell, Saigon" addressed the question of how to maintain a Vietnamese identity despite the likelihood of permanent exile, giving rise to what a writer in the mainland refugee camps called "a fellowship of countrymen away from their homes."⁴⁵ Resettlement officials feared that the company of fellow refugees would only rekindle painful memories, but such was not always the case in Southern California. Having found a space they could call home, Nam Lộc and others put structures of feeling to music, giving rise to an exilic collective memory punctuated by a vow to return and reclaim the lost homeland, no matter the cost. A powerful enough narrative for refugees, exile even permeated the lives of immigrants such as the Irish, who found it more empowering to describe their migration as involuntary.⁴⁶

"Farewell, Saigon" and other songs performed much-needed social work on this side of the Pacific by giving voice to emotions that refugees felt reluctant to express, while listeners back in South Vietnam gravitated to the way the tunes gave voice to memories and emotions they were not allowed to express. "Farewell, Saigon," held a special place in the heart of one man who remained in Vietnam until 1991: "How can one forget a day like April 30, 1975? Once we knew the war was lost, we all cried."[47] Residents of what was now known as Hồ Chí Minh City felt a greater social distance than ever from the Vietnam they once knew: recalled musician Ngô Thụy Miên, "There was no communication whatsoever between us and the outside world save a once or twice a day, we listened to, in clandestine settings of course, the Voice of America (VOA) or BBC to catch a few comments or a few old songs here and there to soothe our soul."[48] And therein lay the infrastructure for a transnational circuit of communication.

These foreign radio services of course engaged in propaganda, but the stations also engaged in social work by communicating the whereabouts and well-being of the diaspora back to the homeland and reassuring listeners that they had not been forgotten. The Voice of America began cultivating a transnational Vietnamese community as early as the 1960s, when native-language broadcasts based in Washington aired throughout Vietnam. Behind the microphone was a young Georgetown University graduate, Lê Văn, a native of Hanoi whose background made him one of the few people qualified at that time to translate into Vietnamese programs such as *The Story of Jazz*, *Freedom of Intellect*, and *Music from America and Vietnam*.[49] More than 80 percent of South Vietnam's population listened to radio, and the VOA hoped a good chunk of them would appreciate three hours of daily Vietnamese-language programming devoted to American culture and society.[50]

However, the South Vietnamese preferred the BBC, which was perceived as offering better world news, commentary, and overall objectivity. One listener recalled tuning into "the BBC broadcasts two times daily exactly at 6 a.m. and 9 p.m." for definitive reports from the theater.[51] The VOA's lower ratings reflected the fact that in 1966, only 42 percent of Saigon's population had a favorable opinion of the United States, and the number was even lower among educated people.[52] That distrust was validated during the final month of the war. For years the U.S. government had warned of a communist bloodbath, but as defeat drew near, American officials inexplicably tried to keep the South Vietnamese in the dark.

Under the post-1975 government, radio stations such as VTVN and ARVN ceased to exist, leaving a gigantic information vacuum that only foreign stations like VOA and BBC could fill. The criminalization of noncommunist culture meant that people had to listen in secret and pass along news in coded mnemonic phrases such as, "Did you hear what *Vinh's **O**ld **A**unt* [Vợ Ông Anh] said last night?" or "Do you know what the *Babe **B**artering **C**lothes* [Bà Bán Cam] told me?" A 1987 survey of 262 former boat people revealed that more than 70 percent listened to the two stations despite the state ban. As one listener noted, "The local people were getting bored with domestic news that continually repeated the same propaganda. However, we were all deeply interested in the VOA and BBC broadcasts three times daily."[53] When Vietnam invaded Cambodia in 1978, the foreign broadcasters provided a much-needed alternative to state media denials of the conflict. Strictly censored Vietnamese state media explains why radio listeners also looked forward to any news about the diaspora, Vietnamese music, and news about the United States, three programming priorities that the VOA was now very well equipped to meet.

Intentionally or not, the VOA played a large part in constructing a transnational imagined community whose metropolises included Santa Ana and San Jose, California; Houston, Texas; New Orleans, Louisiana; and Falls Church, Virginia. Just as Monterey Park became a common reference point among Chinese throughout the world, so too did Ca-li, San-ta A-na, and Te-xat—as the Vietnamese transliterated American place-names—become extensions of the diasporic imagination. Familiarity with the United States reached the point that in 1984 a man from the West Coast testified to a U.S. Senate panel that he used a money transfer service in Texas based on the recommendation of his wife, who had never set foot outside of Vietnam.[54]

The radio stories regarding the diaspora bordered on the melancholic, leaving little doubt that refugees had not forgotten their roots and their brethren. Such accounts sounded nothing like the class enemies the Hanoi government exhorted its people to hate. As stories of Vietnamese taking to the open sea to seek asylum reached critical mass in the late 1970s, the VOA could persuasively define the diaspora as a new phenomenon, implying that centuries of war, struggle, and foreign domination could not scare so many to risk their lives on a journey that many would not survive. While many of the first-wave refugees struggled to deal with their loneliness, VOA listeners on the other side saw an opportunity to be reunited with family and friends and saw refugee status, based on the magnitude of the exodus before them and the new songs they heard, as the real majority. Once the VOA received approval for a Saturday evening music program in 1976, representatives flew to Southern California to investigate the grassroots culture taking shape.[55]

The area featured an emerging public sphere connected in large part by the refugee press.[56] In March 1976, one of the first refugee newspapers, *Trắng*

Đen (The Truth), hit newsstands in Vietnamese markets and restaurants across the country, including such far-flung locales as Kansas City's Saigon Market and Minneapolis's Oriental Foods. The refugee version of the old Saigon newspaper, now based in Southern California, described itself as the "Voice of the Noncommunist People" and brought news from Vietnam, the Vietnamese refugee diaspora, general U.S. news, and contributions from unpaid guest writers. In the absence of a large local ethnic economy, Trắng Đen's business model depended mostly on six thousand subscribers scattered across the United States. The newspaper's editor acknowledged early on that "fifty-two cents out of every dollar goes to postage and taxes alone" and that "without volunteers, this paper would never have gotten off the ground."[57]

The first weekly edition published a refugee song written from the point of view of a wife left behind in Vietnam, articles about resistance in Vietnam to communist rule, reports of community activities across the United States, ads from people seeking to reconnect with friends and family, and entertainment in the form of cartoons and essays. An article on "Super Refugee" told the story of a forty-six-year-old man who resettled in Brooklyn in 1975 but secretly returned to Vietnam a year later to rescue his wife and children.[58]

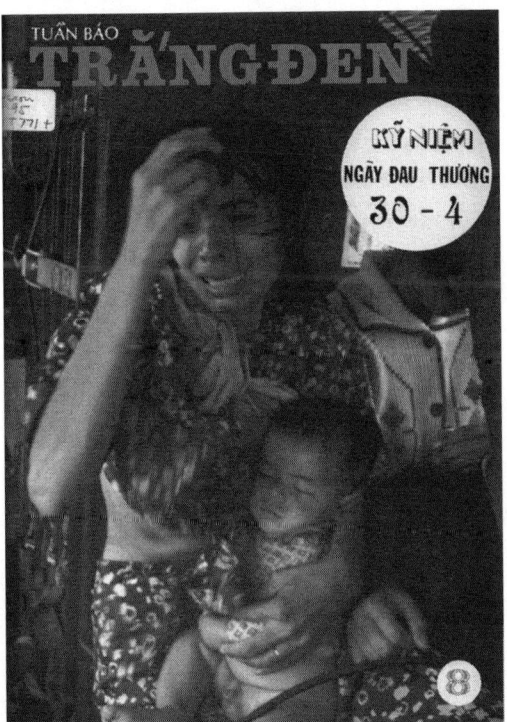

Figure 3. Trắng Đen [The Truth], a Vietnamese American magazine, depicted refugees as the central figures in Vietnamese history.

The editorial tone was clear: conditions in communist-ruled Vietnam were as bad as or even worse than the first-wave migrants had feared, and something needed to be done. The uncertain prospect of reuniting families motivated Vietnamese Americans to collective action, and *Trắng Đen* and other newspapers furnished the instructions. The paper printed a form letter that readers (presumably males whose wives and children remained in Saigon) could send to the International Red Cross: "I find myself hard to live farther without my beloved [wife] and children here. But I do not know how to have them here because the government of VN does not let them leave, and I cannot afford to pay for their travel tickets supposing they are permitted to, either." Readers were told that convincing their sponsors—American citizens—to join in the letter-writing campaign could lead to "better results."[59] *Trắng Đen* also instructed readers how to directly petition the U.S. State Department to negotiate an agreement to bring the relatives of Vietnamese Americans over to the United States.[60] Without bilateral relations between Hanoi and Washington, families were unlikely to be reunified through legal immigration procedures. Almost no one anticipated that the people of South Vietnam would take matters into their own hands. The exodus of the late 1970s and early 1980s constituted the second wave of Vietnamese refugee migration. Their firsthand testimony of life under communism confirmed what many in the West suspected.

The Boat People Crisis

As the Associated Press aptly observed in 1977, "Vietnamese who dislike Communism cannot escape it by skipping across the border, because opposite Vietnam's borders are China, Laos and Cambodia, all Communist. So they leave by sea."[61] Despite the conditions the boat people were fleeing, other countries often responded to them with hostility or indifference, a reminder of the blurry line separating political refugees, who are exempt from deportation, from illegal immigrants, who are its prime targets. Assuming that these claims to refugee status were legitimate, many people had little choice but "to sail from one unwelcome port to another," as the *Los Angeles Times* put it.[62] The plight of the boat people first garnered mainstream media attention in early 1976, when the government of Thailand threatened to deport more than one hundred thousand undocumented Indochinese, a flow by land and sea that had begun after the fall of Saigon and was continuing nearly a year later.[63] In another incident that received press coverage in the United States, eight men sailed from the southern coastal town of Vũng Tàu on December 15, 1976, only to be denied entry to Malaysia, Singapore, Indonesia, and

Singapore again before their boat finally broke down on the way to Thailand. Four of the men drowned; the other four were jailed by Thai authorities.[64] A front-page headline in the *Los Angeles Times* in late 1976 describing the murders of one hundred boat people off the coast of Cambodia, read, "Viet Refugees Butchered."[65] Vietnam's neighbors tried their best to avoid pointing fingers at Hanoi while addressing the question of what conditions could compel people to brave the South China Sea in old fishing boats.

Denying asylum or refugee status had less to do with ideology and more to do with the pragmatic fact that none of these countries could afford unilaterally to take a stand against its communist neighbors. Fearing reprisals from Hanoi, the Japanese government strongly discouraged defector Nguyễn Công Hoan from holding a press conference detailing the horrors of post-1975 Vietnam until the former antiwar official secured a visa to the United States.[66] The former member of the Vietnamese National Assembly subsequently testified before the U.S. Congress about the hundreds of jailings and killings that had occurred since the end of the war.[67] "I escaped from Vietnam to tell the truth about what is happening in my country," he later wrote in *Newsweek*. "Vietnamese listen attentively to the Voice of America and the BBC. The cause of human rights comes up very often in conversations. Where hope is a rare commodity, the news that the world is watching, and cares, provides moral sustenance."[68] In 1977, U.S. House of Representatives hearings on human rights in Vietnam established that dissatisfaction with the new regime extended far beyond members of the old regime and the Christian minority.[69] The United States, which had cut off formal diplomatic and economic ties with the unified Vietnamese government, had greater incentive to holding its wartime enemies responsible for this humanitarian crisis. Testimonials by the second wave of refugees from Vietnam bolstered the claim, however problematic, that the boat people crisis was the inevitable result of Communist Party rule.

Word of the second wave dominated the pages of the refugee press, but *Trắng Đen* engaged in the most social work. As a service to its readers, the paper published the names of camp arrivals. In September 1976, *Trắng Đen* sent checks for two hundred dollars to refugees in Malaysia and three hundred dollars to camps in Thailand and the Philippines.[70] By month's end, the paper sent another two thousand dollars to help the refugees to a Roman Catholic priest, Thomas Đỗ Thanh Hà, himself a boat person who had fled from Saigon to Thailand in April 1976 to avoid imprisonment.[71]

Vietnamese émigrés in the United States, the paper reported, had written letters urging Congress to admit the new refugees.[72] The State Department replied in January 1977 that "the only way large numbers of Indochinese refugees will be able to reach America will be through normal immigration when those already here change their status to resident alien or citizen and can petition for preferential visas for their relatives."[73] Touched by stories of their fellow Vietnamese waiting in limbo, readers wrote to *Trắng Đen* volunteering to sponsor families.[74] In the absence of a comprehensive plan of action, the United States admitted only one hundred Vietnamese per month in 1977—a tiny fraction of the eighty thousand displaced Indochinese in makeshift refugee camps in Thailand alone.[75] By the fall, just as the United Nations was urging the rescue of boat people at sea who might be in distress, Washington had created a new program to admit fifteen thousand people.[76] It would not be the last such program.

Vietnamese Americans worked actively on behalf of the boat people, staging protests at which people held signs that read, "Sending the Refugees Back Is Murder" and "Please Do Not Send Vietnamese Refugees Back to Vietnam," urging America not to turn its back on an old ally in need. Hundreds of demonstrators at a time congregated on the streets of downtown Los Angeles. City councilman Art Snyder, who represented a majority-Latino district, spoke at an August 19, 1978, demonstration near City Hall that was also covered by the VOA and BBC Radio. Fourteen Vietnamese refugees in Santa Ana participated in a hunger strike to protest human rights violations in Vietnam, hundreds of others in front of the White House. At these protests, Yến Đỗ distributed copies of his newspaper, *Người Việt Daily News*. Originally published in San Diego on a shoestring budget, *Người Việt* [The Vietnamese People] initially survived with the support of a network of friends and volunteers. After spending two years as a traditional social worker in Texas, Yến Đỗ founded *Người Việt* on the principle of social work: "To help resettle and educate the newcomers and to continue the collective memory of our group of refugees."[77] Consequently, he filled the pages of *Người Việt Daily News* with articles on "how to get jobs, how to apply for welfare, how to apply for a driver's license, even how to buy insurance."[78] He also utilized an extensive web of sources—from material already published in the mainstream press to letters from Vietnam "that arrived through France or Hong Kong"—to keep his viewers informed about the homeland and the boat people crisis.[79]

The boat people exodus also created a new social type, that of loved ones in Vietnam glued to their radios for updated reports from the camps, a daily drama captured in a song, "Người Ở Lại Quê Hương" [Those Who Remain in the Homeland], heard often on the VOA. Nguyệt Ánh's metatextual wife-as-social-type listens to the VOA "behind closed doors" [lén nghe] for news about the "countless thousands" [Hàng vạn người dân] who "have crossed the ocean" [ra đi], only to discover that their loved ones had not survived the journey to the "Promised Land / Where freedom awaits" [Thiên / Đường tìm về Tự Do].[80]

The Vietnamese who remained in their homeland had an insatiable appetite for this and others songs by Vietnamese Americans. Unbeknownst to Vietnamese communist officials, the VOA established a post office box in Hong Kong where listeners could send feedback on the station's programming, which was then forwarded to Washington. The VOA received numerous requests to play traditional South Vietnamese music as well as American rock and roll.[81]

Dissident musicians who remained in Vietnam quickly realized that the VOA provided one of the best modes of sharing their work with others in the country, provided they could first smuggle the music out. One of the first songs that reached the diaspora, "Anh Giải Phóng Tôi Hay Tôi Giải Phóng Anh?" [Who Liberated Whom?], argued that the newly discovered upward economic mobility North Vietnamese cadres enjoyed came at the expense of the "liberated" South Vietnamese dispossessed of their homes and banished to new economic zones or reeducation camps. The song's composer, Nhật Ngân, was expecting that fate and thus had a friend, singer Ngọc Minh, memorize the lyrics prior to escaping by boat. Two years later, the song made its way back into Vietnam via the VOA, with singer Ngọc Minh telling her listeners that the unidentified composer still lived in Vietnam.[82] Even people incarcerated in reeducation camps stayed in the loop by using their Sundays off "to discuss secretly . . . the news from the VOA and BBC brought in by visiting relatives."[83]

Convincing the world that the Indochinese boat people deserved refugee status still presented a challenge. Southeast Asian countries generally sought to avoid recognizing the boat people as legitimate refugees not only for fear of angering a neighboring government but also because under international law, doing so would require them to accept all new arrivals. The Hanoi government, in the midst of tensions with China and the United States, declared the boat people part of a "vast anti-Vietnamese campaign launched throughout the world by the mass media of Peking and the West in a well-orchestrated manner."[84] By manufacturing mass panic and mass exodus, Hanoi contended, the United States could defeat North Vietnam on the terrain of human rights, using the spectacle of drowning boat people as their prop. In a July 17, 1981, cover story, the *Far Eastern Economic Review*, a weekly public affairs magazine based in Hong Kong, cited "a growing conviction among diplomats and relief workers" that refugees are "drawn by the siren song of the easy life on foreign shores, a song broadcast daily by Voice of America and the BBC."[85] While the Western powers indeed reaped the political benefits of the boat people crisis at minimal cost and the boat people may have been a little too optimistic about their chances of receiving asylum, that does not mean that the boat people did not fit the universally recognized criteria for refugees: people whose "race, religion, nationality, membership in a particular social group or political opinion" makes them the object of persecution and thus forces them to seek asylum elsewhere. That objective consumed a young Roman Catholic musician, Việt Dzũng, whose first composition, "Một Chút Quà Cho Quê Hương" [A Gift for the Motherland] (1978), painstakingly documented the suffering in post-1975 South Vietnam. Though living in Missouri, the nineteen-year-old son of a politician engaged in his own social work, alleviating through song the suffering of his people. "At that time," he recalled, "everybody over here is going to work and saving money, sending it to Vietnam. A lot of people were telling stories about Vietnam at that time. It is a very dark, very bleak period. So I just listened to their stories and put it to music."[86]

> Con gởi về cho cha một manh áo trắng
> Cha mặc một lần khi ra pháp trường phơi thây
> Gởi về Việt Nam nước mắt đong đầy
> Mơ ước một ngày quê tôi sẽ thanh bình
>
> [To my father, I send one white dress shirt
> For him to wear on the day of his execution
> For Vietnam, I send all my tears
> In hope that one day, there will be peace.]

Each verse talked of the material things—from candy to sleeping pills—that émigrés could send back to Vietnam to ease, even temporarily, the suffering of family and friends. Việt Dzũng included lyrics about refugee Americans sending their wedding rings, which would pay for unauthorized passage out of the country. One smuggler in Saigon, which was not located on the coast and thus presented additional challenges, charged twenty-five ounces of gold per person for this service in 1977.[87]

Facing accusations from U.S. politicians and Vietnamese officials that the VOA was "recruiting" refugees into the United States, Lê Văn argued that would-be refugees interpreted VOA news as they saw fit. "If I said the weather would be clear and sunny for the next few days," he recalled, "somebody might think it is a good time to go."[88] In fact, VOA and BBC announcements, such as Jimmy Carter's decision to pick up any refugee boats in the South China Sea, merely "encouraged" those already determined to escape "to think that their chances of reaching safety were enhanced"—but that certainly did not equate to any sort of guarantee.[89] A Buddhist monk who escaped Vietnam in 1978 recalled how the VOA broadcast of Carter's statement on human rights provided a "new gem of hope" for the Vietnamese people.[90] When the U.S. Committee for Refugees interviewed hundreds of boat people in 1983, "almost all indicated that they knew from Voice of America broadcasts or other sources that pirate attacks should be expected. They also knew it was possible, if they landed in Thailand, that they would be interned for a period of years." Despite the dangers, only one of those interviewees, a woman whose daughter had been raped and abducted, regretted embarking on the journey.[91] Testimony from the boat people made it clear that songs like Việt Dzũng's "Tha Chết Trên Biển Đông" [Better to Die at Sea] were not mere hyperbole. Regardless of whether such claims proved true, Southeast Asian nations were unfairly bearing the burden of someone else's Cold War. The United States clearly needed to do more about the boat people crisis than just gloat.

America Reacts

The first major turning point in American public opinion came in December 1976, when outspoken antiwar activists such as singer Joan Baez, American Civil Liberties Union founder Roger Baldwin, and beat poet Allen Ginsberg publicly campaigned against the "grievous and systematic violations of human rights" taking place in Vietnam.[92] Their appeal suggested that American humanitarian intervention and refugee gratitude had the potential to restore people's shattered faith in American exceptionalism by rewriting post-1975 as an opportunity for a nation to redeem its soul. In early 1978, a coalition led by Leo Cherne of the International Rescue Committee urged the U.S. government to "adopt a coherent and generous policy for the admission of Indochinese refugees over the long range."[93] Their vision came closer to reality in Congress as restrictionists Joshua Eilberg and James Eastland lost their positions as committee chairs at the end of the year. Succeeding them on the House Immigration Subcommittee and Senate Judiciary Committee, respectively, were the far more immigrant-friendly Representative Elizabeth Holtzman of New York and Senator Ted Kennedy of Massachusetts. Furthermore, President Carter's State Department bore little resemblance to the antirefugee and anti-Semitic bureaucrats serving under Franklin Roosevelt. Given these huge shifts among social liberals and antiwar activists, the Indochinese boat people were benefiting not just from the machinations of calculating Cold Warriors but also from social movements toward inclusivity that culminated in progressive legislation on civil rights, immigration, and now refugees.

With stakes so high, organized labor and African Americans, the two Democratic Party groups most vulnerable to an influx of cheap labor, spoke passionately in support of asylum for the four thousand people leaving Vietnam each month during 1978. The AFL-CIO, the largest and most powerful union, rebuffed fears that a refugee influx would negatively affect the already tight labor market. In early 1978, the AFL-CIO called on the president "to work with other countries, using both example and persuasion, to guarantee all these refugees a home."[94]

In another statement, eighty-nine leaders of the black community—among them Bayard Rustin, Ralph Abernathy, A. Philip Randolph, Jesse Jackson, Vernon Jordan, and Coretta Scott King—flatly rejected any suggestion of deporting "our brothers and sisters in the refugee camps" back to Vietnam, a policy that would "result in almost certain death." Instead they called on the U.S. government "to facilitate the entrance of these refugees into the United States" because African Americans' "continuing struggle for economic and political freedom is inextricably linked to the struggle of Indochinese refugees who seek freedom."[95]

At the peak of the exodus in 1979, when departures exceeded ten thousand per month, U.S. television viewers witnessed CBS News correspondent Ed Bradley, an African American, rescuing Vietnamese boat people off the coast of Malaysia. His report described the South Vietnamese as "the people we left behind but cannot escape," and his concluding words strongly suggested that the United States had a moral obligation to open the golden door for all the boat people. According to the Federal Indochinese Resettlement Task Force, of the nearly 300,000 refugees resettled between 1975 and 1978, 52 percent called the United States their new home, and America remained the preferred destination of the boat people.[96]

In early 1979, America's monthly entry quota stood at seven thousand refugees, a figure achieved by way of executive action. By June, as thousands of demonstrators, including Baez, gathered in Washington to demand action, President Carter preemptively doubled the quota. When the United Nations High Commissioner on Refugees invited international leaders to Geneva the following month to formulate a global consensus on the refugee crisis, the United States boldly compared the human suffering on the South China Sea with the Holocaust of World War II. On July 21, 1979, in a speech written by a liberal Jew and approved by Holocaust survivor Elie Wiesel, Vice President Walter Mondale reminded the international community how its indifference four decades earlier had allowed Hitler's Final Solution to become a reality: "If each nation at Evian had agreed on that day to take in 17,000 Jews at once, every Jew in the Reich could have been saved. At Evian, they began with high hopes. But they failed the test of civilization. Let us not be the heirs to their shame." He continued, "History will not forgive us if we fail. History will not forget us if we succeed."[97] By the end of 1979, the UN commissioner had persuaded the Eastern nations to not deport the boat people, Western nations to offer them final resettlement, and Vietnam to initiate an "orderly departure program" to enable people to join their relatives in the United States without having to risk their lives at sea. It was not a perfect arrangement: the Southeast Asians were obliged to accept all entrants, while Western nations enjoyed the option of cherry-picking the "good" refugees from the camps, but it provided the small Southeast Asian countries valuable political cover against reprisals from Hanoi. Vietnam's communist party, once the darlings of the anticolonial movement, were now well-known human rights violators, and the refugees from Indochina, once considered the corrupt losers of a civil war, were suddenly heroes of the postwar.

Little Saigon Proper

Thanks to the boat people, the Vietnamese American population doubled between 1975 and 1980. This new cohort of exiles, influenced by refugee popular culture and their own harrowing journeys, envisioned diasporic identity in heroic terms, thus erasing the perception of refugees as losers or criminals. As newspaper publisher Yến Đỗ remembered, "The boat people rekindled the political spirit of Little Saigon because they were survivors of the communist regime."[98] Indeed, between January 1980 and March 1981, nearly 48 percent of all new Southeast Asian arrivals to California landed in Los Angeles and Orange Counties.[99] Intellectuals among the boat people quickly published memoirs about their time in reeducation camps, such as Tạ Ty's *Đáy Địa Ngục* [This Is Hell], Phạm Quốc Bảo's *Cùm Đỏ* [Red Chains], and Hà Thúc Sinh's *Đài Học Máu* (Bloody College).[100]

When Yến Đỗ arrived in 1979, Orange County had only twelve Vietnamese businesses, including one supermarket (Saigon Market at 2329 West

First Street in Santa Ana, which had opened in the summer of 1976) and two restaurants. Although the presence of the Saigon market meant that Orange County residents no longer had to travel to Chinatown in Los Angeles to buy groceries, the rest of the business district comprised bean fields, strawberry patches, and Anglo-owned family businesses. By 1980, however, more than one hundred Vietnamese businesses had sprung up all over Orange County, transforming a majority-white suburb just as Chinese entrepreneurs were doing in the suburban San Gabriel Valley.[101]

Secondary migration brought thousands more first-wave and second-wave refugees to Orange County, ushering in a new kind of economy. Rather than struggling in the mainstream economy, refugees could start their own businesses in Little Saigon, which had enough Vietnamese to constitute a viable labor and consumer market. By 1986, when the City of Westminster alone had more Vietnamese businesses than all of Los Angeles County, the *Người Việt Daily News*, with its ad-based business model, had supplanted *Trắng Đen* and its subscriber-based model as the region's dominant Vietnamese newspaper.[102] Accompanying ads for restaurants and doctors were those for brand-new tract housing starting at forty thousand dollars and new shopping centers in need of tenants, reflecting Orange County's growth potential.[103]

California's vast reservoir of housing and health insurance subsidies for the poor, along with ethnic mutual assistance associations and strong religious and educational resources, gave Vietnamese further incentive to gravitate toward Orange County.[104] A 1975 law signed by Governor Jerry Brown exempted Vietnamese refugees from out-of-state tuition charges, making community college and California state universities virtually free.[105] In 1975, tuition in the University of California system remained just $630 per year, within the average person's reach. With free child care services, community colleges provided incentives for Vietnamese women to enroll as well.[106]

One of the most prominent refugees confessed that gaming the system and pooling resources enabled Vietnamese to afford houses so quickly: "It may look like fraud, but that's the way they survived."[107] The Refugee Act of 1980 not only defined refugees as victims of persecution in accordance with United Nations precedent but also gave Vietnamese access to more sources of public assistance in California than in any other state.[108] Medi-Cal, the state's two-billion-dollar-per-year health insurance program for the poor, helped create an ethnic economy in Little Saigon, especially as mainstream doctors increasingly denied care to Medi-Cal patients.[109] With thousands of low-income and limited-English-speaking refugees suddenly possessing the means to pay for medical care, Little Saigon was a potential gold mine for any of the three hundred refugee doctors and dentists across the United States willing to set up shop there.[110] And virtually every doctor setting up shop in the Vietnamese community accepted Medi-Cal patients.[111]

When Phạm Duy had landed at the Florida refugee camp in 1975, he had told local reporters, "I sing about my country. Where's my country now?"[112] By 1977, two major mass migrations—the boat people exodus and secondary migration across the United States—told him, "We hold our country in our heart / We carry our nation in our soul."[113] He moved west to Orange County, reinventing himself as an exile and continuing his prolific career with songs such as "Ta Chống Cộng Hay Ta Trốn Cộng?" [Did We Fight or Did We Flee?], "Tháng Tư Đen" [Black April], "Người Việt Cao Quý" [With Dignity the People of Vietnam]; "1954 Cha Bỏ Quê-1975 Con Bỏ Nước" [The Exiles of a Father and His Son]; and "Hát Trên Đường Vượt Biên" [Song for the Boat People]. These and other songs of the period interpreted exile as the mark of a chosen people:

> Ôi! Cao quý thay những người Việt sống ở nghìn phương
> Vẫn còn nuôi tình tự quê hương
> Nắm tay nhau trên đoạn đường trường
> Hẹn mai về giải thoát quê hương
> Bằng cả tình thương của đời Việt Nam.
>
> [With dignity, all the people from Vietnam
> Though they're spread throughout the earth,
> Love the country of their birth
> Someday, hand in hand, they'll come
> Back to liberate their Vietnam.][114]

Social Work and the Meaning of Exile

Post-1975 diplomatic tensions between Hanoi and Washington fueled refugee nationalism, and vice versa. Before leaving office in early 1977, President Gerald Ford again vetoed Vietnam's entry in the United Nations and denied Hanoi's claim that his predecessor, Richard Nixon, had promised billions in economic aid. Vietnam gained UN membership the following September, but tempers flared a year later, as Washington expelled Vietnam's UN ambassador on espionage charges. Families of American service members missing in action wanted information about their loved ones from Hanoi, a situation that ultimately gave the United States sufficient moral and legal cover to admit additional Vietnamese as "refugees."[115] But considering the wealth of oral testimony exposing the atrocities committed by the communist government, it is also fair to conclude that refugee nationalism played a small but significant role in shaping Washington-Hanoi relations.

But pressing the United States to punish Vietnam by starving it had a potentially hazardous effect on those who could not escape the country. Instead of promoting democratic reforms or an accounting for all missing U.S. personnel, the economic embargo nearly crippled the Vietnamese economy. It also contributed to the extreme liberalization of economic life, with individual remittances from overseas Việt Kiều subsidizing a significant portion of Vietnam's already struggling economy.

In the interim, the noncommunist world's recognition of the boat people—and by extension other post-1975 émigrés from communist Indochina—as "genuine" political refugees represented a bittersweet victory of sorts for Little Saigon. Only as refugees on the run could they shame the world—especially former antiwar activists—into admitting that the Việt-Cộng had committed an alarming number of human rights violations. The newfound virtue and heroism in refugee cultural identity explains why Little Saigon was never merely pre-1975 Saigon transplanted onto foreign soil. To suggest so would be to ignore the centrality of exile, rescue, and gratitude in shaping the orientation of the refugee community. They were a community of survivors whose admission into the country had been made possible by exposing the contradictions of post-1975 Vietnam, by turning the refugee crisis into an opportunity for America to redeem its humanitarian image, and by projecting an image as model minorities worthy of rescue that was nowhere to be seen during the Vietnam War. But promises of asylum did not address the root causes of the boat people crisis, which partly explains why the politics of rescue and Little Saigon became far more militant during the 1980s.

4 The Anticommunist Việt-Cộng

*Freedom Fighters and the
New Politics of Rescue*

> They are our brothers, these freedom fighters, and we owe them
> our help. . . . They are the moral equal of our Founding Fathers
> and the brave men and women of the French Resistance. We
> cannot turn away from them for the struggle here is not right
> versus left; it is right versus wrong.
> —Ronald Reagan on the Nicaraguan Contras, 1985

> We the Vietnamese people are determined to fight until the
> Vietcong has been completely overthrown, until the Russian
> imperialists have been expelled from the national territory and
> their military bases abolished, and until peace, independence and
> freedom for our country are attained.
> —National United Front for the Liberation of Vietnam, 1982

Becoming Refugee American took a strikingly extremist turn after 1980. The Vietnamese American population had doubled to 250,000, thanks in large part to a generous admissions policy enacted in the wake of the boat people crisis. Many Americans expected grateful refugees to forget about the past and focus on individual assimilation, but the exiles continued to dream of reclaiming their lost homeland. As a result of America's fear of losing yet another war—a condition dubbed the Vietnam Syndrome—the refugees were on their own in this effort. Well aware of this state of affairs, ethnic newspapers such as *Trắng Đen* [The Truth] devoted space to the underground anticommunist resistance movement in the jungles of Southeast Asia. In January 1980, one young staffer, overcome with nationalist fervor, contemplated joining that movement in Vietnam rather than enjoy what she termed a pointless middle-class future in exile, declaring, "Better to die there fighting." Her editor, desperate to offer his people any glimmer of hope—and presumably sell more papers—reached out to a little-known resistance agitator currently in Australia, informing Võ Đại Tôn that Vietnamese Americans were ready to join the movement to reclaim their homeland.[1]

The story of the resistance movement, mainly its rise and fall, is well known in Vietnamese communities throughout the world, but this seemingly trivial underground history of notoriously bad refugees has a larger significance for American studies. Conventional wisdom has depicted freedom fighters as wild-eyed zealots who brought the Vietnam War to American shores and deluded themselves into believing that they could do on their own what the world's mightiest military had failed to accomplish: defeat the Việt-Cộng. But they were not an isolated crowd of zealots who refused to assimilate. Rather, Refugee Americans increasingly saw it their duty as Vietnamese *and* Americans to continue the war against communism by other means. As Vietnamese, they had an opportunity to reshape their image from that of wartime losers who fled like cowards to that of the ultimate heroes of their nation. The resistance movement reflected acculturation insofar as the 1980 election of Ronald Reagan had suddenly conferred mainstream legitimacy to an unabashedly imperialist foreign policy that treated Vietnam as a war America chose not to win. Reagan's overt support and covert funding of anticommunist freedom fighters such as the Nicaraguan contras and Afghan mujahideen had powerful sway over an ethnic community constantly under pressure to justify its cost in American dollars, lives, and reputation. This was a path to model minority status many impoverished Vietnamese American men found appealing.

In short, the rescued had become the rescuers. In 1980, to help counter America's reluctance to engage in conventional warfare, President Jimmy Carter authorized the expansion of covert special operations units accountable only to the executive branch. What on the outside appeared to represent a scaling-back of military force was in fact a further shift to secret extrajudicial warfare. In this context, freedom fighters constituted an addition to the advanced mobilization of a permanent secret army consisting more than ever of mercenaries. As a result, refugees who were not far removed from appealing to American guilt and charity were now boasting that they could take out the Việt-Cộng all by themselves.

The new politics of rescue also featured a racial component. At the same time that America underwent its own remasculinization in films to compensate for the crisis in masculinity that defeat in Vietnam had wrought—a point made by cultural critic Susan Jeffords—the image of the freedom fighter enabled Vietnamese refugees to think of themselves as equal partners with America in the war on communism.² Even though Vietnamese in the United States often worked menial jobs, this shift in worldview gave the refugees, particularly men, a second chance to command the basic respect and admiration Americans had denied them during the Vietnam War. The remasculinization of Vietnamese America featured military heroes destined to reclaim the lost nation, the women who loved them, and a nation that idolized them. A people who had gotten used to expressing eternal gratitude to the United States for rescuing them from a life without freedom were now claiming that they could save the United States from the shame of defeat in Vietnam.

As a result, the resistance movement attracted more than its share of wild-eyed extremists, many of them former members of the military full of hope that a successful homegrown uprising against the Hanoi regime would propel them to transnational glory. Defining Vietnamese identity in extremely narrow terms, this demographic enforced an authoritarian ultranationalism. The ironic inability of so-called freedom fighters to tolerate dissent in their own ranks led to the murder of five Vietnamese American journalists accused of communist ties and to the silencing of many others. The freedom fighters' legacy of intimidation and violence against their critics explained why at least one researcher in the 1990s shied away from interviewing these people.³ To defeat the Việt-Cộng, refugees created an anticommunist Việt-Cộng.⁴

Despite the overlap with neoconservative foreign policy, the dangers of dissent, and the general hatred of communism among the refugee population, the resistance movement's meteoric rise was no foregone conclusion. Many refugees had initially avoided politics, knowing full well that Hanoi's reprisals would fall most heavily on relatives who had remained behind. In addition, participation in the resistance movement virtually guaranteed that ultranationalists would be jailed or killed if they ever showed their faces in communist-run Vietnam again. The resistance represented a new instance of becoming Refugee American to the extent that ultranationalists, the quintessential bad refugees, were allowed by First Amendment rights and encouraged by the Reagan Doctrine to continue the Vietnam War by the most violent of means. The best way to convince ordinary people to take such a risky undertaking was to present victory as inevitable.

Vietnam's Vietnam War

Stories about the resistance surfaced as early as June 1975, when Camp Pendleton's nearly seventeen thousand refugees woke up to the improbable news of Vietnam's "large-scale search for possible resistance troops" hidden throughout the former South Vietnam. Quoting official sources from Vietnam, the camp newsletter indicated that nearly three hundred thousand former South Vietnamese troops had failed to meet the May 31 deadline for registering with the new government.[5] A communist newspaper, *Liberation Daily*, excoriated the "small number of soldiers of the puppet army" for having "murdered cadres and revolutionary fighters," "spread reactionary propaganda," and formed "bandit gangs that rob the people."[6] Nevertheless the government insisted that new registrants would still receive "amnesty": that is, they would receive only time in the reeducation camps. Resistance fighters, by contrast, would face "severe punishment."[7]

The mainstream U.S. press offered various assessments of a potential counterrevolution.[8] The *Los Angeles Times* estimated the number of resistance fighters in the thousands, though the "long-range prospects for the anti-Communist forces appear virtually hopeless."[9] The *New York Times* indicated that the new government's acknowledgment of "security problems" across South Vietnam "could indicate a more serious and widespread resistance."[10]

Seizing another opportunity to redeem his tarnished legacy, former South Vietnamese premier Nguyễn Cao Kỳ told a gang of reporters in Fullerton, California, that he was the people's choice to lead the estimated twelve thousand resistance fighters in Vietnam.[11] "I really would prefer to die gloriously on the battlefield than to live here in exile," he declared.[12]

Working out of the Orange County home he purchased in 1977, Phạm Duy composed a rousing anthem, "Hat Cho Người Ở Lại" [Song for Those Who Stayed], reminding refugees that the purpose of exile was to better the lives of those in Vietnam. The melody, which sounded like a country western cover, reflected Phạm Duy's attraction to folk styles, while lyrics lionized the resistance movement and reflected Vietnamese refugee nationalism.[13]

> Hát cho người hùng đang cầm súng
> Âm thầm đang phục quốc
> Hát cho người ở vùng nông thôn
> Hay người đang ở ngay phố phường
> Đồng bào ơi! Vùng lên tranh đấu!
> Ngày chiến thắng sẽ không lâu.
>
> [I sing for those, arms in hand,
> Fighting underground in the resistance
> I want to sing for villagers
> For city dwellers.

Fellowmen! Let's fight
Until our victory.]¹⁴

In April 1976, the thousands who subscribed to *Trắng Đen* discovered the first overseas organization dedicated to the resistance. Calling itself the Force of Renaissance, the San Diego–based group's ultimate goal was to recruit and train soldiers to join the allegedly sixty-thousand-strong insurgency back home. Even though the Force had just two hundred members, it had attracted the support of three respected community organizations: the Vietnamese Association for Culture Preservation, the Vietnamese Community Foundation, and the Vietnamese Catholic Committee. But many refugees refused to join the Force because they feared that taking such a hard-line political stand would jeopardize the safety of family members still in Vietnam.¹⁵ Even Nam Lộc and other single men fretted more about sending money to family than cursing the communists. Others, such as Mỹ-Bình, a devout Catholic mother in Orange County, cast a cynical eye on the potential of politics to deliver anything more than conflict, pain, and death. She found sanctuary in church and family, praying for her father's release from the reeducation camps.¹⁶

Even if the early Vietnamese refugees had pushed for an aggressive anticommunist agenda that resembled a continuation of the Vietnam War, they would have been swimming upstream against the American political climate of the post-Vietnam period.¹⁷ Americans generally opposed the entry of Vietnamese refugees until the advent of the boat people crisis, which eventually drew bipartisan support because it relied on soft power to address Vietnam's human rights abuses and cited America's moral obligation to help those escaping by boat.

After the 1970s, however, militant anticommunism briefly supplanted victim-based anticommunism as the dominant identity of the Vietnamese refugee community. This change occurred in the wake of a series of potential quagmires for Eastern Bloc countries intent on occupying their neighbors. Facing unanticipated resistance in Afghanistan, the Soviet Union found itself unable to provide Vietnam with significant material support. That left Hanoi on its own in its wars against Cambodia and China. These endless conflicts drained scarce resources—including human labor—from the rest of the Vietnamese economy. With productivity below subsistence levels, millions of Vietnamese civilians reached the brink of starvation. In addition, the rise of militant anticommunism among Vietnamese Americans was facilitated by President Ronald Reagan's support of secret guerrilla insurgencies against communist-run countries.

The Reagan Influence and Secret Armies

Although the former Hollywood actor started his adult life as a New Deal Democrat, Reagan's thirst for fame and power steered him toward neoconservatism and the Republican Party.[18] Neoconservatism, informed in large part by Social Darwinism, patriarchy, and nationalism, cynically believes that Americans must aggressively and unilaterally arm and defend themselves against an innately hostile world.[19] It is also informed by greed, given the vast wealth it has generated for the military-industrial complex. Ironically, this coalition of warmongers was spearheaded by Reagan and others who spoke like charismatic warriors despite never having seen combat.

On the stump, Reagan painted the political establishment as weak and effeminate so he could position himself as strong and masculine. Echoing the talking points of the emergent neoconservative movement, with its unshakable faith in U.S. global hegemony and disdain for multilateral institutions such as the United Nations, Reagan repeated his misguided belief that American military might was "the greatest guarantee for peace and freedom for this country."[20] Positioning himself as a populist outsider, Reagan argued that three decades of "weakness and indecision" in Washington had resulted in concession after concession to the communists, making defeat in Vietnam almost inevitable. In the aftermath of the Korean War, he argued, "our country decided for the first time that victory was not necessary."[21] The man those in his own party accused of being a warmonger countered that the "peace at any price" alternative would lead only to a Soviet-dominated world.[22]

In 1976, Reagan had led the neoconservative charge to secure some semblance of post-Vietnam victory by accusing current president Gerald Ford, a fellow Republican, of surrender if he normalized relations with the Hanoi government.[23] When Reagan received his party's presidential nomination four years later, he told a gathering of the Veterans of Foreign Wars that the Vietnam War was indeed a "noble cause."[24] Reagan's America, in which veterans deserved nothing less than the nation's undying gratitude, was as much about reasserting traditional masculine values as it was about validating conservativism.[25] Just as important, Reagan's vision reinvigorated the conservative line of argument that a combination of weak-willed leaders in Washington and the peace movement had lost the war in Vietnam. His emphasis on manipulating American faith and public opinion sounded like the China Lobby all over again.

Reagan still had to get around the problem of the Vietnam Syndrome. Defeat in Vietnam had amplified doubts about America's purpose and power in the world in ways not too different from those experienced by Europe in the postcolonial era. Reagan exploited this crisis of confidence by increasing U.S. dependence on counterrevolutionary guerrillas to fight the Cold War in vulnerable zones across the globe. He had flirted with the idea as early as 1975, meeting in Florida with exile leaders from Panama and Cuba ready to give the failed Bay of Pigs invasion another shot.[26]

As president, Reagan trained his sights on communism in Latin America, authorizing nineteen million dollars for the creation of a secret anticommunist army, known popularly as the contras, to bring down the populist regime that had overthrown Nicaraguan dictator Anastasio Somoza. "They are our brothers, these freedom fighters," Reagan said, "and we owe them our help."[27] His brand of help, known as the Reagan Doctrine, constituted a radical—and technically illegal—departure from the prior Cold War containment policy.[28] Neoconservatives blamed Jimmy Carter for the "fall" of Nicaragua in 1979 and invoked a Latin American domino theory. Testifying under oath before the U.S. Senate in early 1982, one Reagan State Department official echoed the rationale for going to war in Vietnam: "There is no mistaking that the decisive battle for Central America is under way in El Salvador. If, after Nicaragua, El Salvador is captured by a violent minority, who in Central America would not live in fear?" General William Westmoreland, who had previously served the top American military official in Saigon, doubled down on the earlier testimony by stating, "The domino theory has validity in Central America. If El Salvador falls, after Nicaragua, then Guatemala, Honduras, and Costa Rica could go. After that, there's nothing standing in the way of the Panama Canal."[29]

Neoconservatives' obsession with American strength and military redemption, now through extralegal channels, knew no boundaries. In 1983, U.S. Special Forces illegally invaded the Caribbean island of Grenada in an effort to reverse the recent coup d'état that had put Marxists in power. Clint Eastwood's 1986 warrior flick, *Heartbreak Ridge*, described the episode as the military's first "victory" against the communists, counting Korea as a tie and Vietnam as a loss. Grenada's new leadership created a Thanksgiving holiday to commemorate the anniversary of the invasion. Speaking at the 1985 gathering of the National Conservative Political Action Committee, Reagan called the mighty unsavory band of Nicaraguan contras "the moral equal of our Founding Fathers," fighting the good fight of "right versus wrong."[30] Without the knowledge of Congress, Lieutenant Colonel Oliver North helped arrange the covert and illegal sale of weapons to Iran in exchange for U.S. hostages and extra funding for the contras. Ever the protector, Reagan vowed to keep Americans forever safe by authorizing billions for an outer space missile defense shield—dubbed Star Wars—that never actually saw the light of day.[31]

Policy aside, Reagan's promilitary, promasculine message resonated with a large swath of veterans still waiting to be showered with glory and honor for their service in Vietnam. In keeping with Reagan's "noble cause" speech, one veteran took issue with the winning design for the Vietnam Veterans Memorial.[32] Testifying in 1981 before the commission in charge of designing the memorial, he stated that Maya Lin's proposal for an abstract monument reflected the home front perception of the war. Instead of honoring all of those who served, he contended, its roll call of the deceased concentrated too much on the costs of war. He objected to the granite V-shaped wall as "a black gash of shame and sorrow," surrounded on the Washington Mall by "well-known edifices of white marble rising in massive splendor to honor great American heroes."[33] He argued in favor of a more typical commemoration such as the Seabee Memorial, the 101st Airborne Division Memorial, and the Marine Corps' Iwo Jima Memorial:

> These [memorials] show heroic figures rising in triumph on top of black pedestals, while the proposed Vietnam memorial is anti-heroic—a black hole, the reward we get, and the place we have been given in our national garden of history, for faithful service in a confused and misunderstood war. Black walls, the universal color of sorrow and dishonor, hidden in a hole, as in shame. Is this really how America would memorialize our offering? It may be that, in the future, all memorials to American heroes will be black and underground. I doubt it, but even if that's true, why should we Vietnam veterans have to be the first? The only underground memorial I know of is a tomb. Yes, we lost 57,000, but what of the millions of us who rendered honorable service and came home? Why cannot we have something white and traditional and above ground?[34]

Despite such objections, Lin's design was retained, and the Vietnam Veterans Memorial was dedicated on November 13, 1982. However, a more conventional statue, *The Three Soldiers*, was built alongside the wall and was dedicated on November 11, 1984.

The Resistance Movement Takes Flight

If Reagan's bellicose foreign policy alarmed the mainstream media and a political establishment weary of war, it delighted Little Saigon and other refugee communities. After all, Reagan promised a stronger America finally capable of putting the Soviet bloc "on the moral defensive, the intellectual defensive, and the political and economic defensive."³⁵ An obscure organization, the Vietnamese American Republican National Federation, tried to get coethnics on board the 1980 Reagan-Bush ticket by linking it to the resistance movement in Vietnam.³⁶ Another refugee organization likened the Vietnamese resistance to the rest of the Reagan Doctrine:

> Resistance movements are an effective bulkhead to impair and contain the spread of Soviet hegemonism. This approach is also commensurate with the American ethical standard of human rights. It is also obviously, an economical measure. Blocking Soviet expansion in Afghanistan by assisting the Afghanistan Resistance is certainly less costly than any other measure of a military build-up. The Vietnam case requires similar consideration. Freedom-fighters around the world have actually eroded the expansionist capability of the Soviet and their henchmen. Weakening the Soviet Union by adequate assistance to these resistance movements is an effective course of action, because it is morally right and it is the least expensive alternative.³⁷

Only in the context of neoconservatism and the increasing U.S. dependence on secret counterrevolutionary guerrillas to fight the Cold War can we more fully understand the meteoric rise of the resistance movement in Little Saigon. And Reagan's alliance with some of the more barbarous elements of humanity in the name of anticommunism set the precedent for the increasing right-wing authoritarian climate associated with freedom fighters.

Võ Đại Tôn, a former colonel in the South Vietnamese army, vaulted to notoriety in 1980, when he founded the Overseas Vietnamese Volunteer Forces for the Restoration of Vietnam. He answered *Trắng Đen*'s call and volunteered to lead an overthrow of the communist regime. He first agreed to visit Los Angeles on July 19, bringing with him an exiled Laotian general, Vang Pao.³⁸ The general, who had been employed by the U.S. Central Intelligence Agency during the Vietnam War, claimed to have three hundred thousand Hmong resistance fighters under his command already situated in the jungles of Laos, awaiting orders for the next mission.³⁹ The event in Los Angeles was followed by rallies in Anaheim and San Diego organized by the local college student organizations. Attendees hoped their support of the resistance would help reunite them with family and put a much-desired end to the observance of April 30 as the day their country had perished.⁴⁰ Tôn's influence faded after he was captured a year later on his way from Laos to Vietnam, but he electrified the refugee community one last time, refusing Hanoi's orders to implicate the United States, China, and Thailand in a prepared public confession and instead vowing to "liberate Vietnam once and for all."⁴¹

While Võ Đại Tôn languished in a communist prison cell, other resistance organizations tried to win over his large following. Nguyễn Cao Kỳ, speaking in Tokyo in December 1982, told those in attendance that Vietnamese Americans were training for combat in America's national parks. And like other resistance types, Kỳ proclaimed that the potential for counterrevolution in Vietnam negated the need for U.S. troops: "With 75 to 80 percent of the people against the regime, we do not need [U.S. troops]. Give me guns, and we'll kick them out!"[42] But refugees paid closer attention to another organization as footage of its exploits began to surface. The February 5, 1982, issue of Seattle's *Đất Mới* newspaper featured a photograph of an M16-toting guerrilla allegedly training just outside of Vietnam. He was dressed in the same black pajamas and had the same initials made famous by the Việt-Cộng's leader. His organization had a similar name and appropriated much of the Việt-Cộng's rhetoric. Hoàng Cơ Minh was an admiral in the Vietnamese navy who had commanded a fleet of ships to safety as the war was ending and then received passage to the United States. There, he initially worked as a self-employed painter, earning a decent living but suffering severe status depreciation. In 1980, he cofounded the National United Front for the Liberation of Vietnam with the belief that "supporting a liberation movement is a mandatory duty . . . not a charitable act."[43] By March 30, 1982, CBS News had attained a copy of the video footage and correspondent Morley Safer was commenting on the uncanny resemblance between the Front and its nemesis except that

> these Vietcong are the new anti-communist Vietcong. A rag tag of refugees who have taken it upon themselves to liberate South Vietnam, to do to the present regime what the present regime did to them. . . . They return to the jungle from places like Arlington, Virginia, and Sacramento, California. They dress in camouflage and the black pajamas that were the trademark of their enemies . . . They even called the jungle path they have cut *The Hoàng Cơ Minh Trail*. *Giải phóng*—"*liberation*"—is the way these would-be insurgents salute each other. Their form of address is *"comrades."* They spend their evenings in political education and indoctrination. It is unclear how much actual fighting they have done. They say in their speeches that they are the nucleus around which an entire nation will rally and throw off the chains of Communism.[44]

The Front ultimately failed in its mission, and Hoàng Cơ Minh, commanding an army of far fewer than ten thousand men, lost his life in 1987 trying to lead an incursion through the jungles of Laos. By 1991, the U.S. Justice Department had prosecuted the Front's top brass for tax evasion, conspiracy, and other offenses, but for a brief period during the 1980s, they had the full attention of the refugee community. They had an extensive operation designed to raise money from Vietnamese refugees around the world and to promote awareness of the Front's activities among government officials through their political party, Việt-Tân [Reform Party], a name that reflected Hồ Chí Minh's influence on the movement.

Người Việt Daily News publisher Yến Đỗ, hardly an extremist, acknowledged that "in 1982, the second phase of the newspaper began with the appearance of the National Liberation Front of Hoang Co Minh . . . a group that provided a lot of local news for the newspaper to report."[45] During 1982 alone, the Front held five of its twenty-nine rallies in Southern California.[46] With the help of popular Vietnamese actress Kiều Chinh, the Front recruited 150 artists to participate in the largest event yet at the Los Angeles Shrine Auditorium on July 3, 1982.[47] More than four thousand guests paid between five and eight dollars each to attend the sold-out event. Later that year, more than five thousand people paid five dollars each to pack the Anaheim Convention Center.[48]

On the surface, the attendees did not appear to be fanatics. A respected Anaheim physician handled Southland fund-raising duties. Some attended merely to enjoy the musical performances. The front row included high-ranking Saigon officials and Catholic priests and nuns. Front members stood out in their trademark brown shirts and beige slacks.[49] Otherwise, most performers wore conventional Western dress or traditional Vietnamese clothing, while the one-hundred-member all-woman chorus sang from songbooks resembling the South Vietnamese flag.[50] "I must have sung in 50 places," said one of the choir members. "The crowds were screaming and cheering. There were speeches and patriotic songs." Capturing the spirit of the times, she recalled, "You felt that soon you'd be back in Vietnam."[51]

Inevitable return was part of the sentiment on April 17, 1983, when an overflow crowd of five thousand converged on Garden Grove High School to see Hoàng Cơ Minh in person. Although they came from different parts of the West Coast, all had invested their hopes and their funds in the Front's promise to reunite them with their loved ones. Front members often boasted an army of ten thousand, recruited from the ranks of Vietnamese Americans and recent refugees still in Thailand. When audience members heard from Chairman Hoàng Cơ Minh that the Front had made progress, they went home happy enough. One young attendee proclaimed, "The battle can never end," despite the fear that her support for Minh would jeopardize her family's safety in Vietnam.[52] The Front's popularity reached its height in 1984, when eleven thousand people packed the Anaheim Convention Center on March 17 to catch a glimpse of Khánh Ly and other singers and to celebrate

Figure 4. Hoàng Cơ Minh, leader of the National United Front for the Liberation of Vietnam, waves to a crowd of five thousand in Garden Grove, April 17, 1983. Photo by Debora Robinson, Copyright 1983, *Los Angeles Times*. Reprinted with Permission.

the event's theme: Liberating Vietnam. Organizers used the opportunity to talk about the Resistance Radio, which had begun beaming to Vietnam in December 1983, urging young people to defect from the regime and join the underground resistance movement.[53]

Vietnamese American organizations wanted the United States to take the resistance movement seriously because they already saw their struggle as part of a larger united popular front against communism.[54] Readers of the refugee press found inspiration in the anticommunist struggle in Poland or other parts of Eastern Europe.[55] In the mold of the anticommunist Polish Solidarity Party, the Front founded a political party in opposition to the Vietnamese Communist Party. An April 30 observance in Seattle included representatives from the Polish Anti-Communism Organization, the Free China Foundation, the Christian Anti-Communism Crusade, and the Laotian Refugee Association.[56] For its part, the Front's newsletter claimed that much could be learned from the exploits of the Nicaraguan contras.[57]

Economic concerns also underlay the resistance movement in Little Saigon. Rank-and-file ultranationalists, especially the men, had less economic incentive to stay in the United States. By the mid-1980s, the infusion of less urbanized refugees and reduced public benefits meant that somewhere near four hundred thousand Vietnamese Americans were competing in a tight job market. In 1985, the Indochinese unemployment rate in Orange County had reached 36.4 percent, which was better than the rate for their brethren in Chicago and Seattle but much worse than the national average. Moreover, a staggering 44 percent of Indochinese men had no jobs. Though women were more likely to be employed, they earned just eighty-three cents for every dollar men earned.[58]

According to Nazli Kibria, Vietnamese American families had a difficult time adapting to women breadwinners, low household incomes, and patchwork family structures. Women felt compelled to balance their traditional roles as subservient wives with their new roles as economic authority figures, while men suffered from depression and dysfunction as a consequence of their inability to fulfill their gendered obligations. This combination of a shaky family structure and scarce material resources had the potential to restrict the life chances of members of the next generation.[59] But in light of the fact that if these Vietnamese had remained in their home country, they would have remained poor, refugee identity may have helped them to make sense of their predicament. The situation could be blamed on the communists. Not surprisingly, resistance-style refugee nationalism, with its embrace of the exiled masculine warrior plotting a heroic return, provided a more appealing worldview than did identification as a fearful refugee. Like the rest of America, refugee nationalism underwent its own remasculinization.[60] The Front's shady fund-raising certainly provided wealth for its top brass, but its mafia-like operation also provided rank-and-file refugees with jobs. Just as important, its connections with U.S. politicians gave refugee men the respect and dignity they had been denied during the war.

Robert Dornan and the Front's American Sympathizers

Little Saigon was part of the Thirty-eighth U.S. Congressional District, virtually the only California House seat in which a competitive election would occur in 1984. Republican candidate Robert Dornan, a typical neoconservative hawk who had never seen combat, had represented west Los Angeles County from 1976 until 1982, when he chose not to run for reelection. Two years later, he took aim at the only Democratic congressman left in heavily Republican Orange County, ten-year incumbent Jerry Patterson. The campaigns combined to spend $1.5 million on the race, making it one of the nation's costliest, and Dornan cruised to victory in November with 53 percent of the vote.⁶¹

Dornan pandered for votes wherever he could, and his extreme anticommunism found a receptive audience among Vietnamese Americans. When the Front invited Dornan to speak at a September rally, he told the eight hundred in attendance "that he was ready to support policy of the refugee groups. That made him the only candidate until now to support them. If he is in Congress, he will be the spokesman for that policy."⁶²

Dornan was not the only major U.S. official supporting the Front. The organization's literature quoted future Republican vice presidential candidate Jack Kemp's declaration that "all Americans admire [the Front's] devotion to the freedom of Vietnam and [the] Vietnamese people, just as we appreciate the rich contributions you have made to America."⁶³ Colorado Republican senator William Armstrong praised Hoàng Cơ Minh's willingness to leave "his family and safety in the West to turn clandestinely to Vietnam to lead the freedom fighters there in their unequal struggle with Communist despots."⁶⁴ In early May 1983, just prior to a major Front gathering, the organization's second in command met in Washington with United Nations ambassador Jeane Kirkpatrick, deputy undersecretary of defense for policy Richard G. Stillwell, and deputy assistant secretary of defense for East Asia and Pacific affairs Richard Armitage.⁶⁵ Armitage, a veteran of the Vietnam War who had given himself a Vietnamese nickname, Trần Văn Phú, had developed a good relationship with Hoàng Cơ Minh.⁶⁶ According to the senior Front official, Armitage secretly persuaded the Thai government to allow the Front unrestricted movement within the country's borders.⁶⁷ Such meetings represented a huge symbolic victory for Vietnamese Americans, who were used to being treated as far less than equals by their American counterparts.

Popular Culture of the Resistance

Resistance organizations placed a premium on propaganda and popular culture that appealed to the heroic masculine theme of the times. The Front's second in command realized the importance of popular culture while attending the group's first culture night on April 3, 1982, in Washington, D.C. Attendees watched a play, *The Prisoner*, that provoked tears and outrage over all the freedoms people in Vietnam had lost at the hands of the communists.⁶⁸

For six dollars, supporters could purchase cassette tapes with titles such as *Kháng Chiến Ca* [Resistance Songs] and *Em Vẫn Đợi Anh Về* [I Still Await My Man's Return] and cases that featured photos of gallant freedom fighters marching through jungles or beautiful women clad in *áo dài* dress waiting to be rescued.⁶⁹ This musical genre subsequently gave rise to a class of woman warriors whose presence and voices challenged traditional South Vietnamese gender roles. Appearing nearly as uninterested in sentimental love songs as their Việt-Cộng counterparts, vocalists Nguyệt Ánh and Ngọc Minh performed songs tailor-made for a male military audience, often oceans apart from their spouses. Resistance-era music often encouraged listeners to see themselves as the heirs of the Vietnamese independence movement.

To sustain their movement beyond the refugee generation, the Front reached out to young children. Front members operated booths at Tết lunar new year festivals and organized autumn festivals all over the world. Underneath banners that read "Vì Các Cháu Thiếu Nhi Toàn Dân Kháng Chiến" [Because Children Are Part of the Resistance, Too], young boys and girls in ethnic dress made their parents proud by singing Vietnamese songs. The Front published popular books such as *Anh Hùng Nước Tôi* [Heroes of the Nation] (1986) that invariably included former South Vietnamese president Ngô Đình Diệm. Though dismissed by the Hanoi government and many Western scholars as an impotent dictator, Diệm received near-universal adoration from the refugee generation for making unpopular but necessary choices during his presidency.⁷⁰ In case their revolution succeeded, the Front invented national holidays such as the National Day of Founding, commemorating occasions unrelated to either the Hanoi or Saigon regimes but instead going back to the days of Emperor Hùng Vương in 2880 BC. These annual festivities continued through the 1990s in Vietnamese communities not only in Orange County but also across the United States (San Jose, Phoenix, Houston, Hawaii, Oklahoma, Atlanta, Chicago, St. Paul, Denver, Seattle, Portland, Pennsylvania, Washington, D.C.) and around the world (Tokyo, Vancouver, Toronto, Montreal, Hong Kong, London, Birmingham, Paris, Berlin, Munich, Melbourne, Sydney, and Norway).⁷¹ As a result, children in refugee communities became accustomed to a form of Vietnamese nationalism banned in their parents' homeland.⁷²

The Front's newsletter, a propaganda piece that bore some resemblance to the procommunist *Thái Bình* tabloid published in Santa Monica, kept readers abreast of the latest offensives supposedly taking place in Vietnam. The November 1986 newsletter alleged an assault on a reeducation camp, the sabotage of a chemical plant, and a cascade of defections from the Việt-Cộng.⁷³ By 1986, the organization had released six videotapes that purported to show Chairman Hoàng Cơ Minh's men setting up bases in Vietnam and taking over one village after another.⁷⁴ "The Front knew people would not contribute money for a long time if they did not see some progress," confessed a former member.⁷⁵

The Front sponsored beauty pageants in San Jose and Long Beach to showcase its own version of idealized femininity.[76] Contestants had to be older than age fifteen and be nominated by an active member of the resistance movement.[77] One contestant from Garden Grove explained that she participated because "if we cannot fight on the battlefront, then we can still make a difference from the home front."[78] Another contestant confessed, "It was not until I attended college and participated in political activities that I fully understood the significance of the resistance movement and my role within it."[79] Even the 1982 winner of one of the regular Vietnamese American beauty pageants, Dương Ngọc Huê, "support[ed] the struggle" by donating half her prize money to the Front.[80] Students at the University of Southern California invited senior Front member Trần Minh Công to join them in Taper Hall on October 5, 1984.[81] One student, twenty-three-year-old Quân Nguyễn, had no doubt that the struggle would last for years and require "lots of sacrifice" but nevertheless believed that Vietnamese Americans must not shy away from their "duty and destiny."[82]

Tired of seeing the world "feel pity for the 'boat people' tragedy" every April 30, the Front preferred to shift the focus to more heroic characteristics, such as "the endeavors of the Vietnamese people to liberate their country, and about the Vietnamese resistance."[83] Thanks to all the violent red-baiting and political assassinations taking place in Little Saigon, the Front got its wish.

Conformity at All Costs and by All Means

Unlike the boat people crisis, which brought people across all different social backgrounds together in solidarity with Vietnam's newest refugees, the resistance movement gained little traction among the general population outside those who had served in uniform or supported the Vietnam War. Mainstream publications referred to the Front as a largely "longshot," "symbolic," or "quixotic" effort.[84] The Front denied receiving any aid from the U.S. government, and fund-raising proved one of the greatest challenges. In addition to the admission fees charged at concerts, the Front's members canvassed neighborhoods for donations, with some families happily contributing as much as twenty dollars each month when the collection people arrived.[85] Others contributed less happily: saying no could have dangerous consequences. "We heard some reports about extortion," said Westminster police detective Marcus Frank. "The front was going around to businesses and factory assembly lines asking for contributions. They told Vietnamese if they did not contribute, people might think they're pro-communist."⁸⁶ By the mid-1980s, estimates showed that the Front had raised between five and seven million dollars, a substantial sum, although if the organization had actually been maintaining an army of ten thousand guerrillas, as it claimed, far more money would have been required.⁸⁷

It was common knowledge in the Vietnamese community that the Front had invested some of its funds in a chain of restaurants serving phở, a popular noodle dish.⁸⁸ Hoàng Cơ Minh's brother opened the first franchise in Sacramento as Phở Kháng Chiến [Resistance] but soon changed the name to Phở Hòa [Peace].⁸⁹ Additional restaurants soon opened in San Jose, San Francisco, Los Angeles, Santa Ana, Monterey Park, and San Diego.⁹⁰ In late 1984, Ty Võ moved to Seattle at the Front's request and opened up another Phở Hòa restaurant, with partial financing from the organization. The space once occupied by Kentucky Fried Chicken now sported a painting of soldiers raising the yellow flag and a collection can for donations to the Front.⁹¹ In 1986 alone, the Phở Hòa chain brought in $2.9 million in revenues.⁹² One federal investigator picked up on the rumor that Delta Savings and Loan in Westminster had been launched almost exclusively with funds generated by resistance groups and served as the Front's main financial conduit.⁹³ Residents of Little Saigon did not object as long as the money actually went to the resistance movement, but when Front leaders appeared to be reaping personal profits, two top officials, Phạm Văn Liễu and Trần Minh Công, stepped down in 1985. They escaped violent reprisals, but journalists who raised legitimate criticisms of the resistance movement were less fortunate. This wave of violence and the culture of fear it encouraged in Little Saigon led to the Front's downfall.

None of Little Saigon's seventeen newspapers were immune from the wrath of anticommunist extremists, who engaged in a private grassroots version of McCarthyism, seeing it their duty as new Americans to oust suspected communists in their midst, no matter the cost to a functioning civil society. One editor kept an M16 and two handguns at work in case of attack, precautions he described as "the price of doing business in the Vietnamese community."⁹⁴ In early 1982, an editor of a San Jose–based Vietnamese weekly questioned where the Front's money was going and soon received telephoned death threats. A local merchant was ordered to take that magazine off his shelves.⁹⁵ Later that year, another editor, Kiều Nguyên Tá, received a ferocious beating after his Orange County newspaper, Quê Hương, accused the Front of fraud. As far as Tá was concerned, "The scenes in their film clips of guerrilla fighters looked staged. I also did not like the way they were going around with containers collecting money." Although the controversy destroyed Tá's marriage and bankrupted his newspaper business, he at least walked away with his life.[96]

Beginning in 1981, five other Vietnamese American journalists were not as lucky. The string of murders, all of which remain unsolved, ended after columnist Triet Le and his wife, Tuyet Thi Dang-Tran, were found shot to death in their home near Washington, D.C.[97] A number of non-Vietnamese subjects interviewed by the police and FBI believed that the Front might be involved in the killings.[98] There was no doubt that the organization promoted a climate of fear and violence in Little Saigon. In 1982, Houston police investigating the murder of another journalist, Nguyen Dam Phong, had found Triet Le's name on a hit list next to Nguyen's body. Various terrorist organizations claimed credit for the killings.[99] The Vietnamese Party to Exterminate Communists and Restore the Nation sent a letter explaining that it had carried out the 1987 arson that resulted in the death of Tap Van Pham of Garden Grove in retaliation for Pham's decision to run ads from three allegedly communist-run money collection and remittance centers—Laser Express, Vinamedic, and QTK—as well as a 1985 firebombing at the businesses' Montreal offices.[100] Ads for Laser Express and Vinamedic indeed appeared in the procommunist *Thái Bình*, but other refugee newspapers printed them without incident.[101]

Before his death, Pham had complained that gangs were extorting protection money from him even though journalists made far less money than others.[102] Ironically, many Vietnamese businesses had moved to Orange County to avoid the gangs and violence infesting Los Angeles Chinatown to the north.[103] Fearing retribution, many businesses reluctantly paid between two hundred and three hundred dollars per month to extortionists. In January 1984, syndicated columnist Jack Anderson accused Nguyễn Cao Kỳ of having left Saigon with eight million dollars and of leading the gangs that extorted Vietnamese businesses throughout the Southland. Kỳ certainly had a motive, since he had recently filed for bankruptcy after incurring roughly twenty thousand dollars' worth of gambling debts at Caesars Palace.[104]

Community members seemed to condone political assassinations that weeded out actual communist agents. Front cofounder Phạm Văn Liễu claimed that Hanoi had sent two thousand operatives to America to infiltrate the refugee community: "Their first goal is to destroy the Vietnamese communities. Secondly, to set up financial organizations to get money to send back to Vietnam. The Communists have plans to cause all kinds of troubles in the Vietnamese community so that it will not create a good impression among the Americans." He thus supported the FBI's 1985 program to pinpoint Việt-Cộng hiding in America.[105] Likewise, many community members sympathized with another Front member who confessed to shooting a fellow Vietnamese suspected of promoting normalization with Hanoi. An end to the U.S. embargo would, according to publisher Yến Đỗ, "destroy the dream of returning to a free Vietnam." Đỗ frequently likened Vietnamese refugees to other stateless people, including Cubans and Jews: "Sometimes they look irrational to the average American who has put the events of the past behind. But for Cubans and Vietnamese, it is the meaning of their lives. A lot of them were political prisoners. Revenge lies with them forever."[106] In addition, according to Đỗ, "Young Vietnamese have studied how Jews came back from the Holocaust and built the Israel nation. Through the sorrows of our exodus, young Vietnamese feel the emotional experience of the Jews."[107]

In addition to the journalists, Edward Lee Cooperman, a professor at California State University at Fullerton, was murdered in 1984 by a young Vietnamese student who accused Cooperman of sending high-tech goods directly to the Vietnamese government.[108] Though all exiles sought to reclaim their lost homeland, ultranationalists believed that anything less than complete and unequivocal victory amounted to weakness or surrender to the communists. "I love my country," said a community leader in 1987. "I have a father, mother, five sisters and a brother in Vietnam. But I will not go back. No refugee should."[109]

The Fall of the Front

The resistance suffered many fundamental flaws, the most obvious of which was that, like its neoconservative and communist counterparts, members talked about democracy but seldom practiced it. The demand for blind patriotism constituted a method of social control for the benefit of a small cadre. The resistance had defined itself in radical terms, thus relegating the boat people crisis and human rights reform in Vietnam to secondary status, symptoms of a larger problem that "liberating Vietnam" would ultimately eradicate. The resistance movement claimed that refugees comprised the more peripheral overseas operation, when in actuality, the overseas component was the center of the resistance movement and operations in and around Vietnam itself were peripheral. Conditions in Vietnam, exacerbated by imprisonment or the exodus of potential underground resistance leaders, prevented the creation of a long-term mass uprising against the Hanoi regime. In 1983, the Front counted five thousand official members, a figure that dwarfed the actual number of freedom fighters under Minh's command.[110]

People inevitably doubted that the Front could do on its own what its members had failed to do with the U.S. military by its side, but ultranationalists, like their white counterparts, felt that anything less than blind patriotism jeopardized the movement.

Soon after Phạm Văn Liễu and Trần Minh Công departed in 1985, the organization fell apart. Hoàng Cơ Minh died in battle, and his brother leveraged his way into power. Vietnamese authorities reported killing more than one hundred guerrillas and capturing seventy-seven. Before the end of 1987, eighteen had been convicted of treason, implying they had not obtained U.S. citizenship before joining the Front. Hanoi wanted them to confess to receiving aid from the United States and Thailand but presented no evidence to support those charges. From San Jose, Front spokesman Đông Sơn Nguyễn (originally Nguyễn Xuân Nghĩa) tried to reassure supporters that "Chairman Hoàng Cơ Minh is alive and leading the liberation struggle."[111] Another fourteen years passed before the Front finally acknowledged Minh's death and held a memorial service for him.[112]

But the real tragedy befell average Vietnamese Americans and the rank-and-file members of the Front. "We trusted them and they stole our dream," said a former supporter.[113] In a painful irony, those most passionate about overthrowing the Hanoi regime became the least likely ever to return to Vietnam. A former Front member who had contributed essays for the resistance reflected in 2008 on why he had not returned to his native land since 1975: "I know the Vietnamese government is not pleased with my work and I may be put in jail. Some of my friends have already been put in jail for what they did. All my friends came because they had to visit their ill parents or visit their home village. And they did not do anything wrong on that trip. But they still went to jail." Nevertheless, the man claimed to have no regrets: "I did the right thing. I did nothing wrong." "When things change enough," he and his wife would "go back together, or we will not go at all."[114]

5 Assimilationists and the Postwar
Model Minority Politics in Little Saigon

> I found that Democrats always talk about helping the people with a handout. I said no. I do not like handouts. I never went to Social Services asking for a handout. The first two jobs I worked were as a service station attendant and a shipping and receiving supervisor.
> —Tony Lâm, former Westminster City Council Member, 2007

> Our success in America [is] a direct answer to the failure of the Communists in Vietnam. We may have lost the battle in 1975, but we are winning the Vietnam War.
> —Danh Chau, Vietnamese Chamber of Commerce in San Jose, 1995

When Tony Lâm, the cofounder of the Vietnamese American Chamber of Commerce, became a U.S. citizen in 1982 and a registered Republican the following year, his rationale—"I do not like handouts"—sounded like typical conservative propaganda except for the important fact that memories of Vietnam past, including the magical holiday of Tết, carried with it painful reminders of America's most disastrous foreign policy venture.[1] Whatever Lâm's actual political beliefs, the refugee experience virtually guaranteed a public performance true to the model minority script. Becoming Refugee American, a form of social formation and sense of belonging based on moral obligation rather than legal rights, imposed on the Vietnamese a moral debt that practically demanded perfection in exchange for rescue from communism. Vietnamese refugees, who often testified to entering the United States with little more than the clothes they wore, nevertheless felt immense pressure to climb out of poverty. Many of them inevitably and publicly failed to live up to such unrealistic expectations, leading regret to threaten to overshadow compassion in the American social imagination. In 1980, on the eve of Tết, a *Washington Post* headline declared, "California's Asian

Communities Are Seething with Crime."[2] No one evoked images of model minority valedictorians when, the following year, three young Vietnamese men from Orange County faced more than one hundred years in prison for the kidnapping and rape of six women.[3] The anticommunist witch hunt in Little Saigon resulted not only in death threats but also the murders of those who failed to toe the line. In popular culture, an episode of the hit television show *Magnum, P.I.*, whose title character carried psychological scars from his tour of duty in Vietnam, depicted the Little Saigon area of Honolulu as an unpleasant reminder of a war that veterans would rather forget, while a 1987 neo-noir novel, *Little Saigon*, depicted the Orange County enclave as a violent, gang-infested world with its own set of rules.[4]

Americans wanted to forget the past rather than regret it, but how could they when refugee communities—home to underground counterrevolutionary movements, gang activity, and welfare dependency—had seemingly brought the Vietnam War to America? In a racist society where individual acts could pull down an entire race and vice versa, present-day bad behavior by Vietnamese Americans naturalized the epic failures of the past, reducing the complexity of the Vietnam War and its aftermath to a moral lesson about ingratitude: perhaps South Vietnamese ingratitude and ineptitude made the fall of Saigon a fait accompli. The refugee community found itself in the unenviable position of constantly justifying the sacrifice of fifty-eight thousand American lives. Yet Vietnamese Americans proceeded to do just that, affirming the past by rewriting it.[5] If remembering posed a problem ready to strike at a moment's notice, instantaneously nullifying all the progress made in the name of assimilation, then Vietnamese Americans sought to associate their home country with model minorities and modernity instead of dysfunction and disrepair.

Rewriting the past helps to explain how Vietnamese Americans quickly went from social burdens to model minorities. Social scientists of the 1970s agreed that the biggest hurdle facing Vietnamese Americans was their reluctance to relinquish the past. In the 1980s there emerged a cohort of Vietnamese American assimilationists who enthusiastically embraced the future. In contrast to ultranationalist freedom fighters or the homesick sojourners, middle-class professionals such as Tony Lâm and Yến Đỗ were praised for learning English, launching successful enterprises, becoming naturalized citizens, celebrating the American Dream, and considering the United States their one and only home. In reality, however, they differed little from their stigmatized brethren. Even successful refugees had left behind far too many family and friends to simply forget the past. In addition, news of Vietnamese

Americans running afoul of the law was bound to reflect poorly on their pre-1975 society and thus call into question the wisdom of U.S. involvement with people of questionable moral character and scant self-determination. And what was the enclave of Little Saigon if not an homage to nostalgia? But in this case, idealistic representations of a past that never existed helped both Americans and Vietnamese offset painful collective memories of the war. Without historians on their side to contest past memories, Vietnamese Americans had to reshape their reputation in the present moment.

During a series of racial panics in the early years of Little Saigon's development, an informal and short-term middle-class leadership emerged, representing diverse and divergent interests such as the business sector, religious institutions, students, and social services.[6] Newspaperman Yến Đỗ admitted many years later that "as a media person, I began to understand what we needed to do; we needed to build up a responsible image of the refugees."[7] The assimilationists escaped the grasp of one problematic stereotype by embracing another, except that this model minority stereotype carried revisionist ramifications, as signs of Vietnamese refugee economic success stirred debate regarding who really won the Vietnam War.[8] It was an old strategy with new dimensions and obvious benefits. Vietnamese had transformed a dilapidated suburb into a diasporic mecca where local shops generated hundreds of millions of dollars in annual sales. The Vietnamese refugees felt at home in their new suburban enclave, and many became homeowners.

But these émigrés could not singlehandedly prompt such a rapid image makeover. As a socioeconomically disadvantaged group with limited English skills and political power, they were grateful to have any political allies at all. Historical circumstances convinced many white conservatives, who already had a stake in winning the postwar, to buy into the myth of a Vietnamese American model minority. In 1978, California voters passed Proposition 13, a property tax relief measure that left municipalities with huge budget deficits that sales tax revenue from the emerging refugee business sector filled. In addition, guilt-ridden white conservatives saw a Vietnamese model minority as vindicating America's mission, if not its war, in Southeast Asia and thus were among the first public defenders of Vietnamese Americans against racist attacks. Indeed, the sight of a Vietnamese American middle class in contrast to an impoverished communist-ruled homeland provided conservatives and veterans nationwide with a comforting and powerful antidote to the embarrassment of losing the war. This pro-Western narrative seemed to suggest that via the refugees, the United States and South Vietnam had won the war. Mutual interest in a positive image of the former South Vietnamese, especially in the midst of racial panics locally and crisis abroad, drew Vietnamese Americans and the Republican Party closer together. More important, it showed how an ethnic group succeeded not so much by forgetting the past as by constructing a new one with the help of a heavily invested ally.

However, presenting Vietnamese refugees as naturally industrious provided effective anticommunist propaganda but did little to address long-term poverty, crime, racism, and a widening generation gap in Little Saigon. Conservatives also tended to ignore a major reason so many of these immigrants worked so hard: to send remittances to their impoverished relatives back in Southeast Asia, an obligation that forced many refugees to work multiple jobs yet still collect welfare benefits. If anything, white conservatives and Vietnamese assimilationists disavowed any bad refugee tendencies present among the good refugees as anomalous. Conservative interest in winning the postwar allowed refugee transgressions to be individualized while refugee successes were racialized. This strategy reflected how becoming Refugee American was preferable to being a regular minority and helps to explain why Vietnamese American collective action often avoided the types of confrontation and protest historically essential to social progress. Given the limited alliances available to Vietnamese Americans, model minorityism was perceived as the best available route.

Early Crises and Republican Paternalism

Vietnamese refugees arrived in this country with the support of a small but significant bipartisan coalition in government, education, religion, and social services. With that help, Vietnamese Americans quickly learned to keep popular habits hidden from the wider public. In 1977, for example, Vietnamese refugees in Orange County used their backyards to prepare jerky from fresh-caught squid, as had been the common practice at home. "By all accounts," recounted the *Los Angeles Times*, "the stench was overpowering." Though refugee relief workers and others promptly told the Vietnamese that such customs simply could not be imported to American society and the problem was resolved, hard feelings lingered among those already predisposed to anti-Asian sentiment: "To one policeman, it proved what he had known all along: Vietnamese are dirty, different and do not belong here."[9] That a police officer would openly share such insensitive language with a reporter from a major newspaper indicated the social challenges facing Asians in a majority-white and conservative community.[10]

Stereotypes of filthy Asians reemerged in 1979 when the Centers for Disease Control reported that Orange County's tuberculosis infection rates had grown by 75 percent—from a minuscule .008 percent to a less minuscule .013 percent—and that 20 percent of infected individuals were Indochinese. Orange County's lone Democratic member of Congress, Jerry Patterson did his party no favors by floating a "tentative plan" to reduce by 30 percent the influx of Indochinese refugees to the county. Soon thereafter, the Orange County League of Cities hastily passed a resolution urging county supervisors and health officials to take "whatever steps necessary" to keep the residents of Orange County safe from the new danger introduced by the Southeast Asian refugees. The city councils of Garden Grove and Santa Ana also passed resolutions to address the "new medical problems facing the community," among them "intestinal parasites, tuberculosis and leprosy."[11] But the most negative effect of the tuberculosis scare was the scapegoating of refugees. Bien Qui Le, Chairman of the Vietnamese American Mutual Association, told the *Los Angeles Times* that "children suffered most as playmates refused to play with them," while adults suspected of carrying tuberculosis simply because of their skin color "were refused employment or ostracized in other ways."[12]

Like the earliest generations of Asian Americans, Vietnamese Americans lacked the political and social capital necessary to openly confront white racism on their own.[13] They could not lodge social protests but instead relied on sympathetic mainstream voices to take on that task. A century earlier, Christian missionaries had defended Asian immigrants; in 1979, the *Los Angeles Times* did so, publishing an editorial rebuking Orange County's fearmongers for turning an issue of genuine "concern" into an excuse for a "panic."[14] Nevertheless, the tiny Vietnamese middle class did its part to mobilize against any potential public health scare by constructing a whitened, middle-class past to counter stereotypes of poor, dark-skinned, diseased foreigners. In this case, an ad hoc umbrella organization of doctors and scientists explained that the French method of vaccination that had been in place in Vietnam since the early 1900s would produce false positives in the American testing method. Yến Đỗ remembered the panic as short-lived partly because the Vietnamese "understood the situation immediately and prepared a response and clarification."[15]

Another crisis five years later produced a different response and a different kind of ally. Only a couple of weeks after the lunar new year, California attorney general John Van de Kamp, based on evidence gathered by undercover operatives, ordered the arrest of fifty-one Southeast Asian doctors and pharmacists for allegedly collecting $27.5 million in fraudulent reimbursements from

Medi-Cal, the state-subsidized health insurance program for the poor. In light of the fact that Medi-Cal had paid more than $40 million for refugee medical bills in 1982, public benefits constituted a resource ripe for abuse. According to the prosecution, fraud occurred when refugees sold unused vouchers to health care providers, who then received reimbursement for services never provided, and when physicians wrote phony prescriptions, which pharmacists filled. Van de Kamp acknowledged that the scheme was partly aimed at procuring prescription drugs for "relatives in Vietnam or for sales on the black market in Vietnam."[16]

According to Yến Đỗ's account, "Medi-Cal fraud was the biggest crisis in the community in the early 80s."[17] The controversy received widespread news coverage, including a segment on the Sunday night CBS newsmagazine *60 Minutes*. Linking the misdeeds of several Vietnamese doctors to an unpopular war, though unfortunate, became an unavoidable theme. Feeling community pressure to avoid devoting too much copy space to the guilty parties, Đỗ's paper instead wondered aloud how the matter might affect public perception of the Vietnamese refugees.[18] Meanwhile, the community's ability to craft a model minority image began slipping away: "The fact that there has been a massive police raid, which was statewide . . . made big news all over the nation," recalled the president of the Vietnamese Medical Association of North America. "It has been a terrible blow to our pride as a people, and the general credibility of the Vietnamese in the new land that has adopted us." Without absolving the accused, he noted the racialized dimension of the investigation: "We know that fraud is being committed all the time by many people. It happens all the time, everywhere, and we never see such a police raid."[19] One entrepreneur was happy to see the crooked doctors arrested but remained more concerned that "the American people will think all Vietnamese are bad. We do not want Americans to think that way." Indeed, an Orange County electronic technician received a lecture on the matter from his American coworkers: "Your doctors, your pharmacists, are thieves, and they are the intellectual class and they do that. You are under them. We think you will do something worse than them."[20]

The community again formed an ad hoc committee to respond to the crisis. The committee, which included representatives of forty-two local organizations, held a February 29, 1984, press conference at which it asked Americans to be "fair-minded" and to avoid judging all Vietnamese based on the "misdeeds of a few black sheep."[21] Those "few black sheep" were eventually exonerated, but the members of the Vietnamese middle class did their best to disassociate themselves in every way from the accused.

By immediately disowning the disgraced physicians, the middle classes suggested that welfare fraud and even welfare dependence was anathema to the Vietnamese American way of life. Their rhetoric of disidentification and self-reliance preached a conservative message, and Little Saigon soon benefited almost exclusively from right-wing political support.

As Đỗ recalled, "We fortunately got the help of the Republican party with our first communiqué." And the story did not end there: "It was the beginning of the network between the community and the Republicans. It was a honeymoon period. [California State] Senator Ed Royce sent two of his assistants to monitor the situation and ask what they could do. Finally, we suggested that Royce prepare a statement and have a representative come to the meeting and read it before the Medi-Cal fraud committee. I remembered that it was very emotional for us to have him to appear before the committee, because committee members recognized that they have American support."[22]

That this American support became increasingly concentrated among conservatives and Republicans deserves deeper examination. In the spring of 1984, the *Washington Post* traveled to Orange County to gauge Vietnamese American political participation and concluded that homeland politics steered the older generation toward the Republican Party. However, "when you are thinking about politics right here, you get close to the Democrats," a recently naturalized citizen still torn between the two parties told the paper.[23] But the *Post*'s armchair sociology had mistakenly interpreted "right here" in terms of abstract platform issues without taking into account concrete relationships and alliances. Orange County had very few Democratic politicians, meaning that the Vietnamese were more likely to build relationships with Republicans. The emergence of Asian American suburbs in other parts of the United States often resulted in a conservative white backlash as well as support from Democratic politicians. In conservative Orange County, where Vietnamese Americans were the racialized Other, the backlash from older white conservatives remained the same, while support came mostly in the form of younger, relatively moderate, Republicans such as Ed Royce, Chuck Smith, and Kathy Buchoz.[24] If America's retreat from Vietnam could be viewed as the original sin, then these young conservatives treated their support of the local Vietnamese community as an act of atonement. They saw the demographic transformation of Orange County not so much as a tribute to diversity as much as making amends for broken promises. Buchoz, who served as mayor of Westminster for several years during the early 1980s, was among the early standouts, shopping in Little Saigon when "there were very, very, very few Caucasian people shopping there."[25] In 1990, the Vietnamese American Chamber of Commerce declared that Buchoz had "poured her heart into the community and always showed up to special events in her yellow-colored Vietnamese áo dài dress."[26] Many people wonder why Little Saigon developed in suburban Orange County, but the better question is why it sprang up in Westminster.

Westminster, a sleepy town of seventy-one thousand located just south of Disneyland, would have seemed unremarkable outside of its history of political ineptitude and corruption.[27] After five city officials were indicted on bribery charges in 1961, people knew Westminster as the place where people who served on the city council went to jail. After the 1978 passage of Proposition 13 radically restructured California's municipal wealth, cities such as Westminster found themselves in an economically precarious position.[28] A semirural backwater, Westminster collected relatively little in property taxes and had few retail stores prior to the arrival of Vietnamese businesses. Ed Bynon, the former publisher of the *Westminster Journal*, quipped, "If it were not for the Westminster Mall, there'd be no Westminster."[29]

Buchoz, a small business owner and a Democrat at the time, won election to the city council in 1980, receiving the most votes in Westminster history after a small scandal knocked three conservative incumbents out of office. When she assumed the post of mayor in 1981, she discovered that the city had reached a crossroads. Vietnamese American entrepreneurs had begun transforming Bolsa Avenue from a street "lined with bean fields and half-empty shopping centers" into "the Vietnamese capital of the United States."[30] The 9000 block of Bolsa alone saw the opening of more than twenty-five new Vietnamese businesses between January 1977 and January 1984.[31] The Williamsburg Center, home to Bolsa's first Vietnamese businesses, among them the Hòa Bình Market, Danh's Pharmacy, and Le Croissante Dore, changed its name to the Hòa Bình Center after white-owned businesses had moved out.[32] By the mid-1980s, approximately three hundred Vietnamese-owned businesses lined the streets of neighboring Garden Grove and Santa Ana.[33]

Westminster's nearly 350 Vietnamese businesses represented a potential solution to the city's Proposition 13 problem, but a contingent of angry white citizens disapproved of the cultural consequences. The group touted itself as favoring "slow growth," a loosely knit populist movement that had originated in California in the 1970s, when Petaluma sought to issue no more than five hundred building permits per year, and members' activism ensured that major development projects went to the ballot. Outside of

Figure 5. Asian Garden Mall, also known as Phước Lộc Thọ, opened in 1988 and remains the best-known commercial center in Little Saigon. Photo by author.

America's major urban areas, appeals to preserve local charm, character, and the natural landscape can carry political candidates to victory, especially when progrowth forces are people of color. Westminster's Vietnamese thus faced a local backlash when they moved into existing and abandoned buildings even though the lily-white Irvine Company faced little opposition as it destroyed hundreds of acres of undeveloped land to erect high-rise hotels, housing tracts, and megamalls. In 1981, Westminster residents gathered 150 signatures opposing further Indochinese business expansion.[34] Resentful white businesses owners confided to white reporters that "people are really ticked off" because the Vietnamese were "taking over."[35] "Everywhere you look anymore, it is Viet Cong," said another.[36] Such perceptions did not reflect reality: Vietnamese constituted less than three percent of Orange County's population.[37]

Buchoz, who had campaigned as a slow-growth candidate, had a more positive take: "Almost overnight we saw the emergence of new, brightly colored retail, commercial and professional buildings taking the place of dingy and depressed businesses in a large, undeveloped commercial area."[38] She tried to reach a compromise with angry citizens who demanded that absolutely no more business licenses be issued to Indochinese but found that these opponents were "like being with the Ku Klux Klan. It was very emotional and ugly. They said they were worried about property values, [even though] property values have gone up since the Vietnamese arrived," she said in 1984.[39] The rest of the city council backed her moral stand against racism but likely were swayed even more by Buchoz's post–Proposition 13 vision: "We don't have country cities here anymore. If you want to live in the country, you'll have to go someplace else."[40]

During Buchoz's 1981–82 term as mayor, Buchoz made it her mission "to get totally involved in the Vietnamese community" in ways that exhibited a genuine affection—though paternalistic—toward her new neighbors.[41] Buchoz made it fashionable for other women to start wearing South Vietnamese *áo dài* dresses.[42] She encouraged the Vietnamese to join the mainstream Chamber of Commerce and advocated on their behalf with the white business community. Although the Westminster Chamber of Commerce had only one Vietnamese member prior to the summer of 1981, six were admitted during July alone.[43] Although the neighboring cities of Santa Ana and Garden Grove had larger Vietnamese populations (and, indeed, many Vietnamese from outside the area still refer to Little Saigon's location as Santa Ana), businesses soon flocked to Westminster.[44] Ending Orange County's unofficial slow-growth policy would be the key, Buchoz knew, to Westminster's survival in the post–Proposition 13 political economy. By 1984, the Vietnamese Chamber of Commerce in America estimated that Orange County had 650 Vietnamese businesses generating at least three hundred million dollars in annual sales.[45]

Ironically, Buchoz's strong relationship with the Vietnamese community made her the target of race-baiting by fellow Democrat Al Serrato, a conservative who ran against Buchoz to represent the newly created Thirty-Second District in the State Senate in 1982. In statements decried by Buchoz and others as "blatantly racist," Serrato's campaign mailed out leaflets charging that Buchoz had "marched with Vietnamese in black pajamas," received key financial support from a "Vietnamese businessman," and made "Indochinese refugees" a key issue in her campaign.[46] The desperate xenophobic tactic of lumping refugees with the Việt-Cộng scared enough people to leave Buchoz four hundred votes short of the Democratic nomination, although Serrato finished a distant third.[47] The winner of the primary, whom Serrato labeled a "liberal" with links to antiwar power couple Jane Fonda and Tom Hayden, eventually lost in the general election to Royce, a Republican who later became a strong supporter of the Vietnamese refugees. Buchoz switched to the Republican Party and subsequently returned to the Westminster City Council. Refugee nationalism and the politics of rescue had created an unusual political climate in which Republicans, at least in their dealings with Vietnamese Americans, could claim to be the party of racial tolerance. After learning that Buchoz was stepping away from politics after the 1984 election, the *Người Việt Daily News* put her on the cover of its November 2 issue with a rare English-language headline, "Thank You, Kathy Buchoz."[48]

That Vietnamese, an ethnic group with poverty rates far above the national average, could take advantage of Westminster's opportunities to quickly craft a model minority image resulted in large part from the fact that the Sino-Vietnamese took care of the supply side while the welfare state took care of the demand side. Many big entrepreneurs and landlords, most notably future Godfather of Little Saigon Frank Jao, were first- or second-generation Vietnamese of Chinese heritage. Some had owned businesses in Vietnam and found it advantageous to continue their entrepreneurial ways abroad once they realized that increased refugee migration into Los Angeles, Orange County, San Diego, San Jose, and other places helped make ethnic economies a reality. More important, these business leaders spoke Cantonese, which opened the door to Chinese customers and business contacts all over Asia and North America.[49] During a period when the doors to most communist nations remained closed, the Sino Vietnamese enjoyed a twenty-year entrepreneurial head start over other Southeast Asians, turning minor players in Vietnam into major players in the diaspora.

Saigon's former business class gave Los Angeles's Chinatown a Vietnamese facelift soon after the refugees began to arrive. In 1976, the Man Wah Company, just off College Street, sold bootlegged Vietnamese music cassettes, Chinese herbal medicine, Vietnamese periodicals and books, fish sauce from Thailand, shrimp paste from the Philippines, Chinese sausage from Canada, pickled scallions from Japan, and instant noodles from Taiwan.[50] The shop's owner, Roger Chen, a young Taiwanese developer, joined forces in 1981 with Jao, then a fledgling entrepreneur, to buy up properties on the 9000 block of Bolsa Avenue.[51] With a growing Vietnamese population, affordable property, and local politicians sympathetic to Vietnamese entrepreneurs, Orange County constituted a successful gamble. That year, Duong Huu Chuong, who had been a pharmacist in Vietnam, opened up Orange County's largest Asian supermarket.[52] In 1979, he had opened his first grocery store with five thousand dollars he had smuggled out of

Vietnam. Within five years, he and Chinese friends in Taiwan, Thailand, and elsewhere in the States operated an import/export business that stocked more than one hundred Southern California grocery stores.[53] From 1975 to 1984, developers from Taiwan and Hong Kong had invested ten million dollars along Bolsa Avenue alone.[54] Thus Little Saigon's economic growth mirrored the expanding Chinese American suburb in Monterey Park. The presence of Chinese transnational behemoths soon made obsolete the mom-and-pop grocers like Santa Ana's tiny Saigon Market, which opened in 1976, and the Hòa Bình Market, which opened on Bolsa Avenue in 1978. And the fact that virtually all of these supermarkets accepted food stamps made them a pillar of the ethnic economy (alongside physicians and pharmacists) whose so-called model minority success would not have been possible if the welfare state had not first put money in customers' pockets.[55]

Even Yến Đỗ, who spent a great deal of his newspaper's energy defending Vietnamese Americans against racial profiling after the 1984 Medi-Cal crisis, admitted many years later that welfare fraud was fairly widespread among his people. "For health [care], some people overused Medi-Cal vouchers to obtain prescription drugs for relatives back home [while] some people applied for housing [assistance] in more than one place while the rules say every citizen should apply for housing in only one city. Some refugees applied for their relatives even before the relatives arrived. It may look like fraud, but that's the way they survived."[56] Swept up in a politics of rescue in which immediate success was the only acceptable display of gratitude, Vietnamese Americans felt constrained to deny any dependence on welfare when in fact it was one of the keys to their economic upward mobility. The truth could never come out partly because most conservatives steadfastly refused to acknowledge the link between welfare and prosperity. At the same time, "moderate" conservatives such as Royce, Buchoz, and Chuck Smith felt it their duty as good penitent Americans to oversell Vietnamese Americans as perfect refugees who embodied the classic rags-to-riches story. This model minority narrative, while providing a satisfying new conclusion to the Vietnam War, was no comfort to white xenophobes, of which Orange County had its fair share. Conservatives consequently faced off against each other. It was little wonder then, as Westminster's Mayor Smith sadly admitted in 1987, that the sight of new arrivals, "who came here 10 years ago, boat people out of Camp Pendleton, who are now driving fancy cars and living in nice, big homes," served as a flashpoint for the town's many racists still living in old apartments and mobile homes after so many years.[57]

Little Saigon and the White Backlash of 1989

As the Serrato debacle and everyday interactions revealed, Vietnamese Americans suffered from most Americans' inability to distinguish friend from foe. In 1980, avowed white supremacist and surprise San Diego congressional candidate Tom Metzger warned anyone within earshot about "former Viet Cong guerillas . . . living in the Orange County suburbs."[58] A Japanese American deputy sheriff in Sacramento noted how the "fires of racial hatred" had "flared up against other Asians who've been called 'V.C.' . . . since the refugees arrived."[59] When Nam Lộc, a Catholic Charities refugee caseworker, gave a guest lecture to a classroom of thirty students at UCLA prior to the tenth anniversary of the fall of Saigon, he discovered that only two students knew which side the United States had aided during the war, with one student claiming that the United States had officially gone to war against all of Vietnam. Even worse, the majority of students had no idea why Vietnamese refugees had come to America, with three reporting that their parents had described Little Saigon as an enclave of "illegal immigrants."[60]

Vietnamese Americans had to remind Americans that they were neither the bad guys nor the bad allies. Starting with lunar new year celebrations, college students launched their own Tết Offensive to cleanse Vietnamese culture of any negative associations with the past. In 1978, they organized the first Tết festivals on Southern California's community college campuses.[61] In less than a decade, the Union of Vietnamese Student Associations had moved the festival to off-campus locations such as Santa Ana's Centennial Regional Park, where it attracted at least thirty thousand visitors each year. Whites in attendance included local officials and dignitaries who garnered VIP treatment from an ethnic minority that desperately wanted the event to serve as "a showroom for American people . . . to come and taste our food, and see how we play music and dance."[62] The festival gradually replaced tragic memories of Tết with nostalgic ones.

Students also organized smaller events designed to celebrate a culture unknown to most Americans and outlawed by the government in Hanoi. During the early 1980s, students at California State University at Long Beach organized the first Vietnamese American beauty pageant.[63] Musician Phạm Duy served as one of the judges for the 1984 pageant.[64] Vietnamese student associations also organized major cultural performances that drew from talent on and off campus. With assistance from their counterparts at UCLA, Pasadena City College, Cal State Long Beach, and Cal State

Northridge, students at the University of Southern California held a 1984 show at Bovard Auditorium that featured performances from professional singers Duy Quang (Phạm Duy's son) and Jo Marcell.[65] Renowned vocalist Khánh Ly performed at Pasadena City College's Vietnamese culture night just two weeks later, with proceeds from the event going to the boat people still living in Thailand.[66]

While students enjoyed some success in making Vietnamese culture less threatening to white people, the self-appointed leaders of the business community were less confident that white Americans could be acclimated to Vietnamese names. Businessman Tony Lâm and dentist Phil Trinh exemplified those who adopted English names in keeping with an ethnic politics driven by assimilation rather than advocacy. They founded the Vietnamese American Chamber of Commerce in 1980 partly in response to complaints by Orange County firefighters, police, and other emergency officials that nonfluent readers had difficulty distinguishing among Vietnamese-language business signs.[67] Consistent with a focus on assimilation, the Chamber helped Vietnamese businesses navigate cultural and bureaucratic hurdles and learn how things are done in America, operating from the presumption that their people, not whites, needed education to counter their ignorance.

This strategy of catering to white business elites backfired badly in 1987 when it came to choosing an official name for the Vietnamese enclave in Westminster. Although the refugee business district went by several nicknames—such as *Santa Ana*, *Bolsa*, and *Little Saigon*—Lâm and real estate mogul Jao opted for an obscure title, *Asiantown*, when they unveiled plans for a thirty-million-dollar shopping complex on the 9000 block of Bolsa Avenue that would include the Asian Village and the Asian Garden Mall, which were anticipated to anchor the ethnic economy. Jao, by far the wealthiest of all Vietnamese Americans, claimed that the name *Little Saigon* was "too narrow, too small" and not worthy of his vision of a shopping center "broad enough for different Asian ethnics."[68] Lâm echoed similar assimilationist talking points when he told reporters, "'Little Saigon' is too negative and reminds people of the bad experiences from the war."[69] Their talking points, though in lockstep with white elites, reflected a dismissive attitude toward their fellow ethnics. Lâm and Jao quickly learned that they did not actually speak for the community.

Vulnerable Vietnamese American merchants, especially those located in Santa Ana and Garden Grove, refused to launch class-based critiques against the concentration and centralization of capital and instead invoked race-based populism. One after another, community members painted Jao and Lâm, both of ethnic Chinese ancestry, as racial outsiders akin to the Han, who had colonized Vietnam for several centuries. Jao's insistence on identifying as Chinese did not help his cause, while Lâm's dream of an upscale mall would have squeezed out many family-owned businesses. In reality, rank-and-file grievances encompassed both racial and class dimensions. By favoring the *Asiantown* moniker and housing it in his brand new shopping center, Jao could depict Vietnamese culture as exotic yet respectable. For Jao, identifying as Asian had less to do with solidarity than it did with profitability. In his thinking, Vietnam was less a country and more a damaged brand name that any smart businessman would shun. If successful, Asiantown would forever shift the balance of power in the refugee commercial sector from businesses dispersed throughout Southern California to a concentrated commercial real estate market controlled almost exclusively by Jao and his associates.

The episode revealed how assimilation and accommodation constituted a performance best reserved for white audiences, while protest frequently resulted from internal squabbles. Without popular support, Jao and Lâm went ahead with the shopping center project but withdrew the *Asiantown* moniker in favor of the community's preferred name, *Little Saigon*. Coined by white journalists to describe the American-run refugee camps of 1975, *Little Saigon* nevertheless held sway in the community as a lasting tribute to an extinct capital city the triumphant communists had renamed after their leader, Hồ Chí Minh. Taking their cues from the masses, white politicians in Orange County agreed to the name *Little Saigon* when they designated the profitable enclave a special tourist zone. In addition to providing legal institutionalization, the move implied a degree of reconciliation harkening back to the war. The name *Saigon* was now cause for collective celebration rather than mutual mourning. Community history reached a new high on June 17, 1988, when Governor George Deukmejian visited Orange County to formally unveil the Little Saigon freeway sign to an audience of nearly four hundred awed spectators at Jao's Asian Garden Mall: "Each year, Little Saigon attracts thousands of tourists, shoppers and business people," said the governor to enthusiastic applause. "The dedication of this new freeway sign is further recognition of the importance of Little Saigon as a major cultural, social and commercial center." For a people whose home country had literally erased Saigon from the map, seeing the city's name return brought tears of joy, affirmation, and gratitude. "Only in America is Saigon being resurrected," said Van Tran, a young aide to state senator Ed Royce.[70] Tran's presence foreshadowed the emergence of a new set of cultural brokers who, like the ultranationalist Front, could tap into the rage and populism of his people while cloaked in mainstream respectability.

With the community still reeling from the excesses of the Front and gang violence, the assimilationists cast themselves as the saviors of their people. Nobody relished that role more than Lâm, who likely felt vindicated in January 1989 when unidentified persons trashed the Little Saigon freeway sign and draped an American flag over it. "If the area had been named 'Asiantown' instead of 'Little Saigon,'" he lamented, "then maybe these signs would have been left alone."[71] In reality, not the name but the growth of the enclave had triggered a nativist resurgence. The attack on the sign came just after the Brothers of Viet-Nam, a fringe veterans group based in La Habra, demanded that all five members of the Westminster City Council boycott the Tết festival, which had moved to Westminster for the first time. The Brothers of Viet-Nam argued that Americans should not be celebrating a holiday associated with the 1968 Tết Offensive. Westminster mayor Chuck Smith pointed out the fallacy of that logic: "Imagine if Christmas held horrible memories for a group of soldiers. Should Christmas then be ignored to salve their wounds?"[72] Smith and two council members pledged to attend the festival, but the other two members announced that they would join the Brothers of Viet-Nam in a flag-raising ceremony at City Hall in honor of the 2,383 Americans listed as missing in action in Vietnam. The community had been split between supposedly pro-Vietnamese and pro-American factions, implying, in a theme all too frequent in Asian American history, that Vietnamese and their supporters were not genuine Americans. This rift between old and young conservatives was the brainchild of longtime city council member Frank Fry Jr.

Frank Fry and Racial Politics

Born in 1925, Frank Fry Jr. had moved to Westminster in 1957 and worked as a supermarket manager before winning election to the city council in 1966. He usually campaigned on a basic conservative platform of small government, but he lost his seat in 1980 when rumors surfaced that he was steering city contracts to his own company. His World War II veteran status and membership in the American Legion only reinforced his macho Know-Nothing populism. In 1989, Frey caused an uproar when he uttered some vehemently anti-Asian comments.[73]

Having already achieved a victory when the City Council of Westminster voted four to one against a parade to commemorate the American and

South Vietnamese militaries on June 18, Fry lectured the parade's organizing committee: "It is my opinion that you're American, and you'd better be American. If you want to be South Vietnamese, go back to South Vietnam."[74] Outside of Smith, a Korean War veteran who cast the lone vote in favor of the parade, the members of the council objected to having American veterans share the stage with members of a group that had never been regarded as equal partners.[75] To strengthen his case, Fry leaned on the Brothers of Viet-Nam, whose spokesman declared that Fry "should be commended." "Why should [the Vietnamese] have a different holiday to honor veterans? They're already getting everything they want. It is about time somebody stood up to them."[76]

Fry's remarks suggested that Americans owed nothing more to the South Vietnamese. Furthermore, his attitude reflected larger anti-Asian anxieties exacerbated by crises gripping the nation during the 1980s. Defeated militarily in Vietnam and facing economic competition from Japan and academic competition from Asian American students, many whites perceived the increased visibility and clout of Asians and Asian Americans as cause for alarm. Fry found support among whites for whom centuries of Western imperialism reflected a natural racial hierarchy that placed them permanently atop people of color. Just as important, Fry's remarks indicated that his lifelong commitment to honoring veterans only applied to the U.S. military, and his actions demonstrated the same American disdain for South Vietnamese veterans and their sacrifices that had been evident during the Vietnam War. Fry's statements, issued so close to the annual commemoration of the fall of Saigon, created what Mayor Smith called "a wedge between the Caucasian and the Vietnamese community, and also between the city [government] and the Vietnamese community."[77] This wedge also divided the white community, pitting older, insular conservatives against those willing to see Asians as friends. Among the latter was former Central Intelligence Agency director William Colby, who came to Orange County in April 1989 to praise the Vietnamese as "hardworking" people experiencing the same discrimination that Italian immigrants had suffered.[78] For his part, Fry blamed the Vietnamese for the alleged divisions in Westminster, blind to the point made by the *Los Angeles Times* that no one tells the Irish or Italians to return to Europe if they want their own parade.[79] Editorials in the *Los Angeles Times* and *Orange County Register* rebuked Fry, and the Orange County Human Relations Commission voted unanimously to recommend that Fry apologize to the Vietnamese American community. Vietnamese activists threatened to recall Fry from office but aborted their efforts after Fry issued an apology six days later. Nevertheless, the damage had been done.

Fry had mobilized older white conservatives against their Indochinese neighbors, forcing Vietnamese Americans again to tread ever so lightly. Jao, the most powerful man in the refugee community, opted to express refugee gratitude: "Frank Fry has done too many things that have helped us in the past to make a statement like his affect how we think of him." Another Vietnamese businessman told the *Los Angeles Times* that the Vietnamese are a "very practical people" who more than anything want "Americans to know . . . how thankful we are for living here."[80] After hearing that Fry had agreed to apologize, the spokesman for the short-lived recall effort said it was "a big relief to all of us that this is coming to an end in a very beautiful way" because "any conflict upsets" his people.[81] And Lâm, who went on to become Fry's political rival, concurred that the community "should give him the opportunity to apologize."[82] In casting their lot with white conservatives, Vietnamese Americans had accepted the grand bargain of perfection in exchange for rescue. Any public transgressions in the present would further impugn the Saigon regime of the past. While white people could just be themselves, Vietnamese Americans had to be more because their most ardent mainstream supporters expected nothing less. In this case, their dependence on refugee gratitude and the goodwill of sympathetic—albeit conservative—Anglos worked insofar as Fry apologized and the City Council reconsidered its decision against the parade for Vietnamese veterans. In this light, Vietnamese developed a set of expectations about race relations in America that few other groups could relate to.[83]

The Embargo That Wasn't

Given the enmity between Washington and Hanoi during the Cold War and the refugees' well-known anticommunism, Vietnamese émigrés seemed to have lost any tangible connection to the past and therefore to have fully committed themselves to the future. But reality was more complicated. Newspaperman Yến Đỗ published articles about cultural assimilation at the same time that he dreamed of repatriation. As an anticommunist, he highlighted the effectiveness of the U.S. economic embargo against Hanoi while simultaneously participating in a multi-million-dollar remittance market that far exceeded what was allowed by U.S. law. Testimony by Vietnamese Americans before the Senate Banking, Housing, and Urban Affairs Committee on June 20, 1984, revealed an elaborate grassroots political economy in which virtually all Vietnamese Americans had access to multiple couriers that could be used to send money across the Pacific. Moreover, these remittances helped to fuel the ethnic economy via an endless spate of illicit transactions normally hidden from the mainstream.

The hearings also revealed why refugees living safely in the United States could not afford to stop thinking about the communists. Their loved ones in South Vietnam were being taxed, threatened, and extorted into writing letters begging for assistance. One man, who was known only as Mr. X and who testified while wearing a mask, had set up a secret code with his wife before he escaped alone by boat. When he started receiving letters that lacked her photo and included questions about "what am I doing in America, how much money I make, where I work at," he suspected that the Vietnamese police were "forcing her to write what they want me to do for them and what they need, especially money."[84] A former Vietnamese Marine now living in eastern New Orleans believed that if he stopped sending remittances, "my mother will be put back in the [reeducation] camp forever." Moreover, because there was only one way to get the money to her remote village, he begged authorities not to arrest the currency man with whom he dealt.[85] Echoing the sentiments of early American colonists, Mr. X declared, "Vietnamese here are paying taxes. Also they have to pay an additional tax for the Communists. Is that fair? No."[86] Hanoi of course denied forcing its people to solicit contributions from abroad.[87]

Because refugees sent back goods as well as money, what one police officer called "opportunistic businessmen" trafficked merchandise whose ultimate destination was the black market in Vietnam.[88] U.S. law allowed small shipments of humanitarian goods such as food, clothing, and medicine, but all parties knew that "with the average Vietnamese [in Vietnam] earning $2 to $3 per week, the sale of a $75 cassette radio can earn enough money, even with the high tax, to pay grocery bills for a month."[89] Businesses in every Vietnamese community in the States engaged in this practice, but Orange County businesses grabbed the largest market share. One reporter from the *Orange County Register* discovered a black market in Saigon that was "stocked with the latest products, including Phillips and JVC remote-control color-television sets, Sony stereo cassette recorders, Singer sewing machines, Winston cigarettes, Sheaffer pens, Proctor Silex irons, Remington electric typewriters and Panasonic fans."[90] Danh's Pharmacy, one of the first refugee businesses on Bolsa Avenue, dedicated most of its store space to those nonpharmaceutical items, and its owner confessed to moving ten thousand pounds of goods per month to Vietnam.[91] Despite the embargo, calendars advertising Danh's Pharmacy hung in houses in Hồ Chí Minh City.[92]

To circumvent the four-hundred-dollar limit on individual parcels, AF Express International and other Bolsa Avenue companies accepted orders for expensive items such as nineteen-hundred-dollar Honda motor scooters, which would then be shipped to Vietnam by partner companies in Japan.[93] Yến Đỗ knew from personal experience that "the big items" in 1988 included "water pumps, engines and tillers. Last year it was medicine. Chain saws and motorcycles are good all the time."[94] Vietnamese Freight International of Garden Grove, which reported moving twenty thousand pounds of goods each month, fielded orders from Vietnamese living as far away as Iowa and Minnesota.[95] The Vietnamese Chamber of Commerce in Orange County estimated that the remittance business accounted for a staggering 50 percent of the ethnic economy.[96]

Though engaged in illegal activity, Vietnamese Americans were rarely treated as criminals. For its hearings, the U.S. Senate sought testimony from those perceived as victims, while remittance traffic itself generated scant outrage. One Arlington, Virginia, police detective apprehended a proprietor responsible for routinely shipping more than twenty thousand dollars' worth of pharmaceuticals each week to Vietnam and was shocked when a U.S. Customs special agent shrugged, "No one is interested."[97] A few token crackdowns during the 1980s did not deter most Vietnamese Americans from continuing to violate the terms of the embargo.[98] "How can a box that weighs 150 pounds have goods in it that cost less than $400? Just look at what's being sold," one entrepreneur pointed out. "You send a television over, a stereo cassette radio, a sewing machine, and you wrap it with clothes and fabric. The embargo's a joke. The federal government never checks."[99] As one expert noted, the government would care more if military hardware or high-tech equipment changed hands.[100] Even ultra-right-wing anticommunist member of Congress Robert Dornan believed in the humanitarian principles behind remittances, lobbying to have the old two-hundred-dollar cap raised to four hundred dollars "out of sympathy" for his Orange County constituents.[101] But if Dornan did not seem overly outraged by this violation of Cold War policy, perhaps it was because he was in on the long game, as publisher Yến Đỗ speculated: "The US wants Vietnam to become addicted [to U.S. consumer goods]; That's why it allows the goods to go through."[102] Conservatives' sympathy, along with their desire to win the postwar, made it palatable to portray Vietnamese Americans in a one-dimensionally positive light—that is, as perfect refugees whose upward mobility both affirmed the superiority of capitalism over communism and suggested that the people of South Vietnam were indeed worth fighting for.

Vietnamese for City Council

Assimilationist politics reached its climax in the early 1990s when Vietnamese Americans began running for elected office. The 1990 U.S. Census found that Orange County's Vietnamese American population had grown to seventy-two thousand, enough to sustain an ethnic economy but not a political career. When fifty-six-year-old Tony Lâm decided to run for a spot on the Westminster City Council in 1992, he knew he would need support not only from the sixteen thousand members of the city's Vietnamese community (only 3 percent of which had registered to vote) but also from white voters. Another Vietnamese candidate, Jimmy Tong Nguyễn, age forty-five, entered the race, and the two campaigns registered an additional two thousand Vietnamese voters, but three white candidates also sought the seat. Fearing criticism, none of the Vietnamese organizations dared to endorse either Lâm or Nguyễn.

Because local elections depend so heavily on door-to-door campaigning, Orange County's Vietnamese candidates joined the Republican Party.[103] The Republicans offered much-needed paternalism as well as institutional advantages. By 1984, the county had one hundred thousand more registered Republicans than Democrats, the largest gap in the county's history. Ronald Reagan's landslide victories in the 1980 and 1984 elections depended on former Democrats switching parties, and they did so in droves, claiming that the Democrats no longer represented their values. In addition, the GOP's ten-to-one fund-raising advantage virtually assured a permanent Republican majority. Bruce Sumner, the Orange County Democratic chair, found it quite "ironic if they're saying the Democratic Party is the party of special interests because it is really the Republicans who have the special interests—where do they think the money comes from? It is from all those industries and businesses who want something."[104]

Lâm had spent most of his post-1975 life in Orange County, while Nguyễn had resided in New Orleans prior to moving to Westminster in 1990.[105] Lâm also possessed the perfect model minority biography, often describing himself as "three times a refugee."[106] After missing the boats leaving Hải Phong in 1946, when a French attempt to reclaim colonial territory killed six thousand Vietnamese, the ten-year-old Lâm began supporting himself by singing with an itinerant troupe. In 1954, he joined more than a million North Vietnamese who migrated to Saigon after the Geneva Accords divided Vietnam. And in 1975, he lost everything when he and his family evacuated before Saigon fell.[107] But in case that rags-to-riches tale failed to sway voters, Lâm could tell them he had the support of Mayor Smith, U.S. representative Dana Rohrabacher, the Westminster Police Officers Association, California assembly member Mickey Conroy of Orange, and Representative Dornan.[108] Lâm campaigned as a proud American, and an interview conducted in his office described him being "surrounded by American flags."[109] On November 13, 1992, when all of the votes were tallied, Lâm had won the seat, receiving 7,119 votes.[110] The mainstream media now viewed Lâm, the first Vietnamese American elected to U.S. political office, as the official face of his community. In reality, Lâm's more assimilationist and establishment-oriented identity was quickly challenged by a cohort of self-styled populist Vietnamese American politicians.

A New Model Minority

While it was normal for refugee identity to be tied to the Vietnamese homeland, the assimilationists wanted everyone to believe otherwise. While it was normal to find refugees at the bottom of the socioeconomic ladder, hustling for every dollar, the assimilationists had little choice but to insist that their brethren were superhuman: parents suffered unspeakable horrors to escape Vietnam; children excelled in school; families vacated the slums; refugee gratitude was unrivaled; and Vietnamese had no need to cling to the past. Assimilationists became obsessed with a model minority image because many Americans, especially conservative whites, expected perfection in return for rescuing Vietnamese refugees from communism. White Americans needed as much validation in their collective decision to welcome the Vietnamese as the refugees did in the decision to leave Vietnam forever.

Supporters of the model minority approach were bolstered by data from the 1990 U.S. Census that showed Vietnamese Americans' phenomenal entrepreneurial proclivities. Between 1982 and 1987, the number of Vietnamese-owned businesses in the United States had increased from 4,989 to 25,671, a whopping 415 percent increase that far exceeded the 135 percent growth in their population during the period. And one of out of every eight Vietnamese-owned businesses was located in Orange County. No other Asian American group saw such a dramatic rise in its business sector, and as a representative of Southern California's Vietnamese Chamber of Commerce boasted, people were coming to Southern California because "they realize this is the land of opportunity."[111] Assimilationists neglected to mention the welfare state's impact on the ethnic economy or the importance of remittances in keeping dollars in Little Saigon. They also overlooked the recent arrest of three Orange County gang members charged with extorting protection money from seven coethnic businesses.[112] The modern Asian American model minority stereotype had originated in the 1960s to discredit African American protest as a means for achieving social equality.[113] Three decades later, Vietnamese American history introduced a new context for the model minority myth, rewriting history so that people might forget there ever was a debate over whether South Vietnam and its people were worth fighting for.

6 Divided Loyalties

America's Moral Obligation in the Post–Cold War Era

> The American government instigated the war, so they have a moral and financial obligation to the Vietnamese people today.
> —Vietnamese Major General Tran Cong Man, 1990

> Once they were freed, [South Vietnamese reeducation camp inmates] heard reports that former political prisoners were being venerated in the United States as heroes, given new homes and cars in gratitude for their wartime service.
> —*San Jose Mercury News*, 1992

Until the end of the twentieth century, Vietnamese Americans enjoyed a demographic luxury not available to most of their coethnics across the globe: a refugee majority. Despite protestations by overzealous community members that an abundance of communist spies had infiltrated Little Saigon, U.S. diplomatic, immigration, and refugee policies ensured that very few supporters of the Hanoi regime entered the country. By 1990, the Vietnamese American population had topped six hundred thousand, with the largest concentrations in the suburbs of California and Texas.[1] Safely ensconced in their anticommunist bubble, Vietnamese Americans had assumed that the diasporic population would maintain its refugee orientation and that U.S. foreign policy would always overlap with refugee interests. The former was on full display in early 1999 when more than twenty thousand angry Vietnamese Americans, the largest gathering of its kind, protested a Little Saigon merchant's display of the red flag of Vietnam and a portrait of communist leader Hồ Chí Minh. With Little Saigon serving as their ethnic sanctuary, thousands of Refugee Americans viewed the public display of enemy symbols as a threat to their sovereignty. But by then, their collective anger no longer resonated with U.S. government leaders and intellectual elites: five years after the end of the trade embargo with Hanoi, such protests seemed embarrassing—or worse—from a post–Cold War diplomatic standpoint. The spectacle left mainstream observers wondering how nearly twenty-five years in the States had failed to suppress memories most Americans had allegedly put to rest.[2]

By the late 1980s and early 1990s, even official statements and informal encounters from the Vietnamese people appeared to show that they harbored no grudges against their former enemy. "Everywhere in Vietnam, from Ho Chi Minh City to Hanoi," one American writer recalled, "Americans are met with smiles and appeals for friendship."[3] Calls for war reparations were few and far between. Instead, most observers agreed that the United States had a moral obligation to lift the trade embargo imposed on the communist state since 1954. That act, as they saw it, would usher in a new era of harmonious relations.[4]

Mainstream narratives about postwar reconciliation read like morality tales, with the Vietnamese refugees depicted as petty, vindictive simpletons who should learn to forgive their enemies, as America and Vietnam had evidently done. But overt displays of magnanimity and goodwill ignored all those years America and Vietnam had spent fighting the postwar. For years, conservatives in both countries equated reconciliation with surrender. But after the 1991 collapse of the Soviet Union, money could be made outside of the military-industrial complex. American neoliberals wanted to dominate the world economy even if doing so required recognizing the legitimacy of the Hanoi regime, and Vietnam wanted to move up the Asian hierarchy even if doing so required embracing the same economic system that millions had died fighting. Global free-market evangelists captured the reins of power in both countries, framing reconciliation as a postwar victory for their respective sides, while refugee activists were left with little to feel victorious about.

In this moment of crisis, when U.S. foreign policy and mainstream attitudes no longer overlapped with émigrés' interests, aging refugee activists, including recently arrived former political prisoners, appropriated what David Lloyd refers to as a minority discourse when exercising their local political leverage to ensure that globalization would not transform Little Saigon into Little Ho Chi Minh City. Thanks to their newfound demographic strength in certain pockets such as Orange County, doubling down on the politics of rescue, on saving Little Saigon from extinction, could be couched as a reflection of the democratic process, though never fully detached from the politics of rescue. Refugee activism lent a transnational perspective to a quasi-nativist movement and attracted an unlikely influential ally in Frank Fry Jr., the former xenophobe whose impeccable conservative credentials convinced whites in Westminster to institutionalize refugee nationalism via memorials and heritage flag resolutions so that the refugee generation's collective memory would remain long after they had passed away. History had come full circle, with a community infamous for its unruly anticommunism now on the defensive against Vietnamese capitalism.

Winning the Vietnam War Again

Hanoi's path to state capitalism was slow and unexpected. While Hồ Chí Minh's communist revolution, modeled after Mao's peasant uprising, had energized the worldwide Left, much of Asia, including China, was already undergoing a dramatic transition to a market economy. Between 1973 and 1996, the world's fastest-growing economy belonged to South Korea, followed closely by Singapore, Taiwan, Thailand, China, Hong Kong, and Malaysia.[5] American-backed anticommunist nation building predicated on export-oriented economics, foreign investment, and currency devaluation—essentially a form of self-exploitation—had turned the agrarian frontiers of Southeast Asia into majestic urban skylines rivaling those of America's big cities. As long as these countries offered a surplus of exploitable low-wage, semiskilled, nonunion labor, there was no end to the stampede of multinational corporations relocating their factories there. The World Bank dubbed this twenty-year economic bubble the Asian Miracle.[6]

Not surprisingly, Vietnam sought to join in Southeast Asia's economic boom, especially since internal and external factors left the country isolated and nearly bankrupt through the 1970s and 1980s.[7] The Hanoi government had always distanced itself rhetorically from communism, but economic reforms finally began in earnest after the death of hard-line dictator Lê Duẩn in 1986. The Hanoi government, now led by reformer Nguyễn Văn Linh—the Vietnamese Gorbachev—declared the revolution over and ushered in Đổi Mới, the socialist world's version of the New Deal, introducing free-market reforms to save the communist state.[8] Having seen market-based socialism tested in China, the Vietnamese Communist Party likely moved ahead because the capitalistic paradigm left no other choice. Ideological purity could not resolve the real material disadvantages plaguing much of Southeast Asia. And this time around, with major businesses headed by people of color, capitalism could be depicted as a homegrown Asian phenomenon.

Trade deals with other nations, especially the United States, would provide Vietnam, a small country, valuable leverage against China and other neighboring predatory states.[9]

But the United States, having lost a war to Hanoi in very embarrassing fashion, would only normalize from a position of strength, which it finally achieved after the collapse of the Soviet Union in 1991. Proponents of the so-called New World Order—a euphemism for American economic hegemony—emerged out of the shadows of militaristic Cold Warriors to argue that reconciliation with Hanoi, did not signify weakness but provided an opportunity to win the Vietnam War via free trade.[10] Writing on the fifteenth anniversary of the fall of Saigon, *USA Today* founder Al Neuharth argued that the hard-liners in Washington should stop fighting the last war and concentrate instead on winning the peace.[11] In 1991, as the United States barred its people from attending Vietnam's largest foreign investment conference to date, *Los Angeles Times* business writer Teresa Watanabe seemed to lament seeing "foreign competitors snap up Vietnam's best deals in oil, construction and telecommunications." One of her interviewees, a Vietnam specialist, believed that lifting the economic embargo would be no worse than the status quo: "We have tried for more than 30 years—probably close to 45 years—to use the stick against the Vietnamese [and] they have not changed their way of doing things. I think our greatest strength is our economic system. Maybe we can get to them with the pocketbook where we could not with bombs."[12]

Vietnam came to be seen as vital to securing U.S. hegemony in the New World Order. So important was the mission of reconciliation with Hanoi that its most credible proponent was U.S. senator and former prisoner of war John McCain, the same man who eventually confessed his never-ending hatred of "gooks."[13] Despite concerns that in the absence of an embargo, Hanoi would stop searching for the more than two thousand U.S. personnel still considered missing in Vietnam, McCain and fellow veteran John Kerry expressed satisfaction with their efforts, which included ending its occupation of neighboring Cambodia. President Bill Clinton blocked congressional Republicans' attempts to place a third condition—mostly tied to human rights reforms in Vietnam—on normalization.[14] The United States normalized relations with Vietnam in 1994, and the two exchanged ambassadors the following year. In 1996, President Clinton, the proud face of neoliberalism, confidently asserted that "increased contact between Americans and Vietnamese will advance the cause of freedom in Vietnam just as it did in Eastern Europe and the former Soviet Union."[15]

The End of a Refugee Community?

But the mood in Little Saigon was far more mixed. On the one hand, Orange County became the headquarters of the Government of Free Vietnam and other new exile organizations. Inspired by the downfall of communism in Eastern Europe, these groups believed that "rock and roll diplomacy," without guns and guerrillas, would eventually topple the regime. Some of South Vietnam's disgraced old guard, once aligned with anticommunist guerrilla movements, echoed the sentiments of neoliberals: "Now Marxism is finished," declared Nguyễn Cao Kỳ in 1990. "We should fight [the communists] in the field of politics and economics." Former president Nguyễn Văn Thiệu eagerly predicted a homegrown wave of South Vietnamese rising up to demand the return of land seized in 1975.[16]

The end of the Cold War made it immensely easier—and presumably safer—for Vietnamese Americans to travel to their old homeland but also presented them with problems. Refugee status gave many Southeast Asians a safe haven from communist persecution, while the associated politics of rescue placed them and the American nation on the right side of history. Reconciliation meant an end to refugee admissions as well any attempt by the U.S. government to challenge Hanoi's version of the past. If Hanoi wanted to describe the Second Indochina War as the failed attempt by American imperialists and their puppets to subdue a virtuous albeit communist people's revolution, so be it.

The writing was already on the wall in Washington, where in January 1989, days before leaving office, Ronald Reagan increased the admissions quota for Soviet refugees by 39 percent while decreasing the Southeast Asian quota by 12 percent.[17] With fewer and fewer slots for refugee admissions, crowded tent cities in Hong Kong, Thailand, the Philippines, and other Southeast Asian nations constituted little more than undocumented immigrant ghettoes, with inhabitants subject to repatriation at a moment's notice. With the Hanoi government on more friendly terms with the United States, any claims regarding human rights abuses in Vietnam would fall on mostly deaf ears. If refugees' suffering no longer merited special treatment and if they remained on the wrong side of history, they could never expect Hanoi to even admit that atrocities had occurred, let alone apologize for them.

The era of the boat people and America's moral obligation to Vietnamese refugees was coming to an end. So, too, was the guarantee of an anticommunist Little Saigon as more and more pro-Hanoi immigrants made their way to the West. As the consensus in favor of reconciliation with the former enemy grew, consigning America and its wartime allies to the wrong side of history, the ranks of guilt-ridden Americans still committed to protecting the South Vietnamese from communism grew smaller and more uniformly conservative.

One of the last official acts of moral obligation was the Humanitarian Operation (HO) program of the 1990s, which rid the homeland of nearly one hundred thousand middle-aged former political prisoners, partly at Hanoi's request. This fifth and final wave of Vietnamese refugee migration came on the heels of State Department efforts to admit more than twenty thousand Amerasians born between 1962 and 1976 as refugees. But the former political prisoners, a larger group whose members had been victims of brutal state persecution, had far more incentive to identify as refugees.[18] As members of the military and the intelligentsia, their socioeconomic profile differed little from the predominantly middle-class first wave of refugees airlifted to safety during the final days of the Vietnam War. Consequently, their bodies provided living proof of the horrific fate that the earlier refugees had narrowly avoided. Years of incarceration had left them gaunt, broken, and gray. Inside the camps, they had been trained to confess without equivocation their misguided support of the pre-1975 puppet government, their disdain for the American empire, and their eternal gratitude for having been liberated by Hồ Chí Minh. Even after they had paid their debt to the new utopian society, the HO class and their children could expect no more than second-class citizenship. The best work one former prisoner could find was selling ice cream and lottery tickets on the streets.[19]

Since the earliest days of Little Saigon, the Vietnamese American community had pressed Washington to do something about Vietnam's political prisoners. In 1977, Khúc Minh Thơ, a social worker in Virginia, founded the Families of Vietnamese Political Prisoners Association to advocate on behalf of the release of her husband and others held in reeducation camps.[20] The organization grew quickly, and the sight of military wives asking to be reunited with those who had worked loyally for the United States proved effective enough that Reagan's State Department considered their well-being a "special humanitarian concern," an indication that the nation's guilt had yet to be fully assuaged.[21] The first ten thousand former prisoners were set to arrive in 1984, but, according to the U.S. State Department, "Hanoi withdrew its offer to release the prisoners after making unacceptable demands for guarantees that the prisoners would not engage in anti-regime activities if brought to the United States."[22] Blaming refugee activists for the attacks on a recent Vietnamese mission to the United Nations, a Hanoi diplomat stated flatly, "It is impossible to hand over weapons to be fired against us."[23] Not until five years later, with the Soviet Union on the verge of collapse, did the United States and Vietnam put the finishing touches on the HO program, a derivative of the Orderly Departure Program from the 1980s. Detainees who had spent at least three years in a reeducation camp, as well as their spouses and unmarried dependents, would be eligible. A U.S. diplomat involved in negotiations hailed the pact's goal of "healing the last big wound remaining from the war, which is that these people who were clearly associated with the United States have not been allowed to leave Vietnam and be united with their relatives."[24] Over the next decade, nearly two hundred thousand people—more than twice as many as initial estimates had predicted—made their way to the United States under the program.[25]

For people eligible for the HO program, the chance to resettle in the United States seemed too good to be true: "My uncle did not apply at first because he thought it was a hoax by the VC." Another skeptical former prisoner expected officials to be "rounding us up and punishing us again" but nevertheless took his chances. And when he landed in Thailand, "it looked so much like Vietnam that I really thought they were shipping us to prison!"[26]

Writing in popular Vietnamese-language publications in the United States, many of those released under the HO program revealed the psychological benefits of living in America. After nine years in a communist reeducation camp, former military officer Mai Quốc Linh left Saigon by himself in December 1993, hoping to fulfill his mother's wish that he would somehow "regain the life and dignity that the Communists took away." Within hours of arriving at Los Angeles International Airport, the fifty-one-year-old had already recaptured some of that lost spirit: "I could not stop my eyes from welling or my heart from pounding once I laid eyes on that golden flag of South Vietnam for the first time in eighteen years."[27] Although life in America dealt Linh and others who arrived as part of the HO program far more disappointment than success, their perception of Little Saigon as a refuge from the darkness made it easier to justify their decision to leave Vietnam. Indeed, the preservation of a noncommunist refuge became a critical rallying point at the same time that globalization threatened to introduce to America elements of official Vietnamese nationalism the newest arrivals thought they had left behind.[28]

The cultural compensation afforded HO refugees was vital because economic rewards were few and far between. They were eligible for eight months of public assistance, but many came in expecting much more. Like the refugees who preceded them, many of the HO arrivals interpreted their belonging in the United States as a matter of moral obligation that merited special attention. According to Pastor Nguyễn Xuân Bảo, whose Little Saigon church helped sponsor thousands of those who arrived under the HO program, "Once those Vietnamese military officers or high-ranking civilians arrived here, their dreams were shattered since nobody gave them new houses, and nobody gave them big sums of money, as the Communists had led people to believe!"[29] The early HO refugees also had the misfortune of arriving in the midst of a severe economic recession, and Orange County filed for bankruptcy protection on December 6, 1994. "The prisoners are basically ex-military people who aren't a lot more than farmers and fishermen," bellowed an Orange County social services official. "What are you going to do with someone who worked the rice paddies or killed other people for a living?" One of her colleagues believed that the "health and emotional problems associated with having been in a re-education camp for long periods of time" would absorb large amounts of public resources.[30] Even the ethnic economy had evolved, as the HO arrivals increasingly saw themselves competing for entry-level unskilled jobs against Spanish-speaking immigrants who were twenty or twenty-five years younger.

Most English-language coverage of the HO refugees portrayed them as tragic survivors who faced just as much hardship in the States as in Vietnam. Many of those admitted under the HO program suffered debilitating physical ailments that had gone untreated for years, but the biggest scars were not visible.[31] Without a community of their own, the first of the former prisoners to arrive in America suffered from extreme depression associated with feelings of failure and isolation. Entire families occupied humble accommodations while their first-wave counterparts moved into multistory homes outside of Little Saigon. Less than a month after arriving in Orange County, one former military officer ended his life by riding his bicycle onto Interstate 5 because, as an associate put it, "he saw that his future did not have any light" and "his spirit was tired."[32] But despite their turmoil, the refugees admitted under the HO program did not express harsh words for the United States.

Without hope of rebuilding their individual lives, these émigrés had to justify leaving Vietnam. Former army major Cung Phạm told the *Los Angeles Times*, "There are two beliefs I and my brothers live by. The first is that we willingly left Vietnam because we could not live with the Communist regime. The second is that our youth and usefulness have already passed us by; we now have to live for our children. We came here so that our children could have the chance the war took from us."³³ Phuong Le was one of those children. As a teenager, he had tried ten times to flee Vietnam, and his younger sister drowned at sea in 1987. He embraced refugee nationalism soon after his family finally escaped in 1990.³⁴ "If I look at [South] Vietnam as my blood parents," said Le, "I look at America as my adoptive parents. I love both countries. Both have the same heroic history, and their people have fought for democracy, human rights and freedom."³⁵

Demographics and language barriers helped perpetuate a traditional ethnic business model catering to people who spoke limited English and had low incomes, a situation that benefited ethnic media. The HO refugees were far more dependent on Little Saigon for their economic and cultural sustenance and hesitated to share their new home with Hanoi sympathizers. From a sociological framework, the profile of the HO arrivals seemed to guarantee an intensification of anticommunist sentiment. By 2000, the HO program accounted for one out of every six Vietnamese Americans, far more than supported Hanoi.³⁶

One of the first targets of the HO refugees' activism was the Vietnamese American Chamber of Commerce in Orange County. In 1994, the Chamber cosponsored a trade mission to Vietnam, a potential market of seventy million people, in hopes that "Little Saigon will be the gateway between the United States and Vietnam."³⁷ Furious, the wives and widows of reeducation camp inmates staged a protest around the obstetric clinic operated by the organization's president, Cơ Phạm. Garden Grove resident Andrea Nguyễn, whose husband survived three years in a communist prison, exclaimed, "We're against anyone who will cooperate with the Communists." Her fellow protesters included Châu Tue Phuong, who had left Vietnam just five years earlier, and Nga Phạm, whose husband had died in the camps.³⁸ These women found calls to "forget the past and look toward the future" insensitive at best, since Vietnam faced no similar pressure.³⁹ "In many ways," noted one journalist who visited Vietnam in the 1990s, "Hanoi has had an easier time reaching out to its former enemy the United States than its brothers who fought for the South."⁴⁰

But the HO refugees' proclivity to protest needed institutional support if they wanted their minority discourse legitimized and their ethnic sanctuary protected. Some support remained in Washington, as evidenced by Representative Loretta Sánchez, Orange County's lone Democrat in Congress. Sánchez regularly appeared at public forums and festivals in Little Saigon wearing a custom-made South Vietnamese traditional *áo dài* dress. The FBI advertised in the *Người Việt Daily News* and other ethnic newspapers for recent arrivals "who had worked for, communicated with, or had been asked by the Vietnamese Communist regime to carry out whatever activity, but who no longer believe in, or who are dissatisfied with, the ideas of the Vietnamese Communist regime."[41] The Voice of America increased its editorial programming to Vietnam, with refugee artists contributing new musical compositions such as Việt Dzũng's "Bài Ca Dân Chủ Mới" [Song of New Democracy].[42] In 1991, Congress created Radio Free Asia for the express purpose of reaching listeners in Cambodia, Laos, and Vietnam with far more right-wing propaganda.[43] But those were the exceptions. Refugee politics, no longer a federal priority vis-à-vis Vietnam, would become increasingly local in the post–Cold War era, but only in certain locales. In her research on HO migrants in the Seattle area, cultural studies scholar Maureen Feeney argues that the city's eagerness to embrace free trade with Vietnam in the 1990s made it a less than ideal "Cold War refuge" for exiles desperate to preserve their version of the past. Their lack of political leverage at the local level put refugee nationalism at odds with the University of Washington and transnational entrepreneurs.[44] But more important, the era of normalization finally made it problematic to publicly disparage the Vietnamese government, instantly marking anticommunists as reactionaries and extremists. In conservative Orange County, however, Vietnamese Americans were far more likely to find local allies.

Putting (Vietnamese) Americans First

The political priorities of those admitted under the HO program in the midst of normalization helped to frame Frank Fry's transformation from local bête noire to populist friend of the South Vietnamese. With Little Saigon attracting three hundred thousand visitors annually, both he and political rival Tony Lâm wanted full credit for reshaping the ethnic enclave into a major Orange County tourist destination alongside Disneyland and Knott's Berry Farm.[45] Lâm tried to convince whites that he spoke for the Vietnamese, but his grand schemes demonstrated a greater loyalty to wealthy developers and city boosters than to rank-and-file Vietnamese, and his coethnics responded accordingly. When Lâm suggested honoring South Vietnamese veterans with what he described as the "West Coast Statue of Liberty," Fry, who had once told refugees to go back to Vietnam if they wanted a parade to honor Saigon's veterans, became the idea's champion.[46] By 1996, when he had become Westminster's mayor, Fry told his constituents that the city was "the only place in the world where you'll see an American and a [South] Vietnamese standing side by side on the battlefield."[47] Fry knew that his race and impeccable conservative credentials could insulate the effort from colleagues and citizens skeptical about the prospect of remaking their "All-American City" to "bring the Vietnamese and American communities closer together."[48] In addition, as a white man, Fry had little reason to fear red-baiting and public reprisals from the Vietnamese American community. In professor Nhan Vu's estimation, "The Vietnamese-American community has generally been more lenient on people who are not of Vietnamese descent than on those of Vietnamese descent. Thus, there are few protests against organizations that publicly support trade with Vietnam, so long as those organizations' membership is mainly non-Vietnamese."[49] Indeed, following Fry's announcement, the chair of the Vietnamese Former Detainees Mutual Association, which represented people admitted under the HO program, told the *Orange County Register*, "We support anything related to the former South Vietnamese government, particularly the soldiers who fought for more than 20 years. We would be glad to see a Vietnamese flag at the statue."[50] The idea for the memorial meshed with refugee nationalism's need to publicly treat Americans, especially whites, with deference for fear of losing friends in high places. Fry consequently could become the public face of refugee nationalism in a way no Vietnamese ever could.

In 1998, the selection committee, which included retired senior officers from the U.S. and South Vietnamese militaries, settled on local sculptor Tuấn Nguyễn's representation of a South Vietnamese soldier and a (white) American soldier standing side by side in a show of "collaboration between the two soldiers, the friendship between two countries."[51] Although the committee acquiesced to demands that the American flag and soldier stand higher than their South Vietnamese counterparts, the statue constituted the first time an American audience had seen anything resembling friendship, respect, and equality between U.S. and South Vietnamese veterans. It was a blatant rewriting of U.S. history that reflected the economic and political power of present-day Refugee Americans relative to the collective memory of white Americans. Many whites, especially older veterans, were not ready to embrace their former allies so intimately, and this lack of support further delayed the project. In fact, frustration with Vietnamese refugees, especially among white military types, reached an all-time high in early 1999, when a local video store owner's display of the current Vietnamese flag and a portrait of communist hero Hồ Chí Minh sparked the largest public protests in Vietnamese American history.

The Hi-Tek Episode

The problems began in January 1999, when the owner of the Hi-Tek video store, Trần Văn Trường, decided after a winter trip to Ho Chi Minh City that he would proudly display these communist symbols at his Bolsa Avenue store to "further the dialogue" on how much Vietnam had progressed for the better. Having lost two relatives at the hands of the communists before fleeing Vietnam by boat in the 1980s, Trường surely knew that these symbols would inflame his neighbors. To make matters worse, on the weekend of January 16, he faxed a challenge to his coethnics: "I defy you all . . . if you dare to come to take them off."[52] By one o'clock on the afternoon of Monday, January 18, four hundred protesters had lined up outside the video store, and Trường received several blows to the head while leaving the premises.[53] Protesters waved American and South Vietnamese flags and sang the U.S. and South Vietnamese national anthems.[54] In the evening, demonstrators plastered Tran's storefront with South Vietnamese flags and banners reading, "America and South Vietnam lost Saigon. We together must not lose Little Saigon."[55] Unbeknownst to the general public, they were engaged in a grassroots version of the same political campaign waged by Washington since 1975: to avoid losing to the Vietnamese communists ever again. After nearly two months of protests in front of Hi-Tek that cost the City of Westminster more than $750,000 in overtime pay for law enforcement, city authorities ended the standoff by closing down the store on charges of video piracy.[56] Little Saigon had won this battle in the postwar.

The United States had spent nearly twenty years figuring out how to save face against Hanoi, only to balk when Vietnamese Americans sought a miniature postwar political victory against the communists. The mainstream media denounced the Vietnamese community's crazed behavior over seemingly innocuous symbols, especially since Hanoi had gone to great lengths to repair its image in the minds of most Americans. Confessed Westminster city council member Margie Rice, "I feel like [the Vietnamese] are taking over our city, plain and simple. I would think that after 20 years or so of being here and being given the freedoms that they want, they would calm down. By God, how long can you go on fighting this war?"[57] In a 2004 documentary, *Saigon USA*, filmmakers Lindsey Jang and Robert Winn explored what they saw as a widening generation gap between anticommunist (that is, paranoid) parents and their Americanized (that is, normal) children.[58] A communications study conducted by former Little Saigon beat writer Jeffrey Brody similarly concluded that among American ethnic groups, Vietnamese exhibited the strongest opposition to free speech. During the Hi-Tek protests, Brody penned an op-ed in the *Los Angeles Times* warning Vietnamese Americans against replicating the same oppressive political climate they had risked their lives to escape.[59]

By refusing to view the incident through a transnational lens, the mainstream media left the impression that protesters were ignorant of American laws and customs such as free speech when in fact the protesters were fully aware that only in America could they demonstrate against the Vietnamese government and have their complaints heard around the world. Viewed through a transnational lens, however, refugees were not refusing to become American but rather were taking full advantage of their status as Americans. But they failed to realize that within the framework of American exceptionalism, resettlement was a reward in itself that marked the limits of the nation's moral obligation to its former allies. Convinced of the superiority of American citizenship and culture, most Americans looked askance at what they perceived as Vietnamese ingratitude.

In retaliation for the Hi-Tek episode, Westminster's City Council members except for Lâm and Fry backed the local American Legion's opposition to flying the South Vietnamese flag alongside the American flag on April 30, even in the face of pleas from a Vietnamese American in the U.S. Marines. The council also remained unmoved by the efforts of a local Vietnamese youth group, which went door-to-door offering apologies and flowers to neighbors inconvenienced by the Hi-Tek protests.[60] The city council and white residents wanted the return of their good assimilated refugees, failing to realize the extent to which the Hi-Tek protests had galvanized a large cross-section of local refugees good and bad, young and old. Said *Người Việt Daily News* publisher Yến Đỗ, "This is something special. This is a new era."[61]

Indeed, the protesters seized the opportunity to send an unprecedented and unified message to the Vietnamese government. As Nhan Vũ observed, "They seek to tell the Vietnamese government that it cannot control the Vietnamese-American community the way it controls its own people and that it cannot impose burdens upon them the way it does with its own people."[62] After having chosen to leave Vietnam forever, the protesters were not going to allow their last refuge, Little Saigon, to meet the same fate as its namesake. The ethnic press announced times for work parties and published photographs featuring protesters of all ages and genders plastering the Hi-Tek storefront with South Vietnamese flags. On the evening of February 22, more than ten thousand people filled the parking lot in front of Hi-Tek to partake in a free concert. Between patriotic songs and political speeches, audience members could be heard chanting, "Việt Nam Cộng Hòa Muôn Đời" [Long Live the Republic of Vietnam].[63] A former newspaper writer, Kiều Mỹ Duyên, often joined the protesters and noticed that the demonstrations had an organic character, with no clear hierarchy or leadership or any dominant age group.[64]

These events afforded opportunities for military wives and widows to enter the public sphere and air grievances in a way that had been forbidden back home. Partly on behalf of these women, musician and activist Nam Lộc Nguyễn decided to become active in the seemingly endless fund-raising campaign for the local Vietnam War Memorial, and he was ultimately credited with raising more than one-third of the $1.3 million needed for its completion, an accomplishment he considered his proudest moment as a Vietnamese American. As he recalled, "Over three hundred thousand died and were left behind. What about their souls? You do not have a chance to go back and pray. Why do you not bring the soul here? There were four hundred Vietnam War memorials, but none of them talked about the [South] Vietnamese soldier. So my dream was to build a memorial for them. All I want is to bring their soul here, so I can look at the memorial and see my friend. And a wife can come pray for her husband."[65]

Figure 6. A woman prays for her deceased husband at the Vietnamese-American Memorial in Westminster. Photo by author.

The rest of Westminster did not unite behind the memorial project until the Hanoi government became overtly involved during the summer of 1999. The consul general's office in San Francisco sent a letter that objected to the proposed memorial and suggested replacing the South Vietnamese soldier with a North Vietnamese one, thereby institutionalizing a bond between Americans and the Hanoi government. The act drew Westminster's white and Vietnamese residents into an uncommon show of solidarity. Whatever tensions existed between Americans and South Vietnamese, past or present, were instantly superseded by the threat of a far more distorted collective memory: conservative Americans treating Vietnamese communists as equal partners. The proposed statue "has nothing to do with relations to Vietnam," said Hung Nguyễn, a U.S. Army Ranger and community activist. Fry reiterated the historical basis for choosing to depict South Vietnamese and American soldiers standing side by side: "They were allies during the war. We're not allies with the North." A whopping 78 percent of *Orange County Register* readers felt that the proposed statue would not hurt U.S.-Vietnamese relations.[66] The consul general's objections made bad refugees in Little Saigon American enough. For community insiders, the project itself became a valorization of the democratic process. "The proposed memorial may itself become controversial—even without a North Vietnamese soldier in it," wrote columnist Gordon Dillow. "But that's our business, not Vietnam's. They should butt out."[67] But more was at stake than just the democratic process. A memorial honoring GIs and communists, as requested by the Hanoi representative, threatened to radically rewrite the collective memory of Westminster's Anglo population, a conservative lot who generally supported the Vietnam War and hated communists. Unlike the original statue, which altered the past by depicting South Vietnamese and Americans as equal partners in a just crusade to protect freedom, Hanoi's version would ask almost everyone in Little Saigon to accept their place on the wrong side of history. Vietnamese and Anglos alike found that position untenable. Indeed, on July 13, 1999, the city council, in front of an enthusiastic audience of one hundred, voted unanimously to approve the construction of the memorial.[68] Veterans groups that had spent months opposing the display of the South Vietnamese flag next to the American flag at official events now found themselves rallying in favor of the memorial.

Fry's team commissioned songwriter Lê Quang Anh to compose two English-only patriotic ditties for the memorial's unveiling on Sunday, April 27, 2003, at Westminster's Freedom Park. He titled the first song "Battle Hymn of the Vietnam War Memorial," and like the name, its melody resembled that of the "Battle Hymn of the Republic."

> Come with me to see the Vietnam War Memorial
> To praise the brave for their gallantry
> Come with me to sing a song to honor those, the Heroes
> To praise the Proud who for Freedom sacrificed
> Believing in God and country love led them the way to Hope and Care
> They went to war holding their head high
> Believing in God they're marching on, Vowing to fight the tyranny
> Risking their life to make men Free
> Come with me to proudly hail the men who made the history
> To pay them respect, To pay them tribute.
> Come to see the Stars 'n' Stripes and Yellow Flag both waving
> Through starry nights and never-ending day.[69]

Lê also composed a tourist ditty, "Do You Know the Way to Little Saigon?," whose title echoed Burt Bacharach's 1968 tune, "Do You Know the Way to San Jose?," while its melody and pacing seemed to come from Kurt McKenzie's 1967 hit, "San Francisco."

> Do you know the way to Westminster?
> Do you know the way to Little Saigon?
> Let me tell you how to get there and where to go and where to be
> In order to see the Vietnam War Memorial
> The only monument that you can see nowhere [else]
> How proud the solemn pair of soldiers side by side
> Let's come to praise the brave who fought for human rights
> Let's come to see the Vietnam War Memorial
> And sing a song to honor those, the Heroes
> So proud they stand for Love and Care and for the Free
> Let's come to praise the Brave who fought for you and me.[70]

Despite Little Saigon's changing demographics, the memorial, problematic as it was, enabled the refugee generation to institutionalize its collective memory.

The Centrality of Local Politics

Post Cold War politics in Little Saigon provided the important lesson that nothing was more integral to the fate of refugee nationalism than political allies in the host community. Decades removed from the Vietnam War and no longer eligible for special treatment from the federal government, residents of Little Saigon learned that the local democratic process represented the best avenue for promoting transnational concerns. Without local political power, refugee nationalism faced impossible odds, as was demonstrated in 2005, when memorials erected at former camps in Malaysia and Indonesia were destroyed soon thereafter at the request of the Vietnamese government.[71] To commemorate the thirtieth anniversary of the fall of Saigon, former refugees had staged reunions at Bidong Island, Malaysia, and Galang Island, Indonesia, using the occasion to dedicate memorials to Vietnamese killed while fleeing their homeland. Derek Nguyễn, who had gone on to become an attorney in Southern California, was a teenager when "the Malaysians, especially the people in Terengganu had helped rescue us, and gave a proper burial for those who died at sea."[72]

Each memorial consisted of a simple ten-foot-tall stone plaque with English and Vietnamese inscriptions. The front read,

> In commemoration of the hundreds of thousands of Vietnamese people who perished on the way to freedom (1975–1996). Though they died of hunger or thirst, of being raped, of exhaustion or of any other cause, we pray that they may now enjoy lasting peace. Their sacrifices will not be forgotten.
> —Overseas Vietnamese Communities, 2005

The back read,

> In appreciation of the efforts of UNHCR, the Red Cross and the Indonesian Red Crescent Society and other world relief organizations, the Indonesian/Malaysian government and people, as well as all countries of first asylum and resettlement. We also express our gratitude to the thousands of individuals who worked hard in helping the Vietnamese refugees.
> —Overseas Vietnamese Communities, 2005

Just two months after the Galang Island memorial was dedicated on March 24, the local government quietly tore down the monument after the Vietnamese government complained to the Indonesian president about the "offensive" wording. Hanoi also demanded the destruction of the memorial at Bidong Island.[73] The refugee community protested Hanoi's campaign to rewrite the past, with one organizer declaring, "The monument is part of the Vietnamese people's memory. What happened to our history must be recorded and Vietnam must come to terms with this."[74] From 1978 to 1990, almost 250,000 boat people had landed on at Bidong Island, but the Vietnamese government argued that they fled for economic rather than political reasons. Concerted appeals by the refugee community, including letters from Congresswoman Sánchez and the Vietnamese American member of the U.S. President's Advisory Commission on Asian Americans and Pacific Islanders, failed to move the Malaysian government. With only a hint of resignation in his voice, Malaysia's state secretary told the press, "We have to take into account the relationship between the Malaysian and the Vietnamese government." By the end of October, the memorial at Bidong Island, too, had been demolished.[75] Noted one Vietnamese observer, "It is because they do not want future generations to know the truth about the Vietnamese refugees."[76] Indeed, books published in Vietnam about the history and sociology of the diaspora offer a dramatically different perspective on the exodus, using such terms as *expatriates* and *émigrés* but eschewing *refugees*. In these accounts, people left Vietnam for economically rational reasons: to lift themselves from poverty or to avoid serving in the military.[77]

In the fall of 2000, when the William Joiner Center at the University of Massachusetts at Boston brought two literary scholars from Hanoi to study the diaspora, local Vietnamese Americans, most of them older men bearing U.S. and South Vietnamese flags, flocked to Dorchester Avenue to demonstrate their opposition to the scholarly sanctioning of communist propaganda. "The Vietnamese community here is determined not to allow these two communist writers to tell our story," said one of the protesters. "If they say something different from what the government wants, then they cannot go back," opined another. "They have a mission here."[78]

Whether or not they intended to spread propaganda, the scholars had already won in the court of public opinion. In contrast to stereotypes of communists as demagogues, both scholars came across as quiet, unassuming intellectuals. Meanwhile, members of the refugee community found themselves cast as vindictive reactionaries who "simply cannot imagine finding a shred of good in their old captors. . . . Nor can they embrace any sign of softening that still comes under a banner of Communism."[79] The days of calm anticipated in the postrefugee generation "cannot happen here soon enough," opined a *Boston Globe* staff writer.[80]

The *Boston Globe* account reflected a generic mainstream analysis that internalized the problem while ignoring how history set Vietnamese refugees up to feel betrayed again by their American allies. The Vietnamese presence in the States had always been framed as a matter of moral obligation rather than legal rights. The original sin of losing the Vietnam War delivered such a crushing blow to American prestige and honor that a coalition of liberals and conservatives agreed that sparing multiple waves of migrants a life without freedom constituted a moral imperative, regardless of the cost. To community insiders, Little Saigon's formation is wrapped in a discourse of American guilt and goodwill, with refugees in turn conditioned to be grateful for every American intervention from war to resettlement to a place of their own. Vietnamese Refugee Americans were also conditioned to expect a paternalistic quid pro quo: with the American investment in

South Vietnam having paid off with a "model minority," Americans would continue to protect Vietnamese Americans from racism and communism. In the eyes of the protesters, America had a duty to its allies to keep its enemies out.

With the passage of time, however, the ranks of guilt-ridden Americans committed to helping Vietnamese refugees at the expense of the Vietnamese communists became smaller, older, and more uniformly conservative. The idealistic component of Refugee American identity had accomplished much, but as people—including Saigon's exiles and their progeny—regarded Vietnam in less hostile terms, the politics of rescue shifted its focus from reclaiming old Saigon to preserving Little Saigon. In the post–Cold War era, the Westminster enclave stood out as one of the few remaining spaces where refugees could fly the colors of a defunct regime and recite the national anthem of a country long since fallen. In addition, Little Saigon allowed them a space in which to identify culturally as refugees when doing so was no longer legally necessary, placing them and their American allies on the right side of history. In this framework, Little Saigon represented not just an average ethnic enclave but the least America could do for fallen friends.

Conclusion

Finding Roots in Exile

> If I accept favours, I contract debts which I can never repay, for I can never get on equal terms with him who has conferred the favours upon me; he has stolen a march upon me. . . . I shall always owe him a debt of gratitude, and who will accept such a debt? For to be indebted is to be subject to an unending constraint. I must for ever be courteous and flattering towards my benefactor.
> —Immanuel Kant

> Vietnamese-Americans have been riding a crest of sympathy for over forty years. America realizes that it screwed over Vietnam royally, and we've been cutting its descendants slack ever since that ghastly snafu. The Vietnamese-Americans have this national guilt to thank for their tremendous successes.
> —Kevin Hechinger and Curtis Hechinger, *Hechinger's Field Guide to Ethnic Stereotypes*

Despite all the minivictories achieved in Little Saigon since the 1999 Hi-Tek protests, mainstream institutionalization remained beyond the reach of many important historical and cultural figures of South Vietnamese collective memory. By 1999, Phạm Duy was the lone surviving modern Vietnamese musical legend, and in August 1999, his wife of nearly fifty years, Thái Hằng, died of lung cancer. In 2000, Phạm returned to Vietnam for the first time since he fled a quarter century earlier. Nearly eighty years old, Phạm must have bristled to discover that the Vietnamese government had canonized Trịnh Công Sơn and Văn Cao but refused to recognize Phạm's accomplishments as part of its efforts to marginalize refugee artists. Though bootlegged copies of his recordings were easily obtainable, the official institutions of public memory failed to mention him at all.[1]

A life in exile offered no compensation commensurate with his musical contributions. No one among the refugee generation denied his greatness, but that generation was dying off, and fading memories alone were no substitute for institutionalization. Although more known to Americans than any other Vietnamese composer, Phạm Duy's résumé contained none of the usual benchmarks of musical greatness. He had received no Grammy Awards, no Kennedy Center Honors, no Presidential Medal of Freedom, no lifetime achievement awards. He did not even merit a major encyclopedia entry. Because most Americans viewed the Vietnam War as a foreign policy mistake, fans and scholars of art in the dissident tradition were unlikely to remember him. He was a permanent fixture in Little Saigon, but people there, according to Phạm Duy, "do not ask for autographs. They just look silently. ... They're very shy, I think, my people."[2] Because Vietnamese artists lacked the resources to protect their intellectual property from piracy, Phạm Duy had to continue recording and performing to make money.[3] Even then, none of the major Orange County music labels, now profiting wildly off the sale of concert and karaoke videos, expressed much interest in his more ambitious later work. Phạm's friends put together a series of untelevised concerts and commemorations, *Một Đời Nhìn Lại* [A Life in Retrospective], but they felt miniscule compared to the full-scale spectacle a nation-state could have mustered. Moreover, Phạm noticed that the audiences at these community-based gatherings were aging: language barriers and limited memories of the homeland meant that younger Vietnamese Americans could not relate to the music of their elders.

Such problems illustrate the essential role nation-states have played in making culture and taste intelligible in the global marketplace. Along with exclusive authority to confer political rights, the sovereign nation-state, with its power to institutionalize the past, has the last word in shaping the long-term parameters of popular culture. In the absence of ties to a country, Phạm Duy and other artists have no barometer for measuring their greatness. Being a hero in an exile community has only limited value when exile is intended to be a temporary condition. Because of complex historical circumstances, two formerly stateless populations, the African and Jewish diasporas, eventually became strongly identified with the United States and especially its popular culture. Without that transformation, Phạm Duy's artistic merits remained tied to a country and context that no longer existed and whose target audience was dwindling. As the thirty-year anniversary of the fall of Saigon neared, Phạm made a last-ditch effort to save his legacy, and it put him at odds with the refugee community.

In late 2004, Phạm Duy announced his defection from the refugee community in exchange for a place in official Vietnamese history. The author of "Việtnam, Việtnam," the unofficial anthem of his people, sold all of his copyrights to a Ho Chi Minh City–based entertainment company for nearly half a million dollars. Phạm then revised the story of his hasty retreat from North Vietnam in 1954 and from South Vietnam in 1975, transforming himself virtually overnight from a refugee into an accidental expatriate. In response to Phạm's actions, Hanoi authorized a concert in his honor to be held on April 30, 2005, the thirtieth anniversary of the communist takeover of South Vietnam. Phạm Duy's defection also allowed his children—accomplished musicians themselves—to earn a living in Vietnam with minimal harassment.

Ironically, Phạm Duy's attempt to find a home in communist Vietnam further alienated him from his roots. His songs had officially been banned in North Vietnam since 1954, and despite his passionate denunciations of refugee nationalism, only about two dozen of his compositions were legalized—mostly those from before 1954, when he "carried a guitar in one hand and a gun in the other hand" as part of the effort to oust France from Indochina.[4] He went from being a potential giant in exile to a minor figure in official Vietnamese cultural history. In 2007, his name did not appear in Vietnamese music history books and museums. Thousands of miles to the east, the shops of Little Saigon still sell his music, but he has become at best forgotten and in some cases persona non grata. Younger Vietnamese Americans in search of high art likely gravitate to the "antiwar" music of Trịnh Công Sơn, a contemporary of Phạm Duy who chose to remain in Vietnam.

Desperate to salvage his legacy, Phạm Duy had followed in the unwise footsteps of fellow exile Nguyễn Cao Kỳ, the former prime minister of South Vietnam and self-styled leader of the Vietnamese government in exile, who in 2004 had infuriated the community even more when he swallowed his strident anticommunism and journeyed back to his native country. In 1988, Kỳ had announced, "The only circumstance under which I'd go back is whenever there is freedom and independence for the Vietnamese people."[5] But sixteen years later, with the Cold War long since ended and the Vietnamese Communist Party still in power, Kỳ suddenly exhorted his fellow refugees to "forget the past." When the mainstream media asked if he was waving the white flag, he responded, "If you surrender to your country, what's wrong with that? This is my country, not Little Saigon, not Orange County."[6] For all their conciliatory rhetoric, Kỳ and others who returned seemed to underestimate the cultural concessions the refugee community would have to make in exchange for reconciliation with post–Cold War Vietnam. In short, they were being asked to identify with a nation whose history books and classrooms portrayed the former South Vietnamese as enemies of the revolution and whose national iconography showcased Hồ Chí Minh lovingly cradling a young child in a manner reminiscent of the Madonna and baby Jesus. In spite of all the cruelties the refugees had endured under communism, they were being asked to acknowledge that they were on the wrong side of history.

The overseas Vietnamese community heatedly debated whether Phạm Duy's renunciation of the refugee community constituted an act of treason, since his legacy would now be subsumed under Hanoi's version of the past. None of his albums released in Vietnam since repatriation have included music written after 1954, and one of Phạm's former friends angrily declared in 2007 that "nothing he's done before [2005] matters anymore."[7]

To be fair, many of Phạm's critics have also traveled to Vietnam, often rationalizing their journeys as nonpolitical in nature. But even personal visits have political consequences. Just like Phạm Duy, regular Vietnamese Americans, especially men, found their social status greatly enhanced when they landed in Ho Chi Minh City. Older male travelers had easy access to women seemingly more submissive than their Vietnamese American counterparts, while younger Americanized males, relegated to the bottom of the sexual hierarchy on American shores, reveled in a society where women found them attractive.[8] "This place is heaven!" confessed a twenty-something Vietnamese American male at a Saigon nightclub for expatriates.[9] Back in Little Saigon, several companies specialized in tourist videos targeted at male audiences. Videos featuring young bikini-clad beauties depicted the homeland as the ultimate leisure destination, with great food, scenic vistas, and attractive women.

Even if Phạm Duy and Nguyễn Cao Kỳ were sincere about wanting to spend their last years in their homeland, they had misread the extent to which Vietnamese Americans had turned Little Saigon into a place where refugees could live and die in peace. In 2000, the *Viết Báo Daily News* held its first Vietnamese-language essay competition, Viết Về Nước Mỹ [Writing on America]. One of the eight hundred submissions passionately summed up the competition's purpose: "The refugee generation is reaching its twilight. We forget things or we are forgotten. Some are no longer with us. We need to leave some record of our existence for the next generation. Let's do it before it is too late."[10] In attendance at the November 29, 2000, awards ceremony was Westminster mayor Frank Fry. One hundred of the year's best essays were published in a book sold at Little Saigon's bookstores. In the collective urgency that surrounded the recording of refugee history, not only Phạm Duy but also Nguyễn Cao Kỳ and two major figures from the 1980s resistance movement published their memoirs. *Người Việt* newspaper founder Yến Đỗ published an English-language autobiography that outlined his contributions to Little Saigon and provided a rough social history of the community. In 2001, Đỗ's former partner, Du Miên, moved the three-year-old Vietnam Library and Museum to a thirty-eight-hundred-square-foot space in Garden Grove that eventually held more than fifty thousand books.[11] Among those books were anthologies about the people who arrived as part of the Humanitarian Operation. In 2004, the Viễn Đông newspaper company collected enough personal essays from the wives of former reeducation camp prisoners to fill two paperback volumes. Soon thereafter, the company published a three-volume anthology penned by the former prisoners themselves. And the people of Little Saigon constructed a burial ground so that veterans could have the South Vietnamese flag draped over their coffin, as was done for beloved vocalist and music instructor Duy Khánh when he died in 2003.

Three major barriers separated refugees from younger generations. First, a culture of silence prevailed in many parts of the Vietnamese community despite the efforts of refugee nationalism. When social worker and musician Nam Lộc gave a guest lecture at Georgetown University in 2002, the only Vietnamese student in the audience explained that her parents had never shared their harrowing tale of escape by boat during the 1980s.[12] It is never easy to transform shame into pride, and many refugee families hoped that their children's success would make up for the pain of exile. Second, refugee nationalism's traditional reliance on paternal bonds with the United States did not always sit well with people far less interested in continuing their elders' outpouring of gratitude toward the United States. Raised and educated in America, a society in which communism never truly threatened the status quo and the Vietnam War was viewed as wrongheaded, younger people at times had difficulty believing that the Việt-Cộng had committed such brutal atrocities despite the testimony from the refugee generation.

Finally, language poses the greatest threat to cultural continuity. Very little of the refugee experience has made its way into the English language. Though a few memoirs and novels have been published, scholars have avoided the subject for fear of becoming bogged down in a minefield in which their research is ideologically vetted by various camps. Anticommunist Vietnamese American parents frequently tell their children not to trust most of the published sources on the Vietnam War but have collectively done almost nothing to provide the younger generation with credible English-language material. Few bilingual scholars thus far have translated refugee documents and literature into English.

Such an effort likely awaits philanthropists who care as much as journalist Andrew Lâm does. If he were really rich, Lâm said in 2006,

> I would give lots of money for translation work. I have Vietnamese American college students who came up to me and say: "I can speak a little Vietnamese but cannot read it. I do research on Vietnam and the majority of the texts in English are either from Hanoi and American writers." Where's the history of Little Saigon? They exist in books like *Trại Cải Tạo* and *Vượt Biển*—first person narratives about re-education camps and boat people experiences, written in Vietnamese. But these self same people, who sweated and bled to write these stories and unfortunately, their children cannot access it. Which also means, the rest of America cannot access it. Yet there are a lot of amazing stories waiting to be heard. When we are all gone, it is the text, the stories that survive. And our history cannot survive without care and nurture and a willingness to communicate, to testify. We need to make our history known in everyway possible. That is part of the reason why I became a writer.[13]

More than ten years later, none of these works has been translated into English. In that time, many more Vietnamese Americans have contributed to Vietnamese-language anthologies, a format that preserves the stories but is linguistically accessible to very few people.

Yet Little Saigon continues to exist and to evolve. The younger generation inevitably disrupted the area's conservative dominance after crafting their own spaces in a variety of places, including college campuses, where professors trained in ethnic studies teach courses on Vietnamese Americans, making critical connections between ethnic history and social justice. The annual Tết festival, once a territorial slugfest between competing organizers, is now a single event run by current and former college students. A vibrant cultural renaissance features grassroots activity such as spoken-word salons as well as more institutional fare such as the annual Vietnamese International Film Festival sponsored by the Vietnamese American Arts and Letters Association. In 2014, after years of trying, openly lesbian, gay, bisexual, and transgender activists were finally allowed to march in the annual Lunar New Year Parade along Bolsa Avenue. The parade organizers, long accustomed to bowing to conservative elders, could no longer afford to marginalize younger Vietnamese, and even Westminster's Republican (and Vietnamese American) mayor, Tri Ta, endorsed ending the ban.[14] In that year's elections, thirty-four-year-old school board trustee Bảo Nguyễn, a Democrat, defeated incumbent Bruce Broadwater by just fifteen votes to become Garden Grove's first mayor of Vietnamese descent. The dashing and charismatic Bảo had reached national prominence in 2000 as an undergraduate student at the University of California at Irvine: he wore a T-shirt that read "American Gook" to a John McCain rally, prompting older members of the Vietnamese community to push and spit on Bảo when they misconstrued his act of antiracist agitation as a foolish affront to one of the refugee community's few political allies.[15] Fluent in English, Spanish, and Vietnamese, Bảo represents a new breed of Vietnamese politician whose social work builds alliances with new neighbors and old friends. While born in a refugee camp and respectful of that history, he fosters a gratitude based on paying forward instead of paying back and objects to antiimmigrant rhetoric of any kind.

While no one can predict the future of Little Saigon, the past, too, is far from settled. No one wants to believe that their elders fought and died in vain, but with each succeeding generation comes new debate about how much to glorify the postwarriors or which postwarriors to glorify. Little Saigon has amassed more than forty years of history and culture of its own, even though that was never the intent of the people who settled the enclave. And the various historical and cultural actors have had different views about who and what Little Saigon should be, about refugee gratitude, about institutionalizing their collective memory. Nevertheless, the institutionalization of Little Saigon's culture—in books, in memorials, in Little Saigon—was as close as refugee nationalists would ever come to a postwar victory. Though regime change did not occur in their lifetimes, their collective memories will live on, enabling future generations to learn how and why their elders, treated like not-quite-assimilated immigrants by the majority of Americans, nevertheless identified as refugees who never stopped arguing, however problematically, that the history of the Vietnamese diaspora must include the history of becoming Refugee American.

Notes

Introduction: A Nation of Refugees

1. The literature on the Vietnam War is vast and multifaceted. Some of the canonical texts from the U.S. perspective include Halberstam, *Best and the Brightest*; Karnow, *Vietnam*; Kolko, *Anatomy of a War*. Whereas earlier studies focused their critique on the United States, recent revisionist histories put more effort into critiquing all sides. Examples include Hunt, *Lyndon Johnson's War*; Lind, *Vietnam*.

2. For prior studies of Little Saigon, see Vo and Danico, "Formation of Post-Suburban Communities"; Aguilar–San Juan. *Little Saigons*; Lieu, *American Dream in Vietnamese*; Dang and Vo, *Vietnamese in Orange County*.

3. Kelly, *From Vietnam to America*, 2–3.

4. Takaki, *Strangers from a Different Shore*, 455.

5. For the Cold War politics of U.S. refugee admissions policy, see Loescher and Scanlan, *Calculated Kindness*; Bon Tempo, *Americans at the Gate*.

6. For more on American exceptionalism, see Lipset, *American Exceptionalism*; Rowe, introduction; Lockhart, *Roots of American Exceptionalism*; Etulain and Szasz, *American West in 2000*; Bacevich, *Limits of American Power*.

7. Harwood, "American Public Opinion and U.S. Immigration Policy."

8. The antiforeign sentiment that both propelled Donald Trump to the U.S. presidency in 2016 and was subsequently stoked by his administration represented a profound shift from this longer-term trend but falls outside the bounds of this book.

9. For a more thorough explanation of the various waves of migration, see Sucheng Chan, *Vietnamese American 1.5 Generation*.

10. *Southeast Asian Americans at a Glance*, 5.

11. U.S. Government Accountability Office, *Refugee Program*.

12. Center for American Progress, *Who Are Vietnamese Americans?*

13. Orwell, *Nineteen Eighty-Four*, pt. 1, chap. 3, pt. 3, chap. 2.

14. Zake, *Anti-Communist Minorities.* 47–56.

15. See, for example, Anderson, *Imagined Communities*; Kohn, *Idea of Nationalism*; Gellner, *Nations and Nationalism*; Hobsbawm and Ranger, *Invention of Tradition*; Breuilly, *Nationalism and the State*; Anthony D. Smith, *Ethnic Origins of Nations*; Hobsbawm, *Nations and Nationalism*; McCrone, *Understanding Scotland*; Tanner, *Croatia*; Gilbert, *Philosophy of Nationalism*; Guibernau, *Nations without States*; Anthony D. Smith, *Chosen Peoples*; Zhao, *Nation-State by Construction*; Resendez, *Changing National Identities at the Frontier*; Plokhy, *Origins of Slavic Nations*.

16. Novick, *Holocaust in American Life*, 4.

17. Some of the canonical texts on the Vietnam War include Halberstam, *Best and the Brightest*; Karnow, *Vietnam*; FitzGerald, *Fire in the Lake*; Sheehan, *Bright Shining Lie*; Kolko, *Anatomy of a War*. Whereas earlier studies focused more on passing judgment on the United States only, recent revisionist histories put more effort into critiquing all sides. Examples include Hunt, *Lyndon Johnson's War*; Lind, *Vietnam*.

18. Tom Carhart, "Insulting Vietnam Vets," *New York Times*, October 24, 1981, 23.

19. Halbwachs, *On Collective Memory*.

20. "We Have No Choice," *New York Times*, May 5, 1975, 30.

21. "The Evacuees," *Orange County Register*, April 25, 1975, C6.

22. Sachs, *Life We Were Given*.

23. See Rose, "Tempest-Tost"; Rose, *Dispossessed*.

24. Stanley Karnow, foreword to *Once Upon a Dream*, ed. Tran, Lam, and Nguyễn.

25. Takaki, *Strangers from a Different Shore*.

26. Espiritu, *Body Counts*; Mimi Thi Nguyen, *Gift of Freedom*.

27. In an effort to bridge ethnic studies with new theories of transnationalism, Espiritu, a sociologist, has proposed a critical refugee studies framework that places Vietnamese American history and the politics of rescue—another term related to paternalism—in the context of American imperialism. She hints at the critical but uncredited role the rescued South Vietnamese played in redeeming their American rescuers' faith in American exceptionalism. Nevertheless, her critique of American empire avoids altogether the issue of refugee nationalism. See Espiritu, "Toward a Critical Refugee Study."

28. García, *Havana USA*, 120.

29. Rose, "Tempest-Tost," 10.

30. Jacobson, *Special Sorrows*.

31. Nam Lộc, "Xin Dời Một Nụ Cười."

Chapter 1. Accidental Allies: America's Crusade and the Origins of Refugee Nationalism

1. Kaplan, *Asia's Cauldron*.

2. The term *special relationship* emphasizes a moral, idealistic dimension to alliances and suggests an equality of status between partners. My thesis is somewhat

similar to that of Michael Lind, who describes Vietnam as the "necessary war" (see Lind, *Vietnam*). But unlike Lind, who thinks that policymakers ignored a "third way" to victory, I seek not to justify the war or American intervention but rather to demonstrate how Vietnam was connected to the rest of the Cold War and how Washington's moralist posturing against communism formed the basis for a refugee identity that appealed to American guilt over failing to protect its allies from communism.

3. Matray, *Reluctant Crusade*, 112.
4. Ibid., 206.
5. Brazinsky, *Nation Building in South Korea*, 2.
6. Matray, *Reluctant Crusade*.
7. Believers in modernization theory found their inspiration in Rostow's *Stages of Economic Growth*. Its influence waned in the 1970s, led by critiques such as Frank's *Capitalism and Underdevelopment in Latin America* and Wallerstein's *Modern World-System*.
8. Du Bois, "Talented Tenth," 45.
9. *Korea Reborn*. America's role in the Cold War in general and in Vietnam in particular represented a radical departure from traditional isolationist foreign policy. Until 1946, when British prime minister Winston Churchill instantiated the existence of a "special relationship" between the United Kingdom and the United States, little evidence suggested that Americans would put allies ahead of national interests. All countries wanted the special relationship because it represented an eternal alliance whereby the weaker nation could always count on the protection of the stronger one. In public discourse, there was nothing contradictory about being pro-British and pro-American. In recent years, Israel has come closest to establishing that kind of relationship with the United States.
10. Kennan, *Memoirs*, 547–59.
11. George Kennan, "Review of Current Trends, U.S. Foreign Policy, Policy Planning Staff, PPS No. 23, Top Secret," February 28, 1948 (declassified June 17, 1974), in U.S. Department of State, *Foreign Relations of the United States*, 524–25.
12. Johnson, *Sorrows of Empire*, 151.
13. Herzstein, *Henry R. Luce*, 9.
14. Henry R. Luce, "The American Century," *Life*, February 17, 1941, 61–65.
15. Barrows, *History of the Philippines*, 13.
16. "Letters," *Time*, May 17, 1943.
17. Herzstein, *Henry R. Luce*, 37.
18. *Time*, January 3, 1938.
19. "Letters," *Time*, November 1, 1937.
20. "China: Blunder and Bluster," *Life*, April 5, 1948, quoted in Herzstein, *Henry R. Luce*, 94.
21. Herzstein, *Henry R. Luce*, 110–11.
22. Matray, *Reluctant Crusade*, 236.
23. Truman, *Memoirs*, 333.
24. Garver, *Sino-American Alliance*, 21.

25. The treaties allowed either nation to opt out after giving the other party one year's notice. The Mutual Defense Treaty between the United States and the Republic of China came to an end in January 1, 1980, one year after Washington normalized relations with the People's Republic of China.

26. Garver, *Sino-American Alliance*, 230.

27. Tucker, *Taiwan, Hong Kong*, 54.

28. Ibid., 59.

29. Ibid., 69.

30. "Father of His Country?," *Time*, October 16, 1950.

31. Eul Young Park, "From Bilateralism to Multilateralism," 246.

32. Ibid., 181.

33. Alam, *Governments and Markets*, 44.

34. Ibid., 45.

35. Brazinsky, *Nation Building in South Korea*, 175.

36. Ibid., 179.

37. Ibid., 173.

38. Ibid., 177.

39. Moon, "Between Banmi (Anti-Americanism) and Sungmi (Worship of the United States)."

40. *Korea-USA Centennial*, 37.

41. Nguyễn Cao Kỳ, *Twenty Years and Twenty Days*, 19.

42. Jacobs, *America's Miracle Man*, 223.

43. Herzstein, *Henry R. Luce*, 195.

44. Ibid., 36.

45. Jacobs, *America's Miracle Man*, 221–22.

46. Herzstein, *Henry R. Luce*, 204.

47. Jacobs, *America's Miracle Man*, 264.

48. For the 1954 exodus, see Frankum, *Operation Passage to Freedom*.

49. For U.S. aid and economic development in South Vietnam, see Dacy, *Foreign Aid, War, and Economic Development*; Nguyễn Anh Tuấn, *South Vietnam Trial and Experience*.

50. *JUSPAO Survey: National Urban Public Opinion*, 5–6.

51. Nguyễn Cao Kỳ, *Twenty Years and Twenty Days*, 137–38. In the Vietnamese language, *Việt-Cộng* is merely shorthand for the Vietnamese Communist Party. According to Kỳ, this practice was inaugurated by Ngo Đình Diệm and practiced by Vietnamese refugees to this day. In English usage, *Việt-Cộng* is often used to represent the National Liberation Front, a procommunist guerrilla organization operation throughout South Vietnam. I break scholarly convention and use the terminology familiar to most of the refugee community.

52. Langguth, *Our Vietnam*, 667.

53. Aside from numerous conversations and interviews, the topic of betrayal represented a key subtext of the film *Green Dragon* (2001), the first American movie about the fall of Saigon told from a South Vietnamese perspective.

54. Nixon, "Asia after Vietnam," 121.

55. Joo-Hong Nam, *America's Commitment to South Korea*, 109.
56. "2 Envoys Sought Asia News Curbs," *New York Times*, May 21, 1975, 16; Richard M. Weintraub, "VOA Coverage Limited on U.S. Evacuation," *Washington Post*, April 15, 1975, A12.
57. Heil, *Voice of America*, 168–69.
58. Liu, *Transition to Nowhere*, 16.
59. George McArthur, "Crowds Besiege Embassy," *Los Angeles Times*, May 1, 1975, B5.
60. Bắc Trần, interview by author, San Francisco, April 2007.
61. For more English-language texts on the fall of South Vietnam, see Butler, *Fall of Saigon*; Dawson, *55 Days*; Duiker, *Communist Road to Power*; Hosmer, Kellen, and Jenkins, *Fall of South Vietnam*; Engelmann, *Tears before the Rain*.
62. On January 1, 1959, the exodus began as elites, middle-class professionals, and Batista loyalists left en masse. Cuba's regime change, while worrisome to the American government, was not officially a communist revolution. Not until January 1961, when Castro allied with the Soviets and only a few months before the Central Intelligence Agency's failed assault at the Bay of Pigs, did the United States cut off diplomatic and economic ties with Cuba.
63. García, *Havana USA*, 16. For more on Cuban Americans, see Jorge, Suchlicki, and Leyva de Varona, *Cuban Exiles in Florida*; Rieff, *Exile*.
64. Fagen and Brody, "Cubans in Exile," 391.
65. Liu, *Transition to Nowhere*, 75–76.
66. Le Van Thong, "The Man with a Mustache," *Đất Mới* (Camp Eglin), May 19, 1975, 6.
67. Andrew Malcolm, "Refugee Airlift to Guam Resumes," *New York Times*, April 28, 1975, 17.
68. Refugees could exchange whatever gold they had for U.S. currency. At Camp Pendleton, the official in charge of the exchanges reported transactions no larger than "about $8–9,000 in gold," with the majority exchanging "one or two taels or a few dollars in foreign currency" (Charles T. Powers, "Notes from a Camp Pendleton Diary," *Los Angeles Times*, June 8, 1975, 12).
69. Agamben, *Means without End*, 3–14.
70. Phạm Duy, *Hồi Ký*, chap. 1.
71. Andrew H. Malcolm, "Guam Refugees Mourn for Saigon, Then Face Future," *New York Times*, May 1, 1975, 21.
72. Đỗ Quý Toàn, interview by author, Westminster, May 2007.
73. Paul E. Steiger, "30 Viet Navy Ships Escape," *Los Angeles Times*, May 2, 1975, 1.
74. Mann, *Rise of the Vulcans*, 47

Chapter 2. From Grief to Gratitude: Reaffirming the Past by Rewriting It

1. Nick Thorne, a State Department immigration coordinator for the Vietnamese, said, "There will be no heavy concentrations of placements . . . rather a leavening"

(Eleanor Hoover, "Vietnamese Settlers: Can They Adapt?," *Los Angeles Times*, May 27, 1975, 22).

2. Phạm Duy, *Hồi Ký*, chap. 3.

3. For the refugee camp experience in 1975, see Kelly, *From Vietnam to America*; Liu, *Transition to Nowhere*; Montero, *Vietnamese Americans*.

4. For the argument that the politics of rescue cuts both ways, see Espiritu, "Toward a Critical Refugee Study"; Espiritu, "The 'We-Win-Even-When-We-Lose' Syndrome." See also Espiritu, *Body Counts*.

5. Brehm and Cole, "Effect of a Favor." These insights were brought to my attention in Pérez, *Cuba in the American Imagination*, 179–89.

6. Matthews, *Culture Clash*, xi.

7. T. D. Allman, "Evacuating Refugees: More Self-Deception?," *Los Angeles Times*, April 20, 1975, G1.

8. Liu, *Transition to Nowhere*, 49, 51; U.S. Department of Health, Education, and Welfare, Refugee Task Force, *Task Force for Indochina Refugees*, 30.

9. Evacuee Master File, 1975; Statistical Abstract of the United States, 1981, table 29, in Baker and North, *1975 Refugees*, 28.

10. Eleanor Hoover, "Vietnamese Settlers: Can They Adapt?," *Los Angeles Times*, May 27, 1975, B1.

11. John Nordheimer, "Even in a Refugee Camp, a General Is Still a General," *New York Times*, May 12, 1975, 16.

12. "Ky Denounces S. Viet Evacuees as Cowards," *Los Angeles Times*, April 25, 1975, 2; "Ky Flees to Safe Haven on U.S. Navy Ship," *Los Angeles Times*, April 30, 1975, 2.

13. Dan Oberdorfer, "Refugees Uncertain about Future in U.S.," *Washington Post*, April 24, 1975, A10.

14. "S. Viet Officers on Guam Dodge Angry Refugees," *Los Angeles Times*, May 1, 1975, A2. The 1967–75 presidency of Nguyễn Văn Thiệu was noteworthy for its rampant corruption. See "Firm Confirms It Refused to Fly 16 Tons of Gold Out of Saigon," *Los Angeles Times*, April 15, 1975, 14; Keyes Beech, "Fleeing General Called Vietnam's Biggest Crook," *Los Angeles Times*, May 2, 1975, A2; Kathy Burke, "Ky Seeking Sponsor to Start Him Farming," *Los Angeles Times*, May 6, 1975, A3.

15. Brendan Jones, "U.S. Companies Aid Evacuated Vietnamese Employes," *New York Times*, May 10, 1975, 35.

16. Linda Charlton, "Security Check and Need for Sponsors Delaying Refugee Flow," *New York Times*, May 15, 1975, 14; William K. Stevens, "Nebraska Recruits Vietnamese Doctors," *New York Times*, June 17, 1975, 69; Judy Lee Man, "Many Towns Seek Physician Refugees," *Washington Post*, May 15, 1975, A22.

17. Douglas E. Kneeland, "Sponsors Hard to Find," *New York Times*, May 8, 1975, 1.

18. Liu, *Transition to Nowhere*, 44; U.S. Department of Health, Education, and Welfare, Refugee Task Force, *Task Force for Indochina Refugees*, 26.

19. Kathy Burke, "Newest Pendleton Refugee," *Los Angeles Times*, June 7, 1975, OC-1.

20. Paul E. Steiger, "30 Viet Navy Ships Escape," *Los Angeles Times*, May 2, 1975, 1; "Ford Admits 30,000 More," *Los Angeles Times*, May 2, 1975, A1; "Last U.S. Warship from S. Vietnam at Subic Bay," *Los Angeles Times*, May 7. 1975, 19; *Chân Trời Mới*, May 8, 1975, 1–2; "First of Seaborne Refugees Hit Guam," *Los Angeles Times*, May 7, 1975, 20.

21. Liu, *Transition to Nowhere*, 45–46.

22. "Ford Admits 30,000 More," *Los Angeles Times*, May 2, 1975, A1.

23. Espiritu, *Body Counts*.

24. "Guam 'Tent City'—Refugees Keep Vigil for Families," *Los Angeles Times*, June 1, 1975, 1.

25. Ibid.; "Today's Statistics," *Chân Trời Mới*, June 2, 1975, 3; "Guam's 'Tent City' Calm Despite Dismal Situation," *Los Angeles Times*, May 16, 1975, B9.

26. When sixty-three refugees at Camp Pendleton, California, were asked to name the "most unforgettable event" they had experienced since leaving Vietnam, 36.5 percent responded "lack of food," 22.2 percent responded "seeing misery and defeat," 12.7 percent responded "lost relatives," and 22.2 percent responded "uncertainties." See Liu, *Transition to Nowhere*, 75; Fox Butterfield, "In Saigon, It Is Every Man for Himself, Nobody for Thieu," *New York Times*, April 20, 1975, 199.

27. Liu, *Transition to Nowhere*, 76.

28. Le Van Thong, "The Man with a Mustache," *Đất Mới* (Camp Eglin), May 19, 1975, 6, 8.

29. "Orote Point Không Tiêu Biểu Đời Sống Hoa Kỳ," *Chân Trời Mới*, May 17, 1975, 1.

30. Liu, *Transition to Nowhere*, 82.

31. President's Interagency Task Force, statement, May 19, 1975, published in *Camp Pendleton Newsletter*, June 24, 1975, 5–6.

32. *Time*, May 19, 1975, 9.

33. Letters to the Editor, *Los Angeles Times*, April 29, 1975, C4.

34. However, the refugee controversy generated much less public interest than the issue of gun control legislation. California senator Alan Cranston's office received thirty thousand letters on that issue, compared to about one thousand in response to the Vietnamese refugees. See Bill Boyarsky, "Letters 10 to 1 Negative," *Los Angeles Times*, May 3, 1975, A1.

35. James T. Wooten, "The Vietnamese Are Coming—The Town of Niceville, Fla., Doesn't Like It," *New York Times*, May 1, 1975, 21.

36. Jack Nelson, "Refugee Plans Draw Protests by the Thousands," *Los Angeles Times*, April 30, 1975, A1.

37. David Lamb, "Two Views of the Vietnamese Refugees," *Los Angeles Times*, May 12, 1975, C5; Andrew H. Malcolm, "2,500 Refugees Leaving Guam for U.S. Mainland," *New York Times*, May 2, 1975, 17.

38. Liu, *Transition to Nowhere*, 38.

39. "End of a Tragic Drama," *Chicago Defender*, May 8, 1975, 9; "Eartha Kitt Blasts Ford," *Chicago Defender*, May 13, 1975, 6; "The Refugee Dilemma," *Chicago Defender*, May 15, 1975, 17; Benjamin E. Mays, "I Agree with the President," *Chicago Defender*, May 24, 1975, 6; John W. Lewis Jr, "Caucus Opposes Vietnamese Aid; Wants Program for American Poor," *New Pittsburgh Courier*, May 17, 1975, 1; Robert Flipping Jr., "Black Community Has Mixed Feelings about Vietnamese," *New Pittsburgh Courier*, June 14, 1975, 24; "Viet Refugee Flood," *New Pittsburgh Courier*, November 10, 1979, 6. For Afro-Asian relations, see Prashad, *Everybody Was Kung Fu Fighting*; Pulido, *Black, Brown, Yellow, and Left*; Scott Kurashige, *Shifting Grounds of Race*.

40. Vernon E. Jordan Jr., "Vietnam and the Orphans," *Chicago Defender*, April 19, 1975, 19; J. I. Adkins Jr., "Jordan Criticizes Aid to Viets," *Chicago Defender*, May 14, 1975, 10; Vernon E. Jordan Jr., "To Be Equal," *Chicago Defender*, May 24, 1975, 14.

41. Clyde Taylor, "A Black Teacher's Agonized Message to the Vietnamese Refugees," *Los Angeles Times*, May 26, 1975, B5.

42. Pryor, "New Niggers."

43. Bill Boyarsky, "Letters 10 to 1 Negative," *Los Angeles Times*, May 3, 1975, A1.

44. Paul Housti, "House to Get Bill on Refugees Today," *Los Angeles Times*, June 13, 1975, A12, reprinted in *Thông Báo*, June 17, 1975, 2.

45. "Cheers Drown Out Protests," *Los Angeles Times*, May 2, 1975, A1.

46. "Crowds Greet Viet Refugees in Pennsylvania," *Los Angeles Times*, May 28, 1975, A2.

47. Le Van Thong, "The Man with the Moustache, part 2," *Đất Mới* (Camp Eglin), May 21, 1975, 6.

48. Douglas E. Kneeland, "Many Refugees Are Reluctant to Leave the Security of 4 Camps and Be Resettled," *New York Times*, July 22, 1975, 13.

49. Liu, *Transition to Nowhere*, 96.

50. Phạm Duy, *Hồi Ký*, chap. 2.

51. Lê Quang Anh, interview by author, Midway City, 2007; Liu, *Transition to Nowhere*, 101.

52. Kibria, *Family Tightrope*.

53. "250 Refugee Children Found without Parents," *San Diego Union*, reprinted in *Thông Báo*, July 31, 1975, 1. See also Schulz, *Voyagers in the Land*.

54. Trần Quốc Sỹ, "Chuyện Vui Buồn Trong Đời Tị Nạn," in *Viết Về Nước Mỹ 2001*, 109–16.

55. "Viet Refugees Protest Delay in Return Home," *Los Angeles Times*, June 20, 1975, B2; "Refugees at Chaffee Threaten a Protest," *Los Angeles Times*, May 23, 1975, A1.

56. Kathy Burke, "Families Still There," *Los Angeles Times*, May 18, 1975, A24.

57. Greg Waskul, "Seek Return to Vietnam," *Los Angeles Times*, June 24, 1975, B3.

58. Ngọc Lam, "Viewpoint for Those Who Return," *Tân Dân*, September 9, 1975, 2–3; "Ft. Chaffee Feud Denied as Cause of Refugee Shift," *San Diego Union*, reprinted in *Thông Báo*, June 27, 1975, 1.

59. Vu Thuy Hoang, "Vietnam Refugee Ideological Battle Expected to Intensify," *Washington Post*, December 25, 1977, 10; Nguyễn Nguyễn Phong, "Trại 'Tị Nạn' Pendleton" [Pendleton's "Refugee" Camp], *Thái Bình*, May 1975, 11.

60. During the summer, the hundreds of Vietnamese in the military camps who demanded repatriation staged a flurry of demonstrations, one of which escalated into a riot. When they arrived in Vietnam, the repatriates were incarcerated as prisoners of war. For a theoretically laced analysis of this episode, see Lipman, "Give Us a Ship." For a repatriate's memoir regarding his time as a prisoner, see Trần Đình Trụ, *Việt Nam Thương Tín Con Tàu Định Mệnh: Hồi Ký*.

61. "Notice on Sponsorship and Job," *Thông Báo*, August 27, 1975, 3–4.

62. Quốc Thông, "Nhớ Về Trại Pendleton," in *Viết Về Nước Mỹ 2001*, 408.

63. "Man Offers Jobs to Aid 300 Refugees," *Los Angeles Times*, August 27, 1975. In August, the family-owned Spence Fishing Company sponsored three hundred refugees to work on fishing boats in the Florida panhandle.

64. "24 Viet Refugees 'Rescued' from Base in Fresno," *Los Angeles Times*, October 17, 1975, E10.

65. Frank Del Olmo, "UFWA Says Letter Backs Viet Strikebreaker Claim," *Los Angeles Times*, August 1, 1975, B3.

66. Baker and North, *1975 Refugees*, 51, based on data from Evacuee Master File; "Where Have the First 92,589 Refugees Gone?" *Tân Dân*, October 9, 1975, 1. Refugees likely left with jobs but without sponsors.

67. Rose, "Tempest-Tost," 9.

68. Phạm Duy, *Hồi Ký*, chap. 3.

69. Tran Ly Le, "Goodbye," *Đất Lành*, July 22, 1975, 5 (translated by camp newsletter staff).

70. Le Van Thong, "My Country and Me," *Đất Mới* (Camp Eglin), May 25, 1975, 5.

71. Nguyễn Tuyet Ngan, "Plight of the Refugees," *Thông Báo*, August 19, 1975, 3. This version appeared in the English edition. The original Vietnamese version is not available.

72. Just 14.4 percent of refugees had "good" or better English skills (Liu, *Transition to Nowhere*, 51). Each of the eight camps at Pendleton held between six and eighteen "survival English" classes per day with average enrollments as high as one hundred per class (*Thông Báo*, June 11, 1975, 6). One study indicates that the classes produced mixed results, however (Kelly, *From Vietnam to America*; "Family Waiting for Relatives," *Thông Báo*, September 4, 1975, 4).

73. "Letter to the Vietnamese Refugees," *Thông Báo*, June 11, 1975, 6.

74. "An Open Letter to the Vietnamese Refugees," *Thông Báo*, June 14, 1975, 1. President Nixon, of course, had used the phrase *silent majority* in a November

1969 speech asking for Americans' support for the Vietnam War (Nixon, "Nixon's 'Silent Majority' Speech").

75. "Letter of Welcome from the Mayor of San Diego," *Thông Báo*, June 13, 1975, 5.

76. "Washington Telephone Lines Tied Up by Sponsorship Offers," *Thông Báo*, May 28, 1975, 1–2. According to the Interagency Task Force, approximately 21 percent of the offers of assistance during May and June came from California residents, followed by Florida and Texas with 7 percent each (U.S. Department of Health, Education, and Welfare, Interagency Task Force on Indochinese Refugees, *Report*, 9).

77. Douglas E. Kneeland, "Sponsors Hard to Find," *New York Times*, May 8, 1975, 1.

78. The U.S. Catholic Conference (52,100), Church World Service (17,864), Lutheran Immigration and Refugee Service (15,897), and United Hebrew Immigrant Aid Society (3,531) together resettled 74.7 percent of the 119,591 refugees resettled in the United States in 1975 (Kelly, *From Vietnam to America*, 152). For more on the role of churches in receiving refugees, see Fein, *Congregational Sponsors*; Crittenden, *Sanctuary*; Nawyn, *American Protestantism's Response*.

79. Matthews, *Culture Clash*, x.

80. "Lutherans to Care for 10,000 Viet Refugees," *Los Angeles Times*, May 4, 1975, A7.

81. John Dart, "Southland Churches Gear Up to Aid Asian Refugees," *Los Angeles Times*, May 10, 1975, A26.

82. John Dart, "Churches among Most Reliable Refugee Sponsors," *Los Angeles Times*, August 11, 1975, B3.

83. Approximately 37 percent of the 24,522 families surveyed at Camp Pendleton had five or more members (including extended families) (Liu, *Transition to Nowhere*, 45).

84. Alicia Cooper interview, in *Vietnamese Community in Orange County*, 3:119.

85. John Dart, "Southland Churches Gear Up to Aid Asian Refugees," *Los Angeles Times*, May 10, 1975, A26.

86. Myrna Oliver, "Your Problems Were Ours . . ." *Los Angeles Times*, June 2, 1975, B3.

87. Kathy Burke, "Refugees Get a Home—From Refugees," *Los Angeles Times*, June 4, 1975, B27.

88. "Letter to President Ford," *Đất Lành*, July 4, 1975, 10; "Letter to Mr. Milton Shapp: Governor of Pennsylvania State," *Đất Lành*, July 6, 1975, 1.

89. "Letter of Appreciation," *Thông Báo*, June 4, 1975, 4.

90. "Sponsor Success," *Đất Mới* (Camp Eglin), May 27, 1975, 7.

91. "A Letter from a Refugee," *Đất Mới* (Camp Eglin), July 25, 1975, 6.

92. "Letter," *Tân Dân*, October 31, 1975, 3

93. Donald Harrison, "Refugee Enlistments Proposed," *San Diego Union*, reprinted in *Thông Báo*, May 29, 1975, 5–6; "Ky Suggests Base Jobs for Ex-Saigon Troops," *Thông Báo*, June 18, 1975, 3–4; "Vietnamese Military Can Join U.S. Forces," *Thông Báo*, July 25, 1975, 1.

94. "How to Repay Kindness?" *Đất Lành*, September 22, 1975, 2.
95. "Refugees Fear U.S. Life," *Tân Dân*, October 3, 1975, 1. At Camp Pendleton, by contrast, more than 49,000 refugees had been admitted over that period but only 5,238 remained.
96. Douglas E. Kneeland, "Vietnamese Refugees Seeking to Stay in a Group Pose Resettlement Problem," *New York Times*, November 18, 1975, 24.
97. *Tân Dân*, August 30, 1975, 2.
98. Phạm Duy, *Hồi Ký*, chap. 3.
99. Ibid.
100. Matthews, *Culture Clash*, 124.
101. Hồ Xuân Mai, telephone interview by author, April 2007.
102. Phạm Duy, *Hồi Ký*, chap. 3.
103. Matthews, *Culture Clash*, 25.
104. Minh Nhân, "America and a Contractor," in *Viết Về Nước Mỹ 2000*, 160.
105. Thomas Nguyễn, interview by author, Fountain Valley, September 2008.
106. Matthews, *Culture Clash*, 69.
107. Baker and North, *1975 Refugees*, 146.
108. Matsuoka, "Vietnamese Americans," 120.
109. Baker and North, *1975 Refugees*, 106. As of January 1, 1976, the California governor's office unhappily stated that 20,747 Vietnamese refugees—more than half the state's total—received some kind of welfare assistance ("Half of Refugees on State Welfare," *Los Angeles Times*, January 22, 1976, A3).
110. Further, tight budgets forced social service organizations to use whatever money they had to provide immediate services rather than offer English-language classes and job-related training for the long term.
111. Joan Sweeney, "The Cubans—Making It as Refugees," *Los Angeles Times*, May 12, 1975, B1; B. Drummond Ayres Jr., "Cubans Suggest That the Vietnamese Persevere in Resettlement," *New York Times*, May 24, 1975, 10.
112. B. Drummond Ayres Jr., "Cubans Suggest That the Vietnamese Persevere in Resettlement," *New York Times*, May 24, 1975, 10. William Liu, the director of the Asian American Mental Health Research Center, disagreed vehemently with the official policy of dispersing the refugees. "In comparison with all the immigrants from Europe and from Asia, the Vietnamese people were 'sponsored' and scattered all over the country. Where is the Vietnamese community that they were looking for? Now, after two years, we wonder why there were so many mental health casualties" (Liu, *Transition to Nowhere*, 119).
113. Liu, *Transition to Nowhere*, 119.
114. Jonathan Kirsch, "'Little Saigon'—Another Misconception," *Los Angeles Times*, June 10, 1975, C7.
115. Mỹ-Bình, interview by author, Santa Ana, April 2007.
116. Bùi Xuân Đáng, "Peoria Có Gì Lạ Không Em," in *Viết Về Nước Mỹ 2002*, 461.
117. Tony Lâm, interview by author, Westminster, 2007. Aguilar–San Juan, "Creating Ethnic Places," 119–20, also mentions the practice of calling people whose Vietnamese names appeared in the phone book.

Chapter 3. "Farewell, Saigon, I Promise I Will Return": Social Work and the Meaning of Exile

1. At the time, Florida had the highest rate of Vietnamese refugee departures (9 percent of all secondary out-migration), and California had the highest rate of Vietnamese arrivals (70.9 percent of all secondary in-migration). By January 1978, California's Vietnamese population had reached 42,115, while Florida's had declined to 4,947. See U.S. Social Security Administration, Office of Refugee Affairs, *Indochinese Refugee Assistance Program*, 14.

2. Not all of the "boat people" left by boat. On April 25, 1979, the U.S. State Department reported that 60 percent of new Indochinese refugees had ventured east to Thailand and that many had crossed the dangerous jungles of Cambodia (*Indochinese Refugee Reports*, May 1, 1979, 8).

3. Lieu, *American Dream in Vietnamese*, 90–91.

4. For more on space and place, see Lefebvre, *Production of Space*; Hayden, *Power of Place*; Ma and Cartier, *Chinese Diaspora*; Tuan, *Space and Place*.

5. For more on the boat people, see Grant, *Boat People*; Tsamenyi, *Vietnamese Boat People and International Law*; Cargill and Huynh, *Voices of Vietnamese Boat People*; Brian Doan, *Forgotten Ones*.

6. This section benefits tremendously from the Gramscian school of cultural studies, which holds that popular culture can play a role in oppositional movements by serving as one of the means by which communities or coalitions come together. Stuart Hall, one of the best-known Gramscian thinkers, asked that for analytical purposes we view race and ethnicity as coalitions whose unity exists as a consequence of ongoing crises or trauma that make differentiating factors far less important than the uniting issues. The exigencies of the refugee experience pose such a traumatic experience. See Gramsci, *Selections from the Prison Notebooks*; Hall, "Problem of Ideology"; Hall, "Cultural Studies and Its Theoretical Legacies"; Hall, "Gramsci's Relevance for the Study of Race and Ethnicity." Hall's essays are also available in Morley and Chen, *Stuart Hall*.

7. For more on the Voice of America, see Alexandre, *Voice of America*; Rawnsley, *Radio Diplomacy and Propaganda*; Nelson, *War of the Black Heavens*; Krugler, *Voice of America and the Domestic Propaganda Battles*; Heil, *Voice of America*.

8. Phạm Văn Phổ, "A Lot Changes in 20 Years," *Hiệp Nhất*, April 1995, 17.

9. Nguyễn Duc Tien, "The Vietnamese Catholic Community at 20 (1975–1995)," *Hiệp Nhất*, April 1995, 5.

10. For more on Vietnamese Catholicism and religion in general, see Rutledge, *The Role of Religion in Ethnic Self-Identity: A Vietnamese Community*, vol. 2; Nash, *Vietnamese Catholicism*; Padgett, "Religion, Memory, and Imagination."

11. Vietnamese Friends Club, Santa Ana College, invitation to Community Business Managers, January 12, 1978, Program for Tết, Santa Ana College, February 7, 1978, both housed in Gayle Morrison Collection, University of California at Irvine.

12. Gayle Morrison to U.S. Department of Health, Education, and Welfare Refugee

Task Force, June 27, 1978, Gayle Morrison Collection, University of California at Irvine.

13. *Orange County Child Care Resource Guide.*

14. Vu Thuy Hoang, "Vietnam Refugee Ideological Battle Expected to Intensify," *Washington Post*, December 25, 1977, 10.

15. Sucheng Chan, *Vietnamese American 1.5 Generation*, vii.

16. Students also engaged in other forms of activism, including concerts, such as one held on January 17, 1976, in Long Beach. See *Trắng Đen*, March 6, 1976, 18. In addition, students wrote to President Jimmy Carter to intervene in the boat people crisis. See *Trắng Đen*, March 7, 1980, 29. UCLA offered its first class on the Vietnamese refugee experience in the spring quarter of 1980. See *Trắng Đen*, April 4, 1980, 34.

17. "40 Viet Refugees Protest in Fullerton," *Los Angeles Times*, October 29, 1977, OC-13; "24 Viet Refugees Arrested in Protest," *Los Angeles Times*, October 23, 1977, C6.

18. Kiều Mỹ Duyên, "Giới Thệu Trung Tâm Người Việt Quốc Gia," *Người Việt*, October 28, 1979, 6.

19. Matthews, *Culture Clash*, 12; Virginia Inman, "The Americanization of a Vietnamese Family," *Wall Street Journal*, January 31, 1983, 28.

20. Liu, *Transition to Nowhere*, 16.

21. Phạm Duy, *Hồi Ký*, chap. 3.

22. Việt Dzũng, interview by author, Westminster, April 2007. According to Vinh Phuc, when he was on Bisar Island, Malaysia, in 1979, people valued their music collections too much to share with others: "quý lắm" (quite precious) (Vinh Phuc, interview by author, Westminster, April 2007).

23. Nam Lộc Nguyễn, interview by author, Los Angeles, April 2007.

24. Vietnamese Americans have no preferred term for pre-1975 South Vietnamese music. People sympathetic to refugee nationalism simply refer to it as Vietnamese music, but the music's melancholy tone is unmistakable to even the untrained ear. Vietnamese Americans refer to North Vietnamese wartime music as communist music. See Taylor, *Fragments of the Present*; Olsen, *Popular Music of Vietnam*; Gibbs, "Yellow Music Turning Golden"; Gibbs, "Nhac Tien Chien."

25. Philip Taylor, *Fragments of the Present*, 23–55.

26. Nguyễn Đình San, *100 Bài Hát Việt Nam Hay Nhất Thế Ký 20*, 93; Nguyễn Đình San, *Dư Âm*, 223.

27. Very little if any scholarly literature exists on the reeducation camps, mostly because communist countries either never documented those events or never allowed access to such documents. The closest thing to a scholarly study is Courtois et al., *Black Book of Communism*. Some of those who survived the camps have published memoirs, and films have been made about their experiences. See, for example, Doan Van Toai and Chanoff, *Vietnamese Gulag*; Nguyễn Ngọc Ngạn, *Will of Heaven*; Huỳnh, *South Wind Changing*; Hollander, *From the Gulag to the Killing Fields*; Ham Tran, *Journey from the Fall*.

28. Nguyễn Ngọc Ngạn, *Will of Heaven*, 189.
29. Mỹ-Bình, interview by author, April 2007.
30. Phạm Duy, *Hồi Ký*, chap. 3.
31. Ibid., chap. 5.
32. Xuyên Sơn, "Nên Hoặc Không Nên Gởi Tiền Về Việt-Nam?" [Should We or Shouldn't We Send Money to Vietnam?], *Trắng Đen*, April 9, 1976, 17; "90% of Remittance Money Stolen by Communists," *Trắng Đen*, November 6, 1976, 18.
33. "Money Sanctions Lifted for Cuba, Vietnam Kin," *Washington Post*, January 6, 1978, A13.
34. Do with Brody, *Yen Do and the Story of Nguoi Viet Daily News*, 45. Microfilm of the *Người Việt Daily News* is available at Langson Library, University of California at Irvine
35. Nam Lộc Nguyễn, interview by author, Los Angeles, April 2007.
36. Howard Seelye, "Agencies Take Steps to Ease Overcrowding," *Los Angeles Times*, November 16, 1976, OC-1.
37. Nam Lộc Nguyễn, interview by author, Los Angeles, April 2007.
38. The size and scope of the Southern California community enabled the formation of a Vietnamese public sphere beyond visits to Chinatown and Hollywood Blvd. Despite charging six dollars per ticket, musicians in 1976 sold out two shows at the twelve-hundred-seat Wilshire Ebell Theater to commemorate the one-year anniversary of the "birth of the diaspora." A week earlier, Santa Ana's newly formed Vietnamese-American Mutual Association held a similar event at Anaheim High School, charging two dollars per ticket. With a Vietnamese population of two hundred thousand by 1976, Southern California was one of the few places that could sustain a Vietnamese music concert economy, with the biggest venues in Los Angeles. On a smaller scale, Vietnamese in Huntsville, Alabama, organized two April 30, 1976, events at Protestant churches, and with the help of a Vietnamese professor at the University of Michigan, Ann Arbor's Vietnamese community put together a small event on campus. In early May, the Vietnamese congregation at St. Nicholas Catholic Church in Wilkes Barre, Pennsylvania, scheduled a daylong cultural event featuring singers and screenings of vintage South Vietnamese films. See "Events among the Diaspora," *Trắng Đen*, May 23, 1976, 27–28.
39. K. D., telephone interview by author, February 2009.
40. Hồ Xuân Mai, telephone interview by author, April 2007.
41. The original Vietnamese name for the song was "Sàigòn Ơi, Thôi Đã Hết" [It Is Over, Saigon] because another artist, Lam Phương, had already composed a refugee song, "Sàigòn Ơi, Vĩnh Biệt" [Farewell, Saigon]. Over time, the "Farewell, Saigon" title has become synonymous in popular usage with Nam Lộc's song.
42. "Sài Gòn ơi, Vĩnh Biệt" [Farewell, Saigon], English translation by Phạm Duy.
43. Hồ Xuân Mai, telephone interview by author, April 2007.
44. Nam Lộc Nguyễn, interview by author, April 2007.
45. Ngọc Lam, "Viewpoint: For Those Who Return," *Tân Dân*, September 9, 1975, 2–3.

46. Kerby A. Miller, *Emigrants and Exiles.*
47. Bắc Trần, interview by author, San Francisco, April 2007.
48. Ngô Thụy Miên, email to author, April 2007.
49. Lê Văn, interview by author, Anaheim, May 2007; U.S. Information Service, *VOA Program Schedule, February–April 1965.*
50. *JUSPAO Survey: Media Survey of Urban Vietnam,* ii
51. Lư, *Inviting Call of Wandering Souls,* 31–32.
52. *JUSPAO Survey: National Urban Public Opinion,* 5
53. Lư, *Inviting Call of Wandering Souls,* 152.
54. U.S. Congress, Senate, Subcommittee on Financial Institutions of the Committee on Banking, Housing, and Urban Affairs, *Senate Hearing 98-935, "Vietnamese Currency Transfer Legislation,"* 41.
55. Lê Văn, interview by author, Anaheim, May 2007.
56. The Vietnamese refugee press has enjoyed a longevity unanticipated by theorists of the ethnic press. A 1985 survey found that Orange County had more Vietnamese-language newspapers (fourteen) than it did Spanish (six), Korean (four), and Chinese (one) newspapers combined. See García-Ayvens, *Ethnic Orange County.* For more on the ethnic press in U.S. history, see Robert E. Park, *Immigrant Press and Its Control*; Jordan, *Black Newspapers and America's War for Democracy*; Jaret, "Greek, Italian, and Jewish American Ethnic Press"; Sally M. Miller, *Ethnic Press in the United States*; Olzack and West, "Ethnic Conflict and the Rise and Fall of Ethnic Newspapers"; Yoo, "'Read All about It.'"
57. Việt Định Phương, Editor's Statement, *Trắng Đen,* March 1976, 3.
58. "Super Refugee: From Saigon to America and Back to VN to Rescue His Family," *Việt Nam Tự Do,* reprinted in *Trắng Đen,* July 1, 1976, 6.
59. "For Việt Families' Reunion by Red Cross Int'l," *Trắng Đen,* May 1, 1976, 27.
60. "How to Locate Refugees Still in Thailand?," *Trắng Đen,* April 10, 1976, 25.
61. "Odyssey of the 'Boat People,'" *Los Angeles Times,* August 3, 1977, B4.
62. "The Boat People," *Los Angeles Times,* December 14, 1976, D6.
63. "Thailand to Deport Additional Refugees," *Los Angeles Times,* February 18, 1976, C5; George McArthur, "Sea Claims Many," *Los Angeles Times,* June 13, 1976, 1.
64. Henry Kamm, "Attitude of Asians Hardens toward Indochina Refugees," *New York Times,* June 21, 1977.
65. "Viet Refugees Butchered," *Los Angeles Times,* November 24, 1976, A1.
66. Henry Kamm, "Vietnamese Who Fled to Speak Out Find It Isn't Easy," *New York Times,* June 19, 1977, A10.
67. Dan Oberdorfer, "Jailings, Killings in Vietnam Recounted," *Washington Post,* July 27, 1977, A8.
68. Nguyen Cong Hoan, "Why I Escaped from Vietnam," *Newsweek,* October 31, 1977, 25.
69. U.S. Congress, House, Committee on International Relations, Subcommittee on International Organizations. *Human Rights in Vietnam.*

70. "Vietnam News," *Trắng Đen*, September 25, 1976, 6–7.

71. "4,300 Vietnamese Refugees Remain in Thailand," *Trắng Đen*, October 9, 1976, 6–8.

72. "A Reporter from 'The Truth' Goes to Thailand," *Trắng Đen*, October 16, 1976, 7–10.

73. "President Ford Responds to 'The Truth,'" *Trắng Đen*, January 29, 1977, 5.

74. In 1979, nearly forty Vietnamese Catholic families volunteered to sponsor new refugees by helping them find housing and jobs. In addition, Catholics collected $304 worth of aluminum cans to cover the postage for 140 pounds of reading material being sent to the camps. See Nguyễn Duc Tien, "The Vietnamese Catholic Community at 20 (1975–1995)," *Hiệp Nhất*, February 1996, 52–53.

75. "New Resettlement Openings for Indochina Displaced," *UNHCR*, October 1977, 4; George McArthur, "More Vietnamese Escaping by Boat," *Los Angeles Times*, June 2, 1977, B12; "UNHCR Team Holds Top-Level Talks with Thai Government on Aid to 80,000 Displaced Persons," *UNHCR*, July 1977, 3.

76. "Shipowners Urged to Rescue 'Boat People' in Distress on High Seas," *UNHCR*, October 1977, 1; "New Resettlement Openings for Indochina Displaced," *NHCR*, October 1977, 1; Bernard Gwertzman, "President Approves Plan to Admit 15,000 More Indochinese Refugees," *New York Times*, July 16, 1977, 48.

77. Do with Brody, *Yen Do and the Story of Nguoi Viet Daily News*, 12.

78. Ibid., 15.

79. Ibid.

80. Nguyệt Ánh, *Em Còn Nhớ Màu Cờ*.

81. Lê Văn, interview by author, Anaheim, May 2007; "Youth in VN Love 'Rock,'" *Đất Mới* (Seattle), September 1978, English section, 6.

82. Nhật Ngân, interview by author, Anaheim, April 2007.

83. Lu, *Inviting Call of Wandering Souls*, 93.

84. *Those Who Leave*, 33.

85. Patrick Smith, "Pull Factor Gets the Push," *Far Eastern Economic Review*, July 17, 1981, 5.

86. Việt Dzũng, interview by author, Westminster, April 2007.

87. Peter Arnett, "Refugees from 'Boat with No Smiles' Find New Life in U.S.," *Los Angeles Times*, June 23, 1978, B5.

88. Jim Adams, "Huddleston: State Department 'Recruiting' Indochinese Refugees," Associated Press, June 29, 1981; Lê Vân, interview by author, Anaheim, May 2007.

89. William Chapman, "Carter's Pledge Was Clincher, Vietnamese Refugees Say," *Washington Post*, August 4, 1979, A18.

90. Marjorie Hyer, "Buddhist Monk Tells of Repression in Vietnam," *Washington Post*, February 10, 1978, C10.

91. Roger P. Winter, "Boat Refugees' Horrors," *New York Times*, August 27, 1983, 21.

92. William Claiborne, "Prominent U.S. War Protesters Condemn Hanoi," *Los Angeles Times*, December 30, 1976, 2.

Notes to Chapter 3

93. George McArthur, "Open Door Urged on Indochina Refugees," *Los Angeles Times*, February 19, 1978, A12.

94. "Statements Support Admission of Boat People," *Đất Mới* (Seattle), April 1978, 10.

95. "Black Americans Urge Admissions of the Indochinese Refugees" (International Rescue Committee advertisement), *New York Times*, March 19, 1978, E9.

96. "Refugee Toll Highest Ever," *Đất Mới* (Seattle), April 1978, 11.

97. Walter Mondale, "U.N. Speech," Geneva, July 21, 1979, http://nakbaeducation.com/wp-content/uploads/UNSpeech19MONDALE.pdf.

98. Do with Brody, *Yen Do and the Story of Nguoi Viet Daily News*, 15.

99. California Health and Welfare Agency, Office of Migration and Refugee Affairs, *California State Master Plan for Refugees*, 24–25. Of the 79,957 total arrivals (primary and secondary migration) during this period, 38,309 settled in those two counties.

100. Tạ Ty, *Đáy Địa Ngục*; Phạm Quốc Bảo, *Cùm Đỏ*; Hà Thúc Sinh, *Đài Học Máu*.

101. For more on the San Gabriel Valley's transformation, see Saito, *Race and Politics*; Horton, *Politics of Diversity*; Fong, *First Suburban Chinatown*; Li, "Building Ethnoburbia."

102. According to the 1986 edition of the *Vietnamese Yellow Pages* published by the Vietnamese American Chamber of Commerce, Westminster had 358 Vietnamese businesses, while Los Angeles and Long Beach combined had 215. For *Người Việt*'s transition to an ad-based business model, see *Vietnamese Community in Orange County*, 4:45–46.

103. *Người Việt Ca Li*, April 24, 1980 (ad for Kingsplace tract homes); *Người Việt*, Tết 1982, (ad for the Saigon Shopping Center at the corner of Bolsa and Magnolia, with twenty thousand square feet of retail space and sixty thousand square feet of parking space).

104. For more on the role of Indochinese mutual assistance associations, see Nguyen Van Hien, Bui, and Lê, *Ethnic Self-Help Organizations*.

105. "Education Is Bargain at East Los Angeles College," *Los Angeles Times*, September 4, 1975, K6; Thomas Fortune and Tracey Wood, "Immigrants to Face Out-of-State Fees," *Los Angeles Times*, August 21, 1980, OC-A1.

106. Lorraine Bennett, "Vietnam Refugees Go Back to School," *Los Angeles Times*, August 4, 1975, OC-B8. According to the 1979 *Orange County Child Care Resource Guide*, published specifically for Indochinese refugees, families could find affordable child day care at forty-five facilities, eight of them in Santa Ana.

107. Do with Brody, *Yen Do and the Story of Nguoi Viet Daily News*, 15.

108. Walter Barnes interview, in *Vietnamese Community in Orange County*, 3:26. For more on the 1980 Refugee Act, see Bon Tempo, *Americans at the Gate*; Amnesty International USA, *Reasonable Fear*; Loescher and Scanlan, *Global Refugee Problem*.

109. Robert Fairbanks, "New Reform of Medi-Cal Urged," *Los Angeles Times*, January 1, 1975, A1.

110. "HEW Announces $1.3 Million Program to Help Qualify Viet Refugee Doctors," *Los Angeles Times*, August 8, 1975, B12. As of March 1977, about three hundred Indochinese refugee doctors had taken the certification examination required of all foreign-trained physicians. Nearly half (141) passed the medical section but lacked the English skills to pass the language section on the first try. Also, among the nine institutions authorized to recertify Vietnamese-trained doctors and dentists, only two—Loma Linda University and the University of California at San Diego—were located in California. See U.S. Department of Health, Education, and Welfare, Refugee Task Force, *Task Force for Indochina Refugees*, 69, 73.

111. Nearly every advertisement in Little Saigon's Vietnamese-language newspapers for a doctor, dentist, or pharmacist indicated that they accepted Medi-Cal (Nhận Medi-Cal). Doctors have also constituted the largest professional class in the Vietnamese American population, outstripping entrepreneurial careers such as restaurateurs, real estate agents, mechanics, and nail salon technicians.

112. "I Sing for My Country . . . Where's My Country Now?: Folksinger Has No Country, Vietnamese Singer Laments Loss," *Pensacola News-Journal*, May 11, 1975, A1.

113. Phạm Duy, "Quê Hương Còn Đó Niềm Vui" [Vietnam Is Still There with our Joy] (1979); translated by Mary Nguyễn.

114. Phạm Duy, "Người Việt Cao Quý" [With Dignity the People of Vietnam] (1978); translated by Mary Nguyễn.

115. "U.S. Vetoes Viet Entry into U.N.," *Los Angeles Times*, November 16, 1976, A11.

Chapter 4. The Anticommunist Việt-Cộng: Freedom Fighters and the New Politics of Rescue

1. Việt Định Phương, "Lá Thư Cuối Năm: Chúng Ta Sẽ Không Chết Ở Đây" [Year End Comments: We Will Not Spend Our Whole Lives in Exile], *Trắng Đen*, February 15, 1980, 3–5.

2. Jeffords, *Remasculinization of America*.

3. Aguilar–San Juan, "Creating Ethnic Places." Reyes, *Songs of the Caged*, describes ex-military types as the foundation of anticommunist fanaticism in Little Saigon. Dang, "Anticommunism as Cultural Praxis," also treats the issue as limited to military types.

4. For information on South Vietnamese communist insurgents, see Pike, *Viet Cong*; Pike, "Vietcong Secret War."

5. "News from Vietnam," *Thông Báo*, June 11, 1975, 1–2.

6. "Saigon Tells of Resistance," *Washington Post*, May 22, 1975, A24.

7. "Saigon News," *Thông Báo*, July 17, 1975, 1.

8. Martin Woollacott, "Liberation Troops Attacked in Saigon," *Washington Post*, May 26, 1975, A16; "Vietnamese Admits 'Security Problem' of Armed Holdouts," *New York Times*, July 1, 1975, 8; "Vietnam Radio Cites Resistance in Hue," *Washington Post*, August 29, 1975, A27.

9. George McArthur, "S. Viet Resistance Forces Estimated in Thousands," *Los Angeles Times*, December 8, 1975, A1.

10. David Andelman, "Communist Regime in Saigon Reports Some Military Resistance," *New York Times*, October 19, 1975, 20.

11. Jack Boettner, "Ky Willing to Lead Force of Viet Resistance Fighters," *Los Angeles Times*, July 22, 1975, OC-1.

12. "Ky Willing to Fight Again," *Thông Báo*, July 24, 1975, 1.

13. Phạm Duy published this and other refugee songs in *Thấm Thoắt Mười Năm*.

14. From Phạm Duy's website, now defunct; translated by Mary Nguyễn.

15. Everett R. Holles, "New Front Splits Vietnam Refugees," *New York Times*, March 1, 1976, 7; "Two New Resistance Fronts Spring Up in France and the U.S.," *Trắng Đen*, March 27, 1976, 7.

16. Mỹ-Bình, interview by author, Fountain Valley, April 2007.

17. See Loescher and Scanlan, *Calculated Kindness*; Robinson, *Terms of Refuge*; Bon Tempo, *Americans at the Gate*.

18. For more on Reagan's influence on American politics and culture, see Wilentz, *Age of Reagan*. For a social history of right wing populism in the Sunbelt that Reagan successfully stoked and tapped into, see McGirr, *Suburban Warriors*; Lassiter, *Silent Majority*.

19. For a primer on neoconservatism, see Steinfels, *Neoconservatives*.

20. Jon Nordheimer, "Reagan Says Committed Voters Favor Him in Florida Primary," *New York Times*, March 8, 1976, 29.

21. Lou Cannon, "Reagan Says U.S. Must Act to Halt Communist Gains," *Washington Post*, June 1, 1975, 11.

22. Howell Raines, "Reagan Calls Arms Race Essential to Avoid a 'Surrender' or 'Defeat,'" *New York Times*, August 19, 1980, 1.

23. Philip Shabecoff, "Ford Denies Plans for Ties with Hanoi," *New York Times*, April 24, 1976, 10.

24. Howell Raines, "Reagan Calls Arms Race Essential to Avoid a 'Surrender' or 'Defeat,'" *New York Times*, August 19, 1980, 1.

25. For the gender dynamics of post–Vietnam War America, see Jeffords, *Remasculination of America*.

26. David Binder, "Reagan Met Panamanian and Cuban Exile Leaders in Florida," *New York Times*, December 14, 1975, 54.

27. Ronald Reagan, Speech before the National Conservative Political Action Committee Annual Convention, Washington, D.C., March 8, 1985.

28. For more on the Reagan Doctrine, see James M. Scott, *Deciding to Intervene*.

29. Philip Taubman, "El Salvador as 'Domino,'" *New York Times*, February 20, 1982, 8.

30. Ronald Reagan, Speech before the National Conservative Political Action Committee Annual Convention, Washington, D.C., March 8, 1985; Robert Pear, "Contra Chief Faults Reagan Statements," *New York Times*, October 30, 1988, 3.

31. For a political science analysis of the invasion of Grenada, see Beck, *Grenada Invasion*. For the Iran-Contra Affair (aka Irangate), see Busby, *Reagan and*

the Iran-Contra Affair. For the Strategic Defense Initiative (Star Wars), see Duric, *Strategic Defence Initiative*. For a more critical perspective, see FitzGerald, *Way Out There in the Blue*.

32. See Isaacs, *Vietnam Shadows*; Barroga, "Walls."
33. Tom Carhart, "Insulting Vietnam Vets," *New York Times*, October 24, 1981, 23.
34. Ibid.
35. Ronald Reagan, Speech before the National Conservative Political Action Committee Annual Convention, Washington, D.C., March 8, 1985.
36. Half-page advertisement for the Vietnamese American Republican National Federation, *Trắng Đen*, October 24, 1980, 65.
37. National United Front, *Vietnamese Fight for Freedom*, 42.
38. For more on Vang Pao's past and the "secret war" in Laos, see Warner, *Back Fire*; Hamilton-Merritt, *Tragic Mountains*. For a more recent profile of Vang Pao, including his 2008 arrest on terrorism charges, see Tim Weiner, "Gen. Vang Pao's Last War," *New York Times Magazine*, May 11, 2008, 48–52.
39. *Trắng Đen*, July 18, 1980, 22.
40. Ibid., August 28, 1980, 5.
41. Faber, *Long Road to Freedom*, 113; Nguyễn Van, "Vo Dai Ton," *Justice*, April 1985, 2.
42. Joanne Omang, "'Little Saigons' in U.S. Foster Hopes of Toppling Hanoi," *Washington Post*, January 16, 1983, A6.
43. Joanne Omang, "Vietnamese Emigres Rally Here for Overthrow of Hanoi Regime," *Washington Post*, May 1, 1983, A8.
44. "The Hoang Co Minh Trail" (transcript), *CBS Evening News*, March 30, 1982, reprinted in *Đất Mới* (Seattle), April 5, 1982, 21. Safer was partially correct: "Giải phóng" [Liberate] constituted the first half of a call-and-response greeting among insurgents; the second half was "Vietnam!" See Phạm Văn Liễu, *Trả Tôi Sông Núi*, 197.
45. Do with Brody, *Yen Do and the Story of Nguoi Viet Daily News*, 103.
46. National United Front, *Vietnamese People's Fight for Survival*, 108.
47. Ibid., 105–6.
48. David Holley, "Resistance Movement Has Supporters—but Also Doubters," *Los Angeles Times*, June 27, 1983, OC-A1.
49. National United Front, *Vietnamese People's Fight for Survival*, 101–7.
50. Ibid., 101–2.
51. Jeffrey Brody, "Front Not Upfront, Some Viets Lament," *Orange County Register*, May 20, 1991, B01.
52. Josh Getlin, "5,000 Cheer News of Rebellion in Vietnam," *Los Angeles Times*, April 18, 1983, OC-1, 10.
53. "Người Việt Quyết Đoàn Kết Để Giải Phóng Quê Hương" [Vietnamese United to Liberate the Homeland], *Người Việt Daily News*, March 21, 1984, 22 (translation of an article by John Westcott published in the *Orange County Register*, March 18, 1984). See also Dan Nakaso, "Dream of Return," *Los Angeles Times*, March 18, 1984, OC-A1.

54. For anticommunism during the 1980s, see Osa, *Solidarity and Contention*; Penn, *Solidarity's Secret*; Dillon, *Comandos*; Brown, *Real Contra War*.

55. *Người Việt*, December 26, 1981, 1.

56. "Editorial: Expanding the Struggle," *Đất Mới* (Seattle), May 5, 1982, 20.

57. "Commentary: Lessons from Nicaragua," *Vietnamese Resistance*, November 1986, 7.

58. Caplan, Whitmore, and Bui, *Southeast Asian Refugee Self-Sufficiency Study*, 113, 114.

59. Kibria, *Family Tightrope*. Kibria's study refutes the stereotype of the Asian American model minority but misses out on the way transnationalism affords refugees a level of success unattainable by those in Vietnam. Brimming with survivor's guilt, refugees carry intense obligations to support family members in Vietnam.

60. The nascent field of Asian American literature also underwent a masculinist phase as its pioneers sought to put together an anthology and literary tradition based on stories of heroic Asian American men challenging the constraints imposed by white racism. See Chin et al., *Aiiieeeee!*

61. Karen Tumulty, "Patterson All but Concedes Contest," *Los Angeles Times*, November 7, 1984, 3.

62. David Holley, "Candidates Court Minorities in 38th District Race," *Los Angeles Times*, September 30, 1984, OC-A1.

63. National United Front, *Vietnamese Fight for Freedom*, 47.

64. Ibid., 49.

65. See Cao Thế Dung, *Mặt Trận*; Phạm Văn Liễu, *Trả Tôi Sông Núi*, 322–31.

66. Asked why he chose that name, Armitage explained that the given name *Phú* means "rich," that the middle name *Văn* indicates his gender, and the surname *Trần* was taken from a special clergyman in Vietnam who had blessed his naval group. See Cao Thế Dung, *Mặt Trận*, 149.

67. Phạm Văn Liễu, *Trả Tôi Sông Núi*, 322–31. Liễu's statement corroborates a 1983 statement by an anticommunist Vietnamese American writer who disagreed with the Front: "Although it is tempting to dismiss such people as nothing more than frustrated diehards with a quixotic view of their prospects, the fact is that they are U.S. residents who would have difficulty getting into Thailand without some form of official approbation" (Doan Van Toai and David Chanoff, "Beware of Vietnamese Insurgents," *Los Angeles Times*, August 9, 1983, C5).

68. Phạm Văn Liễu, *Trả Tôi Sông Núi*, 224–25.

69. *Kháng Chiến*, February 1992, inside back cover advertisement.

70. For criticism of Diệm, see Karnow, *Vietnam*; FitzGerald, *Fire in the Lake*; Halberstam, *Best and the Brightest*; Sheehan, *Bright Shining Lie*; Kolko, *Anatomy of a War*. Refugees of all educational and religious backgrounds expressed their adoration of the former leader in interviews and casual conversations with the author.

71. Vietnamese National Founding Day Celebrations, 1987–95, in National United Front, *Mặt Trận Quốc Gia*, 152–70.

72. Children's Activities, in National United Front, *Mặt Trận Quốc Gia*, 126–29; *Kháng Chiến*, December 1987, 42–43.

73. "Resistance Activities," *Vietnamese Resistance*, November 1986, 4.

74. *Anh Hùng Nước Tôi*, 394.

75. Tuấn Phạm, interview by author, Del Rey Oaks, May 2008.

76. For the cultural significance of beauty pageants, see Banet-Weiser, *Most Beautiful Girl in the World*.

77. Half-page advertisement, *Người Việt Daily News*, September 19, 1984, 18.

78. "Tại Sao Tôi Dự Thi Hoa-Khôi Kháng Chiến" [Why I Want to Be Miss Resistance], *Người Việt Daily News*, October 3, 1984, 19.

79. Ibid.

80. National United Front, *National Support Movement*, 64.

81. Half-page advertisement, *Người Việt Daily News*, September 30, 1984, 23.

82. "Người Việt Quyết Đoàn Kết Để Giải Phóng Quê Hương" [Vietnamese United to Liberate the Homeland], *Người Việt Daily News*, March 21, 1984, 22 (translation of an article by John Westcott published in the *Orange County Register*, March 18, 1984). See also Dan Nakaso, "Dream of Return," *Los Angeles Times*, March 18, 1984, OC-A1.

83. "The Vietnamese National Day," *Vietnamese Resistance*, March 1987, 1.

84. David Holley, "Resistance Movement Has Supporters—But Also Doubters," *Los Angeles Times*, June 27, 1983, OC-A1; "The Hoang Co Minh Trail" (transcript), *CBS Evening News*, March 30, 1982, reprinted in *Đất Mới* (Seattle), April 5, 1982, 21; Doan Van Toai and David Chanoff, "Beware of Vietnamese Insurgents," *Los Angeles Times*, August 9, 1983, C5.

85. David Holley, "Resistance Movement Has Supporters—But Also Doubters," *Los Angeles Times*, June 27, 1983, OC-A1.

86. Jeffrey Brody, "Front Not Upfront, Some Viets Lament," *Orange County Register*, May 20, 1991, B01. See also Joanne Omang, "'Little Saigons' in U.S. Foster Hopes of Toppling Hanoi," *Washington Post*, January 16, 1983, A6.

87. "Vietnamese Plot Communist Overthrow, South Seattle Restaurant Is Headquarters," *Seattle Times*, April 29, 1985, D3; "Rebels Keep Vietnam War Smoldering," *Fort Lauderdale Sun-Sentinel*, November 26, 1987, 58A; Tuấn Phạm, interview by author, Del Rey Oaks, May 2008.

88. Việt Dzũng, interview by author, Westminster, April 2007; Tuấn Phạm, interview by author, Del Rey Oaks, May 2008; Phạm Văn Liễu, *Trả Tôi Sông Núi*; Faber, *Long Road to Freedom*. See also Jeffrey Brody, "Front Not Upfront, Some Viets Lament," *Orange County Register*, May 20, 1991, B01.

89. Phạm Văn Liễu, *Trả Tôi Sông Núi*, 300.

90. Advertisements in *Kháng Chiến*, November 1987, 51.

91. "Vietnamese Plot Communist Overthrow, South Seattle Restaurant Is Headquarters," *Seattle Times*, April 29, 1985, D3.

92. Cao Thế Dung, *Mặt Trận*, 488.

93. William Cassidy, "A Study of Vietnamese Involvement in Clandestine International Currency Transfers," in U.S. Congress, Senate, Subcommittee on Financial Institutions of the Committee on Banking, Housing, and Urban Affairs, *Senate Hearing 98-935*, 18.

94. Jeffrey Brody, "Editor's Slaying Heightens Fears in Viet Community," *Orange County Register*, August 23, 1987, B1.

95. Ellen Norman, "Money to Finance Guerilla War," *Peninsula Times Tribune*, June 19, 1982, 1.

96. Jeffrey Brody, "Front Not Upfront, Some Viets Lament," *Orange County Register*, May 20, 1991, B01.

97. B. Drummond Ayres Jr., "Slaying of Vietnamese Exiles in Washington Renews Refugee Fears," *New York Times*, September 25, 1990, B10.

98. Cao Thế Dung, *Mặt Trận*, 23.

99. Carney, "Dangers of Being a Vietnamese Reporter," 15; De Tran, "Painful Past on Trial, Suit Focuses on Reporters' Deaths," *San Jose Mercury News*, December 2, 1994, 1B. For more on Vietnamese American gangs, see Du, *Dream Shattered*. For information about other Asian organized crime, see Posner, *Warlords of Crime*; U.S. President's Commission on Organized Crime, *Organized Crime of Asian Origin*.

100. Steve Emmons and Nancy Wride, "Police Trying to Determine Veracity of Group's Letter," *Los Angeles Times*, August 14, 1987, OC-1; "Text of Letter in Firebombing," *Los Angeles Times*, August 14, 1987, OC-4.

101. Lynn Smith and David Reyes, "Politics, Extortion May Be Behind Viet Journalist's Death," *Los Angeles Times*, August 11, 1987, OC-1.

102. Ibid.

103. Bill Hazlett, "Police Crack Down on Viet Ching Gang," *Los Angeles Times*, June 16, 1982, D1; Jack Jones, "8 Arrested in Extortion Crackdown," *Los Angeles Times*, July 8, 1982, D2; Nancy Wride, "2 Arrested in Suspected Viet Extortion Plot," September 16, 1982, OC-A1; "4 Arrests in Extortion Plot Called Major Breakthrough against Gangs," *Los Angeles Times*, July 16, 1983, OC-A5; Kathy McCarthy, "Asian Crime Network Grows in U.S.," *Los Angeles Times*, January 15, 1984, 5; Roxana Kopetman, "Indochinese Gangs to Be Topic for Police," *Los Angeles Times*, May 20, 1986, OC-A7.

104. "Ky and Wife 'Enjoying Life' Despite Financial Troubles," *New York Times*, January 22, 1984, A18.

105. Ted Bell, "It is Spy vs. Spy among Vietnamese in Sacramento," *Sacramento Bee*, March 27, 1985, A16.

106. Jeffrey Brody, "Editor's Slaying Heightens Fears in Viet Community," *Orange County Register*, August 23, 1987, B1.

107. Buster Sussman, "Vietnamese Publisher Sees Jews, Israel as Example for Vietnam," n.p., n.d., partially reprinted in Do with Brody, *Yen Do and the Story of Nguoi Viet Daily News*, 10.

108. Jeffrey Brody, "Enforcement: U.S. Allows Clandestine Trade to Continue," *Orange County Register*, August 21, 1984, K5.

109. Jeffrey Brody, "Editor's Slaying Heightens Fears in Viet Community," *Orange County Register*, August 23, 1987, B1.

110. Cao Thế Dung, *Mặt Trận*, 32.

111. Dennis Rockstroch, "San Jose Group Admits War against Communist Regime," *San Jose Mercury News*, December 3, 1987, 4A.

112. Jessie Mangaliman, "S.J. Vietnamese Group Admits Leader's Death Fourteen Years after the Fact," *San Jose Mercury News*, July 29, 2001, 1B.

113. Jeffrey Brody, "Front Not Upfront, Some Viets Lament," *Orange County Register*, May 20, 1991, B01.

114. Tuấn Phạm., interview by author, Del Rey Oaks, May 2008.

Chapter 5. Assimilationists and the Postwar: Model Minority Politics in Little Saigon

1. Tony Lâm, interview by author, Westminster, May 2007.

2. Joel Kotkin, "California's Asian Communities Are Seething with Crime," *Washington Post*, February 13, 1980, A6.

3. David Reyes, "100-Year Terms Are Judge's Message," *Los Angeles Times*, April 15, 1981, E1.

4. *Magnum, P.I.*, "Memories Are Forever," Season 2, Episodes 5–6, 1981; Parker, *Little Saigon*.

5. Sociologist Yen Le Espiritu has identified this strategy as a prime barrier to enhanced Asian American panethnic identity. In her analysis, the prominence of American-born Asians resulted in diminished identification with Old World ethnic hierarchies and increased recognition of American ethnic hierarchies—specifically ones that lump people into racial categories. See Espiritu, *Asian American Panethnicity*. Historically, Vietnamese refugees had little personal incentive as Vietnamese or Americans to identify with the Việt-Cộng, a point beyond the scope of Espiritu's study.

6. Trần Minh Công, a spokesman for the National United Front for the Liberation of Vietnam who also worked for the Orange County Housing Agency, wanted to concentrate on homeland politics. Social worker Mai Công focused on mental health and poverty issues. Catholic priests, who potentially represented 30 percent of Little Saigon's residents, were interested in constructing a Vietnamese Catholic Center. The Vietnamese Chamber of Commerce (founded in 1980) has consequently never registered as many as three hundred members.

7. Do with Brody, *Yen Do and the Story of Nguoi Viet Daily News*, 46.

8. Members of minority groups often realize that their individual actions have the potential to be representative of their group as a whole, a burden not necessarily suffered by majority groups. See McIntosh, "White Privilege and Male Privilege."

9. Tracy Wood, "Vietnamese Now Fighting Just to Cope," *Los Angeles Times*, May 29, 1978, A2. According to various interviews I conducted, some early immigrants persisted in the minority Vietnamese habit of eating dog, a practice most common in North Vietnam. Mainstream U.S. newspapers apparently never mentioned the issue, which would have certainly obliterated much of America's goodwill toward the Vietnamese refugees.

10. Tensions between Anglo residents and Southeast Asian refugees in the North Highlands section of Sacramento, California, almost got out of control in 1983 when, as the *Sacramento Bee* newspaper put it, "members of the Hmong tribe from Laos were accused by North Highlands neighbors of ritually slaying chickens in public,

eating dogs, and bathing outdoors" (Hillary Abramson, "Refugees Grapple with a Mystifying New Home," *Sacramento Bee*, April 28, 1985, C7).

11. "Epidemic of Panic," *Los Angeles Times*, October 21, 1979, OC-B2.

12. Bien Qui Le, Letter to the Editor, *Los Angeles Times*, December 16, 1979, OC-B3.

13. For the respectability politics of the early twentieth-century Asian American middle class, see Erika Lee, *At America's Gates*.

14. "Epidemic of Panic," *Los Angeles Times*, October 21, 1979, OC-B2.

15. Do with Brody, *Yen Do and the Story of Nguoi Viet Daily News*, 41–42.

16. Evan Maxwell, "Refugees Charged in Alleged Health Scam: Of 51 Suspects Sought in Medi-Cal Fraud, About Half Are Linked to Orange County," *Los Angeles Times*, February 16, 1984, OC-3. "In some cases, refugees who were not ill sold their [vouchers] to physicians for a kickback of 'several dollars,' according to one investigator. In other cases, according to Van de Kamp, drivers collected large numbers of cards from fellow refugees and turned the [vouchers] over to physicians who submitted fraudulent claims to the state. In addition to false claims on office visits, the investigators said some of the physicians wrote phony prescriptions which were also to be paid by Medi-Cal. Pharmacists involved in the scheme would submit the false drug claims, often allowing the refugees to purchase nonprescription items including food and clothing instead of the prescribed drugs. Van de Kamp said during the press conference that some of the fraudulent prescriptions were actually used to procure drugs 'for shipment to relatives in Vietnam or for sales on the black market in Vietnam.'"

17. Do with Brody, *Yen Do and the Story of Nguoi Viet Daily News*, 53.

18. "Ý Kiến" [Opinion], *Người Việt Daily News*, February 17, 1984, 3.

19. David Holley, "Vietnamese Singled Out in Arrests, Doctor Says," *Los Angeles Times*, February 29, 1984, OC-A1.

20. David Holley, "Arrest of 23 Doctors Stuns the Viets in Orange County," *Los Angeles Times*, February 17, 1984, OC-1.

21. *Người Việt Daily News*, March 4, 1984, 3; David Holley, "Plea Linked to Arrest in Medi-Cal Fraud Case," *Los Angeles Times*, March 9, 1984, OC-A1.

22. Do with Brody, *Yen Do and the Story of Nguoi Viet Daily News*, 58–59.

23. Haynes Johnson and Thomas Edsall, "Asian Americans Torn between Two Parties," *Washington Post*, June 2, 1984, A1.

24. Refugee nationalism worked much differently in Monterey Park, where racism against Chinese immigrant entrepreneurs mobilized Asians, Asian Americans, Latinos, and white liberals in aggressive, far more confrontational solidarity against racial discrimination. Asians in Monterey Park did not wait for either the Democrats or the Republicans to come to their rescue. See Fong, *First Suburban Chinatown*; Horton, *Politics of Diversity*; Saito, *Race and Politics*.

25. John Horn, "American and Vietnamese Cultures Blend in Orange County's Little Saigon," *Orange County Register*, March 13, 1988, 103.

26. See *Vietnamese Business Directory* (1990), 14. Interviewees Tony Lâm and Nguyễn Xuân Bảo gave Buchoz the lion's share of the credit for Bolsa Avenue's emergence as Little Saigon's main thoroughfare.

27. See Orr, "Living along the Fault Line."

28. See California, California Budget Project, *Proposition 13*; Daniel A. Smith, *Tax Crusaders*; Chapman, *Continuing Redistribution of Fiscal Stress*.

29. Andy Rose, "Down on Its Luck: Westminster's Saddled with a Corrupt Past and an Uncertain Future," *Los Angeles Times*, October 19, 1986, OC-A1. The city nearly filed for bankruptcy in 1987. An unpopular but necessary hike in the utility tax enabled the city to forgo laying off thirty police officers and firefighters.

30. Kathleen Day and David Holley, "Boom on Bolsa: Vietnamese Create Their Own Saigon," *Los Angeles Times*, September 30, 1984, 1.

31. Information provided by Westminster City Hall, April 18, 2006.

32. Haynes Johnson and Thomas Edsall, "Asian Americans Torn between Two Parties," *Washington Post*, June 2, 1984, A1.

33. See *Vietnamese Business Directory* (1987).

34. Wayne King, "Asian Immigrants Changing the Character of California's Cities," *New York Times*, September 11, 1981, A16.

35. Steve Padilla, "Vietnamese Businesses Thriving in Southland Despite Some Opposition," *Los Angeles Times*, July 10, 1981, OC-C1.

36. Joe Starita, "American Dream Is Elusive: Culture Shock Poses Problem, but Vietnamese Make Strides in California," *Miami Herald*, April 28, 1985, 9D

37. David Maharaj, "80's Saw a Boom in Viet Populace," *Los Angeles Times*, May 11, 1991, OC-B1.

38. Evan Maxwell, "County, Viet Refugees Coexisting, Panel Told," *Los Angeles Times*, November 18, 1981, OC-A1.

39. Kathleen Day and David Holley, "Boom on Bolsa: Vietnamese Create Their Own Saigon," *Los Angeles Times*, September 30, 1984, 1.

40. Marilyn Kay Kukhler, "Orange County's Women Mayors: The Involvement Began Early," *Los Angeles Times*, November 25, 1981, OC-C1.

41. Ibid.

42. For a photograph of Kathy Buchoz wearing an *áo dài* dress, see *Vietnamese Business Directory* (1990), 14.

43. Steve Padilla, "Vietnamese Businesses Thriving in Southland Despite Some Opposition," *Los Angeles Times*, July 10, 1981, OC-C1.

44. Since 1976, Santa Ana had been the home of the Vietnamese American Mutual Association and Orange County's first Vietnamese stores. Students organized the first Vietnamese American Tết Festival at Santa Ana College in early 1978. The 1986 *Vietnamese Business Directory* of Southern California listed 358 businesses in Westminster, followed by Garden Grove (221), Santa Ana (170), Los Angeles (164), and Long Beach (51). According to a January 1978 Santa Ana College interoffice memo, "160,000 refugees in the US. 20,000 of them are in OC." "Distribution of refugees in Orange County: 28% Santa Ana, 13% Garden Grove, 8% Westminster, 8% Huntington Beach, 7% Orange, 6% Costa Mesa, 6% Fullerton, 2% Buena Park, Less than 1% are distributed elsewhere" (Gayle Morrison Collection, University of

California at Irvine). See also G. M. Bush, "Garden Grove: Buena Clinton, Redevelopment Appear to Be Top Issues," *Los Angeles Times*, November 3, 1984, OC-4.

45. Kathleen Day and David Holley, "Boom on Bolsa: Vietnamese Create Their Own Saigon," *Los Angeles Times*, September 30, 1984, 1. See also Joe Starita, "American Dream Is Elusive: Culture Shock Poses Problem, but Vietnamese Make Strides in California," *Miami Herald*, April 28, 1985, 9D.

46. John O'Dell and Jeffrey Perlman, "Racism Charged after Last-Minute Political Mailers," *Los Angeles Times*, June 7, 1982, OC-A1; Kenneth Reich and Jeffrey Perlman, "Dirty Campaign Tactics Creating Alarm," *Los Angeles Times*, June 14, 1982, B1.

47. Jeffrey Perlman, "Buchoz Says Serrato Apologized for 'Racist' Campaign Mailer," *Los Angeles Times*, June 18, 1982, OC-A5.

48. *Người Việt Daily News*, November 2, 1984, front cover. The *Người Việt Daily News* is available on microfilm at the Langson Library, University of California at Irvine.

49. Penelope McMillan, "It is Chinatown, with Subtitles," *Los Angeles Times*, February 14, 1982, B1; Steve Padilla, "Vietnamese Businesses Thriving in Southland Despite Some Opposition," *Los Angeles Times*, July 10, 1981, OC-C1. For more on the Sino-Vietnamese, see Gold, "Chinese-Vietnamese Entrepreneurs in California"; Ta, "Twice a Minority."

50. Man Wah advertisement, *Trắng Đen*, March 6, 1976, 42.

51. Jeffrey Brody, "Frank Jao: Real-Estate and Power Broker," *Orange County Register*, January 11, 1987, C01.

52. The Reverend Nguyễn Xuan Bào, who founded the Vietnamese Christian Reformed Church, remembered that when he arrived in Orange County in 1982, "the biggest market among many others was Wai-Wai," owned by Duong Huu Chuong (*Vietnamese Community in Orange County*, 2:46).

53. David Holley, "Orange County's 'Little Saigon': Chinese, Vietnamese Feel Tension, but They Coexist," *Los Angeles Times*, October 3, 1984, OC-1.

54. Ibid.

55. According to a 1984 survey of 1,384 Southeast Asian refugees in Orange County, Seattle, Boston, Chicago, and Houston, only 25 percent received no public assistance at all, 58 percent received food stamps, and 23 percent received Aid to Families with Dependent Children money. Researchers calculated that every month, "an eligible family of four officially receives $601 in Orange County, $531 in Seattle, $444.50 in Boston, $368 in Chicago, and $118 in Houston." Those stark differences in public benefits, factored alongside Southern California's favorable political and environmental climate, made the area even more attractive to secondary migrants. See Caplan, Whitmore, and Bui, *Southeast Asian Refugee Self-Sufficiency Study*, 152–53. In 1985, according to the *Sacramento Bee*, "About 14,000 of Sacramento's estimated 18,000 Indochinese (77%) are on welfare" (Hilary Abramson, "Refugees Grapple with a Mystifying New Home," *Sacramento Bee*, April 28, 1985, C07).

56. Do with Brody, *Yen Do and the Story of Nguoi Viet Daily News*, 45–46.

57. "Developers Are Thinking Big about Little Saigon's Future," *Los Angeles Daily News*, April 19, 1987, 7.

58. Nancy Skelton, "Burgener Presses Campaign Attack on Metzger," *Los Angeles Times*, October 1, 1980, SD-A3.

59. Hilary Abramson, "Refugees Grapple with a Mystifying New Home," *Sacramento Bee*, April 28, 1985, C07. Sociologists refer to this concept as racial lumping. See Espiritu, *Asian American Panethnicity*.

60. Nam Lộc, "Xin Đời Một Nụ Cười," *Việt Weekly* (Garden Grove), October 2005.

61. Program for the Tết Festival, Santa Ana College, February 7, 1978; Program for the Tết Festival, Orange Coast College, February 5, 1978; both in Gayle Morrison Collection, University of California at Irvine.

62. David Holley, "Vietnamese Festival Will Ring in the Year of the Buffalo," *Los Angeles Times*, February 10, 1985, OC-A1.

63. Full-page advertisement for eighth annual Vietnamese American Beauty Pageant (August 18, 1984), *Người Việt Daily News*, July 6, 1984, 19. For more about Vietnamese beauty pageants, see Lieu, "Remembering 'the Nation' through Pageantry."

64. *Người Việt Daily News*, August 26, 1984, 1.

65. USC Vietnamese Student Association Culture Night advertisement, *Người Việt Daily News*, April 25, 1984, 19.

66. Pasadena City College Vietnamese Student Association Culture Night advertisement, *Người Việt Daily News*, May 2, 1984, 19.

67. Steve Padilla, "Vietnamese Businesses Thriving in Southland Despite Some Opposition, *Los Angeles Times*, July 10, 1981, OC-C1.

68. "Developers Are Thinking Big about Little Saigon's Future," *Los Angeles Daily News*, April 19, 1987, 7.

69. David Reyes, "Asiantown: Commercial-Cultural Complex Expected to Anchor Southland's Next Chinatown," *Los Angeles Times*, March 16, 1987, OC-1.

70. Richard Paddock, "Governor Courts 'Little Saigon' Votes," *Los Angeles Times*, June 18, 1988, OC-1.

71. Le Kim Dinh, "'Saigon' Signs Targeted: Racism Feared in Posting on Freeway," *Orange County Register*, February 1, 1989, B1.

72. Robert Frank, "Westminster's Role in Tet Festival Angers Vets," *Orange County Register*, January 26, 1989, C1.

73. In many ways, Fry presents a parallel to Barry Hatch, the racist member of the Monterey Park city council who unsuccessfully led a nativist crusade against Asian entrepreneurs during the 1980s.

74. William Boyer, "Viets Denied Parade, Told to 'Assimilate': Angry Veterans Call Council Vote Racist," *Orange County Register*, April 13, 1989, A1.

75. New Orleans and Houston had organized similar parades for the previous three years with little to no opposition ("Vietnamese Parade," *San Francisco Chronicle*, April 14, 1989, A31).

Notes to Chapter 5

76. William H. Boyer, "Apologize to Vietnamese, Panel Tells Councilman," *Orange County Register*, April 14, 1989, B01.

77. David Reyes, "A City Tries to Restore Fragile Fabric of Harmony after Insult," *Los Angeles Times*, April 30, 1989, II-1.

78. David Reyes, "Ex-CIA Chief Defends Role of Vietnamese in Little Saigon," *Los Angeles Times*, April 17, 1989.

79. "Editorial: All Refugees Deserve Tolerance at the Least," *Los Angeles Times*, April 16, 1989, 10.

80. David Reyes, "A City Tries to Restore Fragile Fabric of Harmony after Insult," *Los Angeles Times*, April 30, 1989, II-1.

81. William Boyer, "Fry Will Apologize to Group," *Orange County Register*, April 18, 1989, B1.

82. William Boyer, "Councilman Refuses to Apologize for Remark That Upset Vietnamese," *Orange County Register*, April 15, 1989, B1; Tony Lâm, interview by author, Westminster, May 2007.

83. For more on traditional expectations about race relations within Asian American politics, see Saito, *Race and Politics*.

84. Testimony of Mr. X, in U.S. Congress, Senate, Subcommittee on Financial Institutions of the Committee on Banking, Housing, and Urban Affairs, *Senate Hearing 98-935*, 36–37.

85. Testimony of Sergeant John W. Willoughby Jr., New Orleans Police Department, in ibid., 29.

86. Testimony of Mr. X, in ibid., 61.

87. Vietnam's deputy foreign minister declared, "We see a role for the overseas Vietnamese. We fully welcome any contribution by the overseas Vietnamese toward the fatherland. We encourage them to help their families" (Jeffrey Brody, "Pipeline to Vietnam," *Orange County Register*, August 21, 1988, K01).

88. Testimony of Detective James Bady, Arlington Police Department, in U.S. Congress, Senate, Subcommittee on Financial Institutions of the Committee on Banking, Housing, and Urban Affairs, *Senate Hearing 98-935*, 49.

89. Jeffrey Brody, "Lifeline: Family in Vietnam Lives 'From Package to Package,'" *Orange County Register*, August 21, 1988, K06.

90. Jeffrey Brody, "Pipeline to Vietnam," *Orange County Register*, August 21, 1988, K01.

91. Jean Davidson, "Pipeline to Vietnam Fueled by Family Ties," *Los Angeles Times*, October 31, 1988, 1.

92. Jeffrey Brody, "Lifeline: Family in Vietnam Lives 'From Package to Package,'" *Orange County Register*, August 21, 1988, K06.

93. Jeffrey Brody, "Pipeline to Vietnam," *Orange County Register*, August 21, 1988, K01.

94. Ibid.

95. Jean Davidson, "Pipeline to Vietnam Fueled by Family Ties," *Los Angeles Times*, October 31, 1988, 1.

96. Jeffrey Brody, "Pipeline to Vietnam," *Orange County Register*, August 21, 1988, K01.

97. Testimony of Detective James Bady, Arlington Police Department, in U.S. Congress, Senate, Subcommittee on Financial Institutions of the Committee on Banking, Housing, and Urban Affairs, *Senate Hearing 98-935*, 49.

98. Jeffrey Brody, "U.S. Customs Seizes County Goods, Gold Bound for Vietnam," *Orange County Register*, October 25, 1988, A01.

99. Jeffrey Brody, "Pipeline to Vietnam," *Orange County Register*, August 21, 1988, K01.

100. Jeffrey Brody, "U.S. Customs Seizes County Goods, Gold Bound for Vietnam," *Orange County Register*, October 25, 1988, A01.

101. Jeffrey Brody, "Pipeline to Vietnam," *Orange County Register*, August 21, 1988, K01.

102. Ibid.

103. See Lamb, *As Orange Goes*; Soja, "Inside Exopolis"; Kling, Olin, and Poster, *Postsuburban California*; González, *Labor and Community*.

104. Jeffrey Perlman and Kristina Lundgren, "Registration Trend Cited by Republican Official: 3 Prominent Democrats Join GOP," *Los Angeles Times*, August 8, 1984, OC-A1.

105. "Westminster City Elections," *Los Angeles Times*, October 22, 1992, OC-8.

106. Tony Lâm, interview by author, Westminster, May 2007.

107. Seth Myrdans, "A Vietnamese-American Becomes a Political First," *New York Times*, November 16, 1992, A11.

108. Andrea Heiman, "3 Vietnamese Make History as O.C. Candidates," *Los Angeles Times*, October 8, 1992, OC-1.

109. Seth Myrdans, "A Vietnamese-American Becomes a Political First," *New York Times*, November 16, 1992, A11.

110. Andrea Heiman, Frank Messina, and Rene Lynch, "Countywide Results Unchanged in Final Absentee Tally," *Los Angeles Times*, November 14, 1992, OC-2.

111. "Businesses Up 415% among Vietnamese," *Fort Lauderdale Sun-Sentinel*, August 5, 1991, 33; Ronald Campbell, "Vietnamese-Americans Make Business Their Life," *Orange County Register*, August 2, 1991, A1.

112. "Three Youths Are Charged with Robbery, Conspiracy," *Orange County Register*, July 25, 1991, B6.

113. See Takaki, *Strangers from a Different Shore*; Okihiro, *Margins and Mainstreams*; Cheng and Yang, "'Model Minority' Deconstructed"; Fong, *Contemporary Asian American Experience*; Robert G. Lee, *Orientals*; Kim, *Bitter Fruit*; Chou and Feagin, *Myth of the Model Minority*.

Chapter 6. Divided Loyalties: America's Moral Obligation in the Post–Cold War Era

1. The 1990 U.S. Census counted 617,747 Vietnamese (U.S. Bureau of the Census, 1990 Census Population and Housing: Summary Tape file 1C, February 1992, CD90–1C). The definitive map-based reference books on contemporary Southern

California demographics are Turner and Allen, *Atlas of Population Patterns*; Turner and Allen, *Ethnic Quilt*; Turner and Allen, *Changing Faces, Changing Places*.

2. The 1999 demonstrations ignited a surge in interest in Vietnamese Americans and their supposed inability to let go of past trauma. Most recent scholarship is nonhistorical in its methodology and has focused on Vietnamese American experience since 1990. Reyes's ethnomusicology study, *Songs of the Caged*, mentions Little Saigon's glut of Catholics and former military to explain heightened anticommunist activity there in 1992. Most of this scholarship has been textual or ethnographic in nature, such as Valverde, "Making Transnational Viet Nam"; Feeney, "Freedom to Speak"; Lieu, "Private Desires on Public Display"; Mimi Thi Nguyen, "Representing Refugees"; Lam, "Surfin' Vietnam"; Dang, "Anticommunism as Cultural Praxis." Historical studies of note include Vu Hong Pham, "Beyond and before the Boat People"; Vu, "Rising from the Cold War Ashes"; Tang, "Unsettled."

3. Hall Gardner, "Those Stumbling Blocks to Recognizing Vietnam Do Not Have to Trip Us Now," *Los Angeles Times*, March 14, 1989, 7.

4. Engelmann, *Tears before the Rain*.

5. Crafts, "East Asian Growth before and after the Crisis."

6. See *East Asian Miracle* (which takes a market-oriented approach to success); Stiglitz and Yusuf, *Rethinking the East Asia Miracle* (which does a little more to take government action into account); Ohno, *Beyond the "East Asian Miracle"* (which argues that a hegemonic political culture promoting shared growth pushed governments to make the right choices that would lead to economic growth whose benefits are shared).

7. Dodsworth et al., *Vietnam*.

8. Đổi Mới literally translates as "New Deal," but Vietnam's official English translation for the movement is "Renovation" or "Innovation." Whereas Franklin Roosevelt's New Deal installed socialist measures to ensure the long-term stability of the capitalist order, Đổi Mới essentially installed free-market mechanisms to ensure the long-term stability of the communist regime. Both reforms succeeded at those top-level objectives, though the benefits at the grassroots level are more debatable. See Barbara Crossette, "Vietnam's Party Chief Says Capitalism Can Be Guide," *New York Times*, January 22, 1988, A2.

9. This term is borrowed from Galbraith, *Predator State*.

10. For more celebratory ruminations on U.S. hegemony in the post–Cold War era, see Fukuyama, *End of History*; Huntington, *Clash of Civilizations*. For a critical assessment, see Piketty, *Capital in the Twenty-First Century*.

11. Al Neuharth, "Vietnam: Can USA Ever Win the Peace?" *USA Today*, May 4, 1990, 15A.

12. Teresa Watanabe, "Focus: Is It Time to End Sanctions against Vietnam?," *Los Angeles Times*, March 18, 1991, 3.

13. Other prominent pronormalization politicians included former swift boat commander John Kerry and an entire cohort of conservative and liberal Vietnam veterans who entered the U.S. Congress during the 1980s. Slowly but surely, the United States

made progress in negotiations except on the issue of human rights abuses in Vietnam. In 1989, liberals and conservatives alike had second thoughts about assisting communist nations after China's brutal crackdown on prodemocracy activists in Beijing's Tiananmen Square. See Roger Simon, "A Trip Back to His Future: John McCain's Vietnam Visit Wasn't about Healing; It Was about Ambition," *U.S. News and World Report*, May 3, 2000, 14. During the 2000 presidential campaign, McCain confirmed that he frequently and unabashedly used the term *gook* in reference to his North Vietnamese captors: "I'll call right now my interrogator that tortured me and my friends a gook. You can quote me. I will continue to refer to them in language that might offend some people here, because of their beating and killing and torture of my friends. I hated the gooks and I will hate them as long as I live" (Frank Bruni and Alison Mitchell, "Bush and McCain Scurry toward Showdown," *New York Times*, February 18, 2000, A1).

14. U.S. Library of Congress, *CRS Issue Brief for Congress*.

15. Seth Mydans, "Hanoi Seeks Western Cash but Not Consequences," *New York Times*, April 8, 1996, A3.

16. Sonni Effron, "Ky and Thieu Wage Battle for Hearts, Minds," *Los Angeles Times*, May 20, 1990, OC-1.

17. Robert Pear, "U.S. Raises Quota of Soviet Refugees by Cutting Asians'," *New York Times*, January 12, 1989, A1.

18. Bernard Gwertzman, "More Vietnamese to Get Permission to Enter the U.S," *New York Times*, September 12, 1984, A1.

19. Phạm Hoần Ân, "Job và Tuổi Già," in *Viết Về Nước Mỹ 2001*, 200.

20. See Xuân-Lan Nguyễn, *Legends of the Promised Land*; Martin, "'Freed Vietnamese Have Her to Thank.'"

21. Norman Kempster, "Kin of Missing Vietnamese in Bid to Learn Their Fate," *Los Angeles Times*, May 3, 1987, 5.

22. "Political Prisoners Initiative," *World Refugee Report*, September 1985, 36; "Hanoi Called Hesitant to Let Foes Go," *New York Times*, November 11, 1984, A3.

23. Barbara Crossette, "Inmate Release Hits a Snag in Hanoi," *New York Times*, December 24, 1984, 13. Stephen J. Solarz, the chair of the U.S. House Foreign Affairs Subcommittee on Asian and Pacific Affairs, explained that Hanoi's antidissident demands carried little weight with the United States "because their definition of subversive activities could include anything from writing articles or taking part in demonstrations to sending arms."

24. "Hanoi OKs Exodus to U.S. of Freed Political Prisoners," *Los Angeles Times*, July 31, 1989, 12.

25. Houze, "Remarks."

26. Yvonne Hùynh, interview by author, December 2008. See also Helen Le, "Cha Con Tôi à Đất Nước Hoa Kỳ," in *"Viết Về Nước Mỹ 2000*, 49.

27. Mai Quốc Linh, "Nỗi Buồn Của Tháng . . .," in *Chuyện Người Tù Cảo Tạo*, 319.

28. Feeney, "Freedom to Speak," describes this identification with the United States as rehearsing established narratives—what she calls an "economy of stories"—to obtain permission to enter as a recognized refugee.

29. *Vietnamese Community in Orange County: An Oral History*, 2:55.

30. David Reyes, "County Braces for New Refugees: Immigrants: Officials Will Discuss How to Care for the Expected Resettlement Here of a Number of Freed Vietnamese Political Prisoners," *Los Angeles Times*, October 28, 1989, OC-1.

31. Injuries that Cha Bac suffered in the reeducation camps caused him to fail a physical required for employment at K-Mart (*Chuyện Người Tù Cảo Tạo*).

32. Lily Dizon, "Column One: Wounded by War and Peace: Many Who Survived Vietnam's Prison Camps Sought New Lives in the U.S. but Found Despair," *Los Angeles Times*, April 14, 1995, 1.

33. Ibid.

34. Mai Tran and Vik Jolly, "For Many, a Day of Infamy," *Los Angeles Times*, April 30, 1999, 1.

35. Vik Jolly, "Immigrant Pride Wrapped Up in Two Flags," *Orange County Register*, April 13, 1999, 6.

36. According to the U.S. State Department, nearly 200,000 former political prisoners and their family members had entered the United States as of July 1999, one-sixth of the 1,223,736 Vietnamese living in the United States according to the 2000 Census. See Houze, "Remarks"; Barnes and Bennett, *Asian Population*.

37. Bert Eljera, "Westminster O.C. Trade Mission Protested," *Los Angeles Times*, September 9, 1994, 2.

38. Bert Eljera, "O.C. Trade Mission to Vietnam Protested," *Los Angeles Times*, September 9, 1994, OC-2.

39. John Giddlesohn and Vik Jolly, "Big Changeover in Little Saigon," *Orange County Register*, July 7, 2000, A1.

40. David Lamb, "Column One: A Silent Struggle Haunts Vietnam," *Los Angeles Times*, July 17, 1998, 1.

41. See, for example, U.S. Department of Justice, Federal Bureau of Investigation, "Thông Cáo" [Notice], *Người Việt Daily News*, February 17, 1996; Carey Goldberg, "F.B.I. Using Newspaper Ads to Seek Vietnam Informers," *New York Times*, March 12, 1996, A1.

42. Heritage Foundation 1990 Newsletter.

43. R. Jeffrey Smith, "Task Force Urges Creation of Radio for a Free Asia," *Washington Post*, December 17, 1991, A10.

44. Feeney, "Freedom to Speak."

45. Bert Eljera, "Big Plans for Little Saigon," *Asian Week* (San Francisco), May 17, 1996, 13.

46. Tina Nguyen, "Group to Honor Those Who Died in Vietnam War Memorials," *Los Angeles Times*, April 14, 1995, OC-1.

47. Gail Schiller, "Vietnam War Dead Saluted," *San Jose Mercury News*, April 28, 2003, 13A.

48. Tini Tran and Louise Roug, "Saluting as One: Planned Vietnam Soldier Memorial Brings Westminster's Fighting Factions Together," *Los Angeles Times*, July 18, 1999, OC-1.

49. Mike Whitcomb, "Professor Analyzes Lingering Effects of Vietnam War, *Viet Weekly*, September 15, 2004, 1.

50. Quyen Do, "Westminster Mayor Proposes Vietnam War Veterans Statue," *Orange County Register*, December 3, 1996, B06.

51. Harrison Sheppard, "City Gets Model of Vietnam War Tribute," *Los Angeles Times*, November 5, 1998, OC-2.

52. Vik Jolly, "Little Saigon Display Rips Old Wounds," *Orange County Register*, January 20, 1999, A1.

53. Rachel Tuinstra, "Hundreds Protest in Little Saigon," *Orange County Register*, January 19, 1999, B1.

54. Claire Vitucci, "Ho Chi Minh Poster Angers Vietnamese Refugees," *Contra Costa Times*, January 21, 1999, A12.

55. Larry Gerber, "Mystery Slurs Raise Little Saigon Tension," *Contra Costa Times*, February 27, 1999, A1.

56. Ben Fox, "Proposals Snub Vietnam Visits," *Long Beach Press-Telegram*, April 29, 2004, A9.

57. Steve Schmidt, "Little Saigon Still Reeling from Ho Chi Minh Poster," *San Diego Union-Tribune*, May 3, 1999, A1.

58. The Hi-Tek protests brought out clear divisions among Vietnamese Americans. Most conspicuously, it revealed the growing voice of younger, American-raised ethnics who had no memories of suffering under the communists or any interest in Vietnam. More likely than their parents or grandparents to identify as American, members of this generation did not suffer from refugee nationalism's deference to the host country. They therefore found it easier to vote against Republican candidates without feeling vulnerable to conservative attacks questioning their loyalty to America.

59. Mai Tran, "Poll Finds Paradox among Vietnamese in Orange County," *Los Angeles Times*, April 20, 2000, B5; Jeffrey Brody, "Communist Flag Flies in the Face of Village Unity," *Los Angeles Times*, February 28, 1999, B7.

60. Steve Schmidt, "Little Saigon Still Reeling from Ho Chi Minh Poster," *San Diego Union-Tribune*, May 3, 1999, A1.

61. Ibid.

62. Mike Whitcomb, "Professor Analyzes Lingering Effects of Vietnam War, *Viet Weekly*, September 15, 2004, 1.

63. *52 Days of Resistance* (DVD), purchased at 2007 Tết Festival, Vancouver, British Columbia.

64. Kiều Mỹ Duyên, interview by author, Garden Grove, May 2007; Do Quy Toan, interview by author, Westminster, May 2007.

65. Nam Lộc, interview by author, Los Angeles, April 2007.

66. Mai Tran, "Monuments: The Proposed Westminster Memorial Would Feature South Vietnamese and American Soldiers," *Orange County Register*, July 2, 1999, B2.

67. Gordon Dillow, "Viet Envoy Could Work as a Stand-Up," *Orange County Register*, July 8, 1999, B1.

68. Tini Tran and Louise Roug, "Saluting as One: Planned Vietnam Soldier Memorial Brings Westminster's Fighting Factions Together," *Los Angeles Times*, July 18, 1999, OC-1.

69. Lê Quang Anh, *Andy Quang Le and His Musical Compositions* (DVD, NV Video Production, 2005). Lyrics taken from the sheet music for the song.

70. Lê Quang Anh, *Andy Quang Le and His Musical Compositions*. Lyrics taken from the sheet music for the song.

71. Tran, "Remembering the Boat People Exodus."

72. Salmy Hashim, "Former 'Boat People' Plead to Malaysia Not to Destroy Bidong Memorial," *Malaysia General News*, June 28, 2005, http://www.vnbp.org/vietnamese/memorial/baochi/MNNA-BERNAMA.htm.

73. Fadli, "Vietnam Boat People's Plaque Torn Down," *Jakarta Post*, June 20, 2005, http://boatpeople75.tripod.com/Boat_People_plaque_torn_down.html.

74. "Malaysia to Demolish Memorial Built by Vietnamese Boat People: Report," Agence France Presse, June 30, 2005.

75. "Malaysia Demolishes Vietnamese Refugee Memorial," Bernama News Agency (Kuala Lumpur), October 26, 2005.

76. Danh Nguyễn, interview by author, Long Beach, May 2007.

77. Nguyễn Ngọc Hà, *Về Người Việt Nam Định Cư ở Nước Ngoài*; Trần Trọng Đăng Đàn, *Người Việt Nam ở Nước Ngoài*; Committee on Overseas Vietnamese, *Cộng Đồng Người Việt Nam ở Nước Ngoài*.

78. Marcella Bombardieri, "Battle Lines Remain: Some Vietnamese Refugees Protest Hanoi Scholars in Boston," *Boston Globe*, October 26, 2000, A1.

79. Ibid.

80. Adrian Walker, "Still No Peace on Vietnam," *Boston Globe*, August 27, 2001, B1.

Conclusion: Finding Roots in Exile

1. Phạm Duy's situation brings to light the continued importance of the nation-state in this era of transnationalism. More than just the sole administrator of rights and violence, the nation-state plays a primary role as cultural gatekeeper. See Lowe, *Immigrant Acts*; May, *Homeward Bound*; Whitfield, *Culture of the Cold War*; Von Eschen, *Satchmo Blows Up the World*.

2. Rick VanderKnyff, "His Music Links the Generations," *Los Angeles Times*, March 14, 1995, OC-12.

3. According to Reyes, *Songs of the Caged*, few professionals in Little Saigon's music industry seek permission to use other artists' works or collect royalties because

all of the musicians know each other and draw mostly from pre-1975 songs, which they regard as part of the public domain.

4. Dick Schaap, "Singer from Saigon," *New York Herald Tribune*, April 18, 1966.

5. Joseph N. Bell, "Vietnam's Once-Fiery Ky Now Just a 'Papa-San,'" *Los Angeles Times*, October 13, 1988, 3.

6. Mai Tran and Richard C. Paddock, "Column One: The Tourist Who Ran the Place," *Los Angeles Times*, January 24, 2004, A1.

7. B. L., telephone interview by author, May 2007.

8. See Thai, "Marriage across the Pacific"; Thai, *For Better or for Worse*.

9. The overwhelming majority of Vietnamese American men I encountered enjoyed their elevated social status in Vietnam. For more on the gendered dynamics of Asian American expatriate life, see Danico, "Korean Identities."

10. *Viết Về Nước Mỹ 2000*, 5–6.

11. Deepa Bharath, "Community Support Keeps Doors Open and Shelves Full," *Orange County Register*, November 24, 2006.

12. Nam Lộc, "Xin Đời Một Nự Cười," *Viet Weekly* (Orange County), October 2005.

13. New America Media founder Andrew Lâm, interview, in a 2006 issue of *BN*, a now defunct bilingual Vietnamese American lifestyle magazine. On December 17, 2006, the transcript was posted on New America Media's website: http://blogs.newamericamedia.org/andrew-lam/396/bn-magazines-interview-with-nam-editor-andrew-lam.

14. Anh Do, "A Rainbow-Hued Tet Parade in Little Saigon," *Los Angeles Times*, February 1, 2014.

15. Gustavo Arellano, "Bao Nguyen Is Garden Grove's History-Making Mayor in More Ways Than His Ethnicity," *OC Weekly*, November 25, 2014.

Bibliography

Adams, Romanzo. *Interracial Marriage in Hawaii*. New York: Macmillan, 1938.
Agamben, Giorgio. *Means without End: Notes on Politics*. Minneapolis: University of Minnesota Press, 2000.
Aguilar–San Juan, Karin. "Creating Ethnic Places: Vietnamese American Community-Building in Orange County and Boston." Ph.D. diss., Brown University, 2000.
———. *Little Saigons: Staying Vietnamese in America*. Minneapolis: University of Minnesota Press, 2009.
———. *The State of Asian America: Activism and Resistance in the 1990s*. Boston: South End, 1994.
Alam, M. Shahid. *Governments and Markets in Economic Development Strategies: Lessons from Korea, Taiwan, and Japan*. New York: Praeger, 1989.
Alcaly, Roger E. *The Fiscal Crisis of American Cities: Essays on the Political Economy of Urban America with Special Reference to New York*. New York: Vintage, 1976.
Alexandre, Laurien. *The Voice of America: From Détente to the Reagan Doctrine*. New York: Ablex, 1988.
Alpert, William, ed. *The Vietnamese Economy and Its Transformation to an Open Market System*. London: Sharpe, 2005.
Amnesty International USA. *Reasonable Fear: Human Rights and United States Refugee Policy*. Washington, D.C.: Amnesty International USA, 1990.
Anderson, Benedict. *Imagined Communities: Reflections on the Origins and Spread of Nationalism*. New York: Verso, 1982.
Anh Hùng Nước Tôi [Heroes of the Nation]. San Jose, Calif.: Đông Tiến, 1986.
Aptheker, Herbert. *American Negro Slave Revolts*. New York: Columbia University Press, 1943.
Arneil, Barbara. *Diverse Communities: The Problem with Social Capital*. Cambridge: Cambridge University Press, 2006.

Bacevich, Andrew J. *The Limits of American Power: The End of American Exceptionalism*. New York: Metropolitan Books, 2008.

Baker, Reginald P., and David S. North. *The 1975 Refugees: Their First Five Years in America*. Washington, D.C.: New TransCentury, 1984.

Baldassare, Mark. *When Government Fails: The Orange County Bankruptcy*. Berkeley: University of California Press, 1998.

Banet-Weiser, Sara. *The Most Beautiful Girl in the World: Beauty Pageants and National Identity*. Berkeley: University of California Press, 1999.

Barroga, Jeanie. "Walls." In *Unbroken Thread: An Anthology of Plays by Asian American Women*, ed. Roberta Uno. Amherst: University of Massachusetts Press, 1993.

Barrows, David. *A History of the Philippines*. New York: American Book, 1905.

Basch, Linda G., Nina Glick Schiller, and Cristina Szanton Blanc. *Nations Unbound: Transnational Projects, Postcolonial Predicaments, and Deterritorialized Nation-States*. Langhorne, Pa.: Gordon and Breach, 1994.

Beck, Robert. *The Grenada Invasion: Politics, Law, and Foreign Policy Decisionmaking*. Boulder, Colo.: Westview, 1994.

Black, Earle, and Merle Black. *The Rise of Southern Republicans*. Cambridge: Harvard University Press, 2002.

Blassingame, John. *Slave Community: Plantation Life in the Antebellum South*. New York: Oxford University Press, 1972.

Bodnar, John. *Remaking America: Public Memory, Commemoration, and Patriotism in the Twentieth Century*. Princeton: Princeton University Press, 1993.

Bon Tempo, Carl. *Americans at the Gate: The United States and Refugees during the Cold War*. Princeton: Princeton University Press, 2008.

Bradley, Mark Philip. *Imagining Vietnam and America: The Making of Postcolonial Vietnam, 1919–1950*. Chapel Hill: University of North Carolina Press, 2000.

Brazinsky, Gregg. *Nation Building in South Korea: Koreans, Americans, and the Making of a Democracy*. Chapel Hill: University of North Carolina Press, 2007.

Breuilly, John. *Nationalism and the State*. Chicago: University of Chicago Press, 1985.

Brown, Timothy C. *The Real Contra War: Highlander Peasant Resistance in Nicaragua*. Norman: University of Oklahoma Press, 2001.

Brehm, Jack, and Ann Himelick Cole. "Effect of a Favor Which Reduces Freedom." *Journal of Personality and Social Psychology* 3, no. 4 (1966): 420–26.

Brownlee, W. Elliot. *Funding the Modern American State, 1941–1995: The Rise and Fall of the Era of Easy Finance*. Washington, D.C.: Woodrow Wilson Center Press, 1996.

Busby, Robert. *Reagan and the Iran-Contra Affair: The Politics of Presidential Recovery*. New York: St. Martin's, 1999.

Butler, David. *The Fall of Saigon*. New York: Dell, 1985.

Cacioppo, John, and William Patrick. *Loneliness: Human Nature and the Need for Social Connection*. New York: Norton, 2008.

Cao Thế Dung. *Mặt Trận: Những Sự Thật Chưa Hề Được Kể* [The Front: The Untold Story]. Houston: Văn Hóa, 1991.

Caplan, Nathan, Marcella H. Choy, and John K. Whitmore. *Children of the Boat People: A Study of Educational Success*. Ann Arbor: University of Michigan Press, 1991.

Caplan, Nathan, John K. Whitmore, and Marcella H. Choy. *The Boat People and Achievement in America: A Study of Family Life, Hard Work, and Cultural Values*. Ann Arbor: University of Michigan Press, 1989.

Cargill, Mary Terrell, and Jade Quang Huynh, eds. *Voices of Vietnamese Boat People: Nineteen Narratives of Escape and Survival*. Jefferson, N.C.: McFarland, 2000.

CBS Reports. *The Boat People*. 1979.

Center for American Progress. *Who Are Vietnamese Americans?* Washington, D.C.: Center for American Progress, 2015.

Carney, Eliza Newlin. "The Dangers of Being a Vietnamese Reporter." *American Journalism Review* 15, no. 9 (November 1993): 15.

Chan, Sucheng. *Asian Americans: An Interpretive History*. Boston: Twayne, 1991.

———, ed. *The Vietnamese American 1.5 Generation: Stories of War, Revolution, Flight, and New Beginnings*. Philadelphia: Temple University Press, 2006.

Chang, Gordon, ed. *Asian Americans and Politics: Perspectives, Experiences, and Prospects*. Stanford: Stanford University Press, 2001.

Chang, Robert S. *Disoriented: Asian Americans, Law, and the Nation-State*. New York: New York University Press, 1999.

Chapman, Jeffrey I. *The Continuing Redistribution of Fiscal Stress: The Long Run Consequences of Proposition 13*. Cambridge, Mass.: Lincoln Institute of Land Policy, 1998.

Cheng, Lucie, and Philip Yang. "The 'Model Minority' Deconstructed." In *Ethnic Los Angeles*, ed. Roger Waldinger and Mehdi Bozorgmehr. New York: Sage, 1996.

Chin, Frank, Shawn Wong, Jeffrey Paul Chan, and Lawson Fusao Inada. *Aiiieeeee! An Anthology of Asian-American Writers*. Washington, D.C.: Howard University Press, 1974.

Chou, Rosalind S., and Joe R. Feagin. *The Myth of the Model Minority: Asian Americans Facing Racism*. Boulder, Colo.: Paradigm, 2008.

Choy, Christina, dir. *Who Killed Vincent Chin?* Film News Now Foundation, 1987

Chuyện Người Tù Cải Tạo [Narratives of the Reeducation Camp Prisoners]. Vol. 2. Westminster, Calif.: Viễn Đông Daily News, 2007.

Chuyện Người Vợ Tù Cải Tạo [Narratives from the Wives of the Reeducation Camp Prisoners]. 3 vols. Westminster, Calif.: Viễn Đông Daily News, 2004–5.

Cohen, Lizabeth. *Making a New Deal: Industrial Workers in Chicago, 1919–1939*. Cambridge: Cambridge University Press, 1990.

Committee on Overseas Vietnamese. *Cộng Đồng Người Việt Nam ở Nước Ngoài: Những Vấn Đề Cần Biết* [The Overseas Vietnamese Community: An Essential Guide]. Hanoi: Thế Giới, 2005.

Coolidge, Mary Roberts. *Chinese Immigration*. New York: Holt, 1909.

Courtois, Stéphane, Nicolas Werth, Jean-Louis Panne, Andrzej Paczkowski, Karel Bartosek, and Jean-Louis Margolin. *The Black Book of Communism: Crimes, Terror, Repression.* Cambridge: Harvard University Press, 1999.

Crafts, Nicolas. "East Asian Growth before and after the Crisis." *IMF Staff Papers* 46, no. 2 (June 1999): 139–66.

Crittenden, Ann. *Sanctuary: A Story of American Conscience and the Law in Collision.* New York: Weidenfeld and Nicolson, 1988.

Crunden, Robert M. *Ministers of Reform: The Progressives' Achievement in American Civilization, 1889–1920.* New York: Basic Books, 1982.

Curtis, Gerald L., and Sung-joo Han Un-chan Chung. *The U.S.–South Korean Alliance: Evolving Patterns in Security Relations.* Lexington, Mass.: Heath, 1983.

Dacy, Douglas C. *Foreign Aid, War, and Economic Development: South Vietnam, 1955–1975.* Cambridge: Cambridge University Press, 1986.

Dang, Thuy Vo. "Anticommunism as Cultural Praxis: South Vietnam, War, and Refugee Memories in the Vietnamese American Community." Ph.D. diss., University of California at San Diego, 2008.

Dang, Thuy Vo, and Linda Trinh Vo. *Vietnamese in Orange County.* Charleston, S.C.: Arcadia, 2015.

Danico, Mary Yu. "Korean Identities: What Does It Mean to Be Korean American in Korea?" *Transactions of the Royal Asiatic Society—Korea Branch* (Seoul, Korea: Royal Asiatic Journal) 80 (2005): 115–36.

Daniels, Roger. *The Politics of Prejudice: The Anti-Japanese Movement in California and the Struggle for Japanese Exclusion.* Berkeley: University of California Press, 1962.

Dave, Shilpa, Leilani Nishime, and Tasha G. Oren, eds. *East Main Street: Asian American Popular Culture.* New York: New York University Press, 2005.

Davis, Mike. *City of Quartz: Excavating the Future in Los Angeles.* New York: Verso, 1990.

Dawson, Alan. *55 Days: The Fall of South Vietnam.* Englewood Cliffs, N.J.: Prentice-Hall, 1977.

Dean, John. *Conservatives without Conscience.* New York: Penguin, 2007.

Dillon, Sam. *Comandos: The CIA and Nicaragua's Contra Rebels.* New York: Holt, 1991.

Dluhy, Milan J., and Howard A. Frank. *The Miami Fiscal Crisis: Can a Poor City Regain Prosperity?* Westport: Conn.: Praeger, 2002.

Do, Yen, with Jeffrey Brody. *Yen Do and the Story of Nguoi Viet Daily News.* Fullerton, Calif.: Người Việt, 2003.

Doan, Brian. *The Forgotten Ones: A Photographic Documentation of the Last Vietnamese Boat People in the Philippines.* Santa Ana, Calif.: VAALA, 2004.

Doan, Van Toai, and David Chanoff. *The Vietnamese Gulag.* New York: Simon and Schuster, 1986.

Dodsworth, John, Erich Spitäller, M. Braulke, Keon Lee, Kenneth M. Miranda, Christian B. Mulder, Hisanobu Shishido, and Krishna Srinivasan. *Vietnam: Transition to a Market Economy.* Washington, D.C.: International Monetary Fund, 1996.

Donahue, David M. *The Uprooted: Refugees and the United States: A Multidisciplinary Teaching Guide*. Alameda, Calif.: Hunter House, 1995.

Dower, John. *War without Mercy: Race and Power in the Pacific War*. New York: Pantheon, 1987.

Du, Patrick Phuoc Long. *The Dream Shattered: Vietnamese Gangs in America*. Boston: Northeastern University Press, 1996.

Du Bois, W. E. B. "The Talented Tenth." In *The Negro Problem: A Series of Articles by Representative Negroes of To-Day*. New York: Pott, 1903.

Duiker, William. *The Communist Road to Power in Vietnam*. Boulder, Colo.: Westview, 1981.

———. *Vietnam since the Fall of Saigon*. Updated ed. Athens: Ohio University Center for International Studies, 1989.

Duric, Mira. *The Strategic Defence Initiative: U.S. Policy and the Soviet Union*. Aldershot: Ashgate, 2003.

Dymski, Gary, and Lisa Mohanty. "Credit and Banking Structure: Asian and African-American Experience in Los Angeles." *American Economic Review* 89, no. 2 (May 1999): 362–66.

The East Asian Miracle: Economic Growth and Public Policy. London: Oxford University Press, 1993.

Engelmann, Larry. *Tears before the Rain: An Oral History of the Fall of South Vietnam*. New York: Oxford University Press, 1990.

Espiritu, Yen Le. *Asian American Panethnicity: Bridging Identities and Institutions*. Philadelphia: Temple University Press, 1992.

———. *Body Counts: The Vietnam War and Militarized Refugees*. Berkeley: University of California Press, 2014.

———. "Toward a Critical Refugee Study: The Vietnamese Refugee Subject in U.S. Scholarship." *Journal of Vietnamese Studies* 1, nos. 1–2 (February–August 2006): 410–33.

———. "The 'We-Win-Even-When-We-Lose' Syndrome: U.S. Press Coverage of the Twenty-Fifth Anniversary of the 'Fall of Saigon.'" *American Quarterly* 58, no. 2 (June 2006): 329–52.

Etulain, Richard W., and Ferenc Morton Szasz, eds. *The American West in 2000: Essays in Honor of Gerald D. Nash*. Albuquerque: University of New Mexico Press, 2003.

Faber, Michael. *The Long Road to Freedom*. Sacramento: Faber, 1989.

Fagen, Richard R., and Richard A. Brody. "Cubans in Exile: A Demographic Analysis." *Social Problems* 11, no. 4 (Spring 1964): 389–401.

Feeney, Maureen Patricia. "Freedom to Speak: Vietnamese Reeducation and the Search for Cold War Refuge." Ph.D. diss., University of Michigan, 2002.

Fein, Helen. *Congregational Sponsors of Indochinese Refugees in the United States, 1979–1981: Helping Beyond Borders*. Rutherford, N.J.: Fairleigh Dickinson University Press, 1987.

FitzGerald, Frances. *Fire in the Lake: The Vietnamese and the Americans in Vietnam*. Boston: Little, Brown, 1972.

———. *Way Out There in the Blue: Reagan, Star Wars, and the End of the Cold War*. New York: Simon and Schuster, 2001.

Fong, Timothy. *The Contemporary Asian American Experience: Beyond the Model Minority*. Upper Saddle River, N.J.: Prentice-Hall, 1998.

———. *The First Suburban Chinatown: The Remaking of Monterey Park, California*. Philadelphia: Temple University Press, 1994.

Frank, Andre Gunder. *Capitalism and Underdevelopment in Latin America: Historical Studies of Chile and Brazil*. New York: Monthly Review Press, 1967.

Frank, Thomas. *What's the Matter with Kansas?: How Conservatives Won the Heart of America*. New York: Holt, 2005.

Franklin, Bruce H. *M.I.A., or, Mythmaking in America*. Brooklyn: Hill, 1993.

Frankum, Robert B., Jr. *Operation Passage to Freedom: The United States Navy in Vietnam, 1954–1955*. Lubbock: Texas Tech University Press, 2007.

Freeman, James. *Hearts of Sorrow: Vietnamese-American Lives*. Stanford: Stanford University Press, 1989.

Fukuyama, Francis. *The End of History and the Last Man*. New York: Free Press, 1992.

Galbraith, James K. *The Predator State: How Conservatives Abandoned the Free Market and Why Liberals Should Too*. New York: Free Press, 2008.

García, María Cristina. *Havana USA: Cuban Exiles and Cuban Americans in South Florida, 1959–1994*. Berkeley: University of California Press, 1996.

García-Ayvens, Francisco. *Ethnic Orange County: An Ethnic Resources Directory*. Orange, Calif.: Santiago Library System, 1985.

Garver, John. *The Sino-American Alliance: Nationalist China and American Cold War Strategy in Asia*. Armonk, N.Y.: Sharpe, 1997.

Geertz, Clifford. "The Javanese Kijaji: The Changing Role of a Cultural Broker." *Comparative Studies in Society and History* 2, no. 2 (January 1960): 228–49.

Gellner, Ernest. *Nations and Nationalism*. Ithaca: Cornell University Press, 1983.

Genovese, Eugene. *Roll, Jordan, Roll*. New York: Vintage, 1976.

Gerstle, Gary. *American Crucible: Race and Nation in the Twentieth Century*. Princeton: Princeton University Press, 2002.

Gibbs, Jason. "Nhac Tien Chien: The Origins of Vietnamese Popular Song." *Destination Vietnam* (June–July 1998). Paper presented at the Society for Ethnomusicology, Northern California Chapter, Davis, 1996. Translated into Vietnamese by Nguyễn Trương Quý as "Nhạc Tiền Chiến: Khởi Đầu Của Ca Khúc Phổ Thông Việt Nam." *talawas*, March 9, 2006.

———. "Yellow Music Turning Golden." Paper presented at the Popular Culture Association, San Diego, Calif., 2005. Translated into Vietnamese by Nguyễn Trương Quý as "Nhạc Vàng 'Hóa Vàng.'" *talawas*, June 26, 2005.

Gilbert, Paul. *The Philosophy of Nationalism*. Boulder, Colo.: Westview, 1998.

Gilroy, Paul. *The Black Atlantic: Modernity and Double Consciousness*. Cambridge: Harvard University Press, 1993.

Glewwe, Paul, Nisha Agrawal, and David Dollar, eds. *Economic Growth, Poverty, and Household Welfare in Vietnam*. Washington, D.C.: World Bank, 2004.

Gold, Steven J. "Chinese-Vietnamese Entrepreneurs in California." In *The New Asian Immigration in Los Angeles and Global Restructuring*, ed. Paul Ong, Edna Bonacich, and Lucie Cheng. Philadelphia: Temple University Press, 1994.

González, Gilbert G. *Labor and Community: Mexican Citrus Worker Villages in a Southern California County, 1900–1950*. Urbana: University of Illinois Press, 1994.

Gowlland-Debbas, Vera. *The Problem of Refugees in the Light of Contemporary International Law Issues*. Geneva: Nijhoff, 1996.

Gramsci, Antonio. *Selections from the Prison Notebooks*. Ed. and trans. Quintin Hoare and Geoffrey Nowell Smith. New York: International, 1971.

Grant, Bruce. *The Boat People: An Age Investigation with Bruce Grant*. New York: Penguin, 1979.

Gruber, Ruth. *Haven: The Dramatic Story of 1,000 World War II Refugees and How They Came to America*. New York: Open Road, 2010.

Guibernau, Montserrat. *Nations without States: Political Communities in a Global Age*. Cambridge: Polity, 1999.

Gulick, Sidney L. *The American Japanese Problem*. New York: Scribner's, 1914.

Gutman, Herbert. *The Black Family in Slavery and Freedom*. New York: Pantheon, 1976.

Hà Thúc Sinh. *Đài Học Máu* [Bloody College]. San Jose, Calif.: Nhân Văn, 1985.

Haas, Lisbeth. *Conquests and Historical Identities in California, 1769–1936*. Berkeley: University of California Press, 1996.

Haines, David W. *Refugees as Immigrants: Cambodians, Laotians, and Vietnamese in America*. Totowa, N.J.: Rowman and Littlefield, 1989.

Halberstam, David. *The Best and the Brightest*. New York: Random House, 1972.

Halbwachs, Maurice. *On Collective Memory*. Ed., trans., and intro. Lewis A. Coser. Chicago: University of Chicago Press, 1992.

Hall, Stuart. "Cultural Studies and Its Theoretical Legacies." In *Cultural Studies*, ed. Lawrence Grossberg, Cary Nelson, Paula A. Treichler, Linda Baughman, and John Macgregor Wise. London: Routledge, 1992.

———. "Gramsci's Relevance for the Study of Race and Ethnicity." *Journal of Communication Inquiry* 10, no. 2 (1986): 5–27.

———. "The Problem of Ideology: Marxism without Guarantees." In *Marx: 100 Years On*, ed. B. Matthews. London: Lawrence and Wishart, 1983.

Hamamoto, Darrell Y. *Monitored Peril: Asian Americans and the Politics of TV Representation*. Minneapolis: University of Minnesota Press, 1994.

Hamilton Merritt, Jane. *Tragic Mountains: The Hmong, the Americans, and the Secret War for Laos, 1942–1992*. Bloomington: Indiana University Press, 1993.

Harwood, Edwin. "American Public Opinion and U.S. Immigration Policy." *Annals of the American Academy of Political and Social Science* 487 (September 1986): 201–12.

Hayden, Dolores. *The Power of Place: Urban Landscapes as Public History*. Cambridge: MIT Press, 1995.

Hayslip, Le Ly. *Child of War, Woman of Peace*. New York: Doubleday, 1993.

Hechinger, Kevin, and Curtis Hechinger. *Hechinger's Field Guide to Ethnic Stereotypes*. New York: Simon and Schuster, 2009.

Heil, Alan L., Jr. *Voice of America: A History*. New York: Columbia University Press, 2003.

Hellman, John. *American Myth and the Legacy of Vietnam*. New York: Columbia University Press, 1986.

Herskovits, Melville. *Myth of the Negro Past*. Boston: Beacon, 1958.

Herzstein, Robert E. *Henry R. Luce, Time, and the American Crusade in Asia*. New York: Cambridge University Press, 2005.

Higham, John. *Ethnic Leadership in America*. Baltimore: Johns Hopkins University Press, 1978.

Hill, Patricia Wong, and Victor M. Hwang. *Anti-Asian Violence in North America: Asian American and Asian Canadian Reflections on Hate, Healing, and Resistance*. Walnut Creek, Calif.: AltaMira, 2001.

Hobsbawm, Eric. *Nations and Nationalism since 1780: Programme, Myth, Reality*. Cambridge: Cambridge University Press, 1990.

Hobsbawm, Eric, and Terence Ranger, eds. *The Invention of Tradition*. Cambridge: Cambridge University Press, 1983.

Hofstadter, Richard. *The Age of Reform: From Bryan to F.D.R.* New York: Knopf, 1955.

Hollander, Paul, ed. *From the Gulag to the Killing Fields: Personal Accounts of Political Violence and Repression in Communist States*. Wilmington, Del.: Intercollegiate Studies Institute, 2007.

Horton, John. *The Politics of Diversity: Immigration, Resistance, and Change in Monterey Park, California*. Philadelphia: Temple University Press, 1995.

HoSang, Daniel. "Racial Propositions: 'Genteel Apartheid' in Postwar California." Ph.D. diss., University of Southern California, 2007.

Hosmer, Stephen T., Konrad Kellen, and Brian M. Jenkins. *The Fall of South Vietnam: Statements by Vietnamese Military and Civilian Leaders*. New York: Crane, Russak, 1980.

Hroch, Miroslav. "From National Movement to the Fully-Formed Nation: The Nation-Building Process in Europe." In *Mapping the Nation*, ed. Gopal Balakrishnan. New York: Verso, 1996.

Hubbell, L. Kenneth, ed. *Fiscal Crisis in American Cities: The Federal Response*. Cambridge, Mass.: Ballinger, 1979.

Hufbauer, Benjamin. *Presidential Temples: How Memorials and Libraries Shape Public Memory*. Lawrence: University Press of Kansas, 2005.

Hunt, Michael H. *Lyndon Johnson's War: America's Cold War Crusade in Vietnam*. New York: Hill and Wang, 1996.

Huntington, Samuel P. *The Clash of Civilizations and the Remaking of World Order*. New York: Simon and Schuster, 1996.

Huỳnh, Jade Ngọc Quang. *South Wind Changing*. St. Paul, Minn.: Graywolf, 1994.

Indochinese Refugee Reports. Washington, D.C.: Information Exchange Project, 1979–80.

Bibliography

Isaacs, Arnold R. *Vietnam Shadows: The War, Its Ghosts, and Its Legacy.* Baltimore: Johns Hopkins University Press, 2000.

Jacobs, Seth. *America's Miracle Man in Vietnam: Ngo Dinh Diem, Religion, Race, and U.S. Intervention in Southeast Asia.* Durham, N.C.: Duke University Press, 2004.

Jacobson, Matthew Frye. *Roots Too: White Ethnic Revival in Post–Civil Rights America.* Cambridge: Harvard University Press, 2006.

———. *Special Sorrows: The Diasporic Imagination of Irish, Polish, and Jewish Immigrants in the United States.* Cambridge: Harvard University Press, 1995.

———. *Whiteness of a Different Color: European Immigrants and the Alchemy of Race.* Cambridge: Harvard University Press, 1999.

Jamieson, Neil L. *Understanding Vietnam.* Berkeley: University of California Press, 1995.

JanMohamed, Abdul and David Lloyd. "Introduction: Minority Discourse: What Is to Be Done?" *Cultural Critique* 7 (Autumn 1987): 5–17.

———. "Introduction: Toward a Theory of Minority Discourse." *Cultural Critique* 6 (Spring 1987): 5–12.

Jaret, Charles. "The Greek, Italian, and Jewish American Ethnic Press: A Comparative Analysis." *Journal of Ethnic Studies* 7, no. 2 (1979): 47–70.

Jeffords, Susan. *The Remasculinization of America: Gender and the Vietnam War.* Bloomington: Indiana University Press, 1989.

Johnson, Chalmers. *Sorrows of Empire: Militarism, Secrecy, and the End of the Republic.* New York: Holt, 2004.

Jordan, William. *Black Newspapers and America's War for Democracy, 1914–1920.* Chapel Hill: University of North Carolina Press, 2001.

Jorge, Antonio, Jaime Suchlicki, and Adolfo Leyva de Varona, eds. *Cuban Exiles in Florida: Their Presence and Contributions.* Coral Gables, Fla.: University of Miami, North-South Center Publications for the Research Institute for Cuban Studies, 1991.

Jorion, Philippe. *Big Bets Gone Bad.* San Diego: Academic Press, 1995.

Kahn, E. J. *The China Hands: America's Foreign Service Officers and What Befell Them.* New York: Viking, 1975.

Kaplan, Robert. *Asia's Cauldron: The South China Sea and the End of a Stable Pacific.* New York: Random House, 2014.

Karnow, Stanley. *Vietnam: A History.* New York: Viking, 1983.

Kazin, Michael. *The Populist Persuasion: An American History.* Ithaca: Cornell University Press, 1998.

Kearns, Doris. *Lyndon Johnson and the American Dream.* New York: Harper and Row, 1976.

Keating, Michael. *Plurinational Democracy: Stateless Nations in a Post-Sovereignty Era.* Oxford: Oxford University Press, 2001.

Kelly, Gail Paradise. *From Vietnam to America: A Chronicle of the Vietnamese Immigration to the United States.* Boulder, Colo.: Westview, 1977.

Kennan, George F. *Memoirs, 1925–1950.* New York: Pantheon, 1967.

Kennedy, Rory, director. *Last Days in Vietnam*. Boston: American Experience Films, 2014.

Kibria, Nazli. *Family Tightrope: The Changing Lives of Vietnamese Americans*. Princeton: Princeton University Press, 1995.

Kim, Claire Jean. *Bitter Fruit: The Politics of Black-Korean Conflict in New York City*. New Haven: Yale University Press, 2000.

Kimura, Tetsuburo. *The Vietnamese Economy, 1975–86: Reforms and International Relations*. Tokyo: Institute of Developing Economies, 1989.

Kling, Rob, Spencer Olin, and Mark Poster, eds. *Postsuburban California: The Transformation of Orange County since World War II*. Berkeley: University of California Press, 1990.

Koen, Ross Y. *The China Lobby in American Politics*. New York: Harper and Row, 1974.

Kohn, Hans. *The Idea of Nationalism: A Study of Its Origins*. New York: Macmillan, 1944.

Kolko, Gabriel. *Anatomy of a Peace*. New York: Routledge, 1997.

———. *Anatomy of a War: Vietnam, the United States, and the Modern Historical Experience*. New York: Pantheon, 1985.

Konvitz, Milton R. *The Alien and the Asiatic in American Law*. Ithaca: Cornell University Press, 1946.

Korea Reborn: A Grateful Nation Honors War Veterans for 60 Years of Growth. Salt Lake City: Remember My Service Productions, 2013.

Korea-USA Centennial, 1882–1982. Seoul: Yonhap News Agency, 1982.

Krugler, David. *The Voice of America and the Domestic Propaganda Battles, 1945–1953*. Columbia: University of Missouri Press, 2000.

Kurashige, Lon. *Japanese American Celebration and Conflict: A History of Ethnic Identity and Festival in Los Angeles, 1934–1990*. Berkeley: University of California Press, 2000.

Kurashige, Scott. *The Shifting Grounds of Race: Black and Japanese Americans in the Making of Multiethnic Los Angeles*. Princeton: Princeton University Press, 2007.

Lam, Mariam Beevi. "Surfin' Vietnam: Trauma, Memory, and Cultural Politics." Ph.D. diss., University of California at Irvine, 2006.

Lamb, Karl. *As Orange Goes: Twelve California Families and the Future of American Politics*. New York: Norton, 1974.

Langguth, A. J. *Our Vietnam: The War, 1954–1975*. New York: Simon and Schuster, 2000.

Lasker, Bruno. *Filipino Immigration to Continental United States and to Hawaii*. Chicago: University of Chicago Press for the American Council, Institute of Pacific Relations, 1931.

Lassiter, Matthew D. *The Silent Majority: Suburban Politics in the Sunbelt South*. Princeton: Princeton University Press, 2007.

Bibliography

Lee, Erika. *At America's Gates: Chinese Immigration during the Exclusion Era, 1882–1943.* Chapel Hill: University of North Carolina Press, 2003.

Lee, Robert G. *Orientals: Asian Americans in Popular Culture.* Philadelphia: Temple University Press, 1999.

Lefebvre, Henri. *The Production of Space.* New York: Wiley-Blackwell, 1992.

Leighley, Jan. *Strength in Numbers?: The Political Mobilization of Racial and Ethnic Minorities.* Princeton: Princeton University Press, 2001.

Lê Quang Anh. *Andy Quang Le and His Musical Compositions* (DVD). NV Video Production, 2005.

Levine, Lawrence. *Black Culture and Black Consciousness: Afro-American Folk Thought from Slavery to Freedom.* New York: Oxford University Press, 1977.

Li, Wei. "Building Ethnoburbia: The Emergence and Manifestation of the Chinese Ethnoburb in Los Angeles' San Gabriel Valley." *Journal of Asian American Studies* 2, no. 1 (February 1999): 1–28.

Lichten, Eric. *Class, Power, and Austerity: The New York City Fiscal Crisis.* South Hadley, Mass.: Bergin and Garvey, 1986.

Lien, Pei-te. *The Making of Asian America through Political Participation.* Philadelphia: Temple University Press, 2001.

Lieu, Nhi T. *The American Dream in Vietnamese.* Minneapolis: University of Minnesota Press, 2011.

———. "Private Desires on Public Display: Vietnamese American Identities in Multi-Mediated Leisure and Niche Entertainment." Ph.D. diss., University of Michigan, 2004.

———. "Remembering 'the Nation' through Pageantry: Femininity and the Politics of Vietnamese Womanhood in the Hoa Hau Ao Dai Contest." *Frontiers: A Journal of Women's Studies* 21, nos. 1–2 (March 2000): 127–51.

Light, Ivan, and Edna Bonacich. *Immigrant Entrepreneurs: Koreans in Los Angeles, 1965–1982.* Berkeley: University of California Press, 1988.

Lind, Michael. *Vietnam: The Necessary War: A Reinterpretation of America's Most Disastrous Military Conflict.* New York: Free Press, 1999.

Lipman, Jana K. "Give Us a Ship: The Vietnamese Repatriate Movement on Guam, 1975." *American Quarterly* 64, no. 1 (March 2012): 1–31.

Lipset, Seymour Martin. *American Exceptionalism: A Double-Edged Sword.* New York: Norton, 1996.

Little, Douglas. *American Orientalism: The United States and the Middle East since 1945.* Chapel Hill: University of North Carolina Press, 2008.

Liu, William. *Transition to Nowhere: Vietnamese Refugees in America.* Nashville, Tenn.: Charter House, 1979.

Lockhart, Charles. *The Roots of American Exceptionalism: History: Institutions, and Culture.* New York: Palgrave Macmillan, 2003.

Loescher, Gil D., and John A. Scanlan. *Calculated Kindness: Refugees and America's Half-Open Door, 1945 to the Present.* New York: Free Press, 1986.

———, eds. *The Global Refugee Problem: U.S. and World Response.* Beverly Hills, Calif.: Sage, 1983.

Louis, Steve, and Glenn K. Omatsu. *Asian Americans: The Movement and the Moment.* Los Angeles: UCLA Asian American Studies Center Press, 2001.

Lowe, Lisa. *Immigrant Acts: On Asian American Cultural Politics.* Durham, N.C.: Duke University Press, 1996.

Lu Van Thanh. *The Inviting Call of Wandering Souls: Memoir of an ARVN Liaison Officer to United States Forces in Vietnam.* Jefferson, N.C.: McFarland, 1997.

Lye, Colleen. *America's Asia: Racial Form and American Literature, 1893–1945.* Princeton: Princeton University Press, 2005.

Ma, Laurence J. C., and Carolyn Cartier. *The Chinese Diaspora: Space, Place, Mobility, and Identity.* Lanham, Md.: Rowman and Littlefield, 2003.

Mann, James. *Rise of the Vulcans.* New York: Viking, 2004.

Marchetti, Gina. *Romance and the "Yellow Peril": Race, Sex, and the Discursive Strategies in Hollywood Fiction.* Berkeley: University of California Press, 1993.

Márquez, Benjamin. *LULAC: The Evolution of a Mexican American Political Organization.* Austin: University of Texas Press, 1993.

Martin, Frances P. "'Freed Vietnamese Have Her to Thank': Khuc Minh Tho, the FVPPA, and the Use of Grassroots Diplomacy in the Release, Immigration, and Resettlement of Vietnamese Re-Education Camp Prisoners, 1977–2011." Master's thesis, Texas Tech University, 2015.

Matray, James Irving. *The Reluctant Crusade: American Foreign Policy in Korea, 1941–1950.* Honolulu: University of Hawaii Press, 1985.

Matsuoka, Jon K. "Vietnamese Americans." In *Handbook of Social Services for Asian and Pacific Islanders*, ed. Noreen Mokauu. Westport, Conn.: Greenwood, 1991.

Matthews, Ellen. *Culture Clash.* Chicago: Intercultural, 1983.

May, Elaine Tyler. *Homeward Bound: American Families in the Cold War Era.* New York: Basic Books, 1988.

McClain, Charles J. *In Search of Equality: The Chinese Struggle against Discrimination in Nineteenth-Century America.* Berkeley: University of California Press, 1996.

McCrone, David. *Understanding Scotland: The Sociology of a Stateless Nation.* New York: Routledge, 1992.

McGirr, Lisa. *Suburban Warriors: The Origins of the New American Right.* Princeton: Princeton University Press, 2001.

Mears, Eliot Grinnell. *Resident Orientals on the American Pacific Coast: Their Legal and Economic Status.* Chicago: University of Chicago Press, 1928.

McIntosh, Peggy. "White Privilege and Male Privilege: A Personal Account of Coming to See Correspondences through Work in Women's Studies." In *Gender Basics: Feminist Perspectives on Women and Men*, ed. Anne Minas. Belmont, Calif.: Wadsworth, 2000.

Miller, Kerby A. *Emigrants and Exiles: Ireland and the Irish Exodus to North America.* New York: Oxford University Press, 1988.

Miller, Sally M., ed. *The Ethnic Press in the United States: A Historical Analysis and Handbook*. New York: Greenwood, 1987.

Modell, John. *The Economics and Politics of Racial Accommodation: The Japanese of Los Angeles, 1900–1942*. Urbana: University of Illinois Press, 1977.

Montero, Darrel. *Vietnamese Americans: Patterns of Resettlement and Socioeconomic Adaptation in the United States*. Boulder, Colo.: Westview, 1979.

Moon, Chung-in. "Between Banmi (Anti-Americanism) and Sungmi (Worship of the United States): Dynamics of Changing U.S. Images in South Korea." In *Korean Attitudes towards the United States: Changing Dynamics*, ed. David I. Steinberg. New York: Sharpe, 2005.

Morley, David, and Kuan-Hsing Chen, eds. *Stuart Hall: Critical Dialogues in Cultural Studies*. London: Routledge, 1996.

Nakanishi, Don. "A Quota on Excellence?: The Debate on Asian American Admissions." *Change*, November–December 1989, 38–47.

Nam, Joo-Hong. *America's Commitment to South Korea: The First Decade of the Nixon Doctrine*. Cambridge: Cambridge University Press, 1986.

Nam Lộc. "Xin Dời Một Nụ Cười." *Những Ca Khúc Của Nam Lộc: Sàigòn ơi, Vĩnh Biệt* (CD). Thuý Nga Entertainment, 2015.

Nash, Jesse W. *Vietnamese Catholicism*. Harvey, La.: Art Review Press, 1992.

National United Front for the Liberation of Vietnam. *Mặt Trận Quốc Gia Thống Nhất Giải Phóng Việt Nam và Con Đường Cứu Nước* [The National United Front for the Liberation of Vietnam and the Road to Freedom]. San Jose, Calif.: Overseas Committee, National United Front, 1995.

National United Front for the Liberation of Vietnam. *The National Support Movement for the Resistance in Vietnam*. San Jose, Calif.: Overseas Department, National United Front, 1982.

National United Front for the Liberation of Vietnam. *The Vietnamese Fight for Freedom: An Introduction to the National United Front for the Liberation of Vietnam*. San Jose, Calif.: Directorate of Information, National United Front, 1986.

National United Front for the Liberation of Vietnam. *Vietnamese People's Fight for Survival*. Redwood City, Calif.: National United Front, 1982.

Nawyn, William E. *American Protestantism's Response to Germany's Jews and Refugees, 1933–1941*. Ann Arbor, Mich.: UMI Research Press, 1981.

Nelson, Michael. *War of the Black Heavens: The Battles of Western Broadcasting in the Cold War*. Syracuse: Syracuse University Press, 1997.

Ngai, Mae. *Impossible Subjects: Illegal Aliens and the Making of Modern America*. Princeton: Princeton University Press, 2005.

Nguyễn Anh Tuấn. *South Vietnam Trial and Experience: A Challenge for Development*. Athens: Ohio University Center for International Studies, 1987.

Nguyễn Cao Kỳ. *Twenty Years and Twenty Days*. New York: Stein and Day, 1976.

Nguyễn Chí Thiện. *Flowers from Hell*. Trans. Huỳnh Sanh Thông. New Haven: Yale Southeast Asian Studies, 1984.

Nguyễn Đình San, ed. *100 Bài Hát Việt Nam Hay Nhất Thế Kỷ 20* [The 100 Greatest Vietnamese Songs of the 20th Century]. Hanoi: Thanh Niên, 2007.

———, ed. *Dư Âm: 100 Ca Khúc Đặc Sắc của 100 Nhạc Sĩ Thế Kỷ 20* [Echoes: 100 Selections from the 100 Greatest Vietnamese Songwriters of the 20th Century]. Hanoi: Thanh Niên, 2007.

Nguyen, Mimi Thi. *The Gift of Freedom: War, Debt, and Other Refugee Passages*. Durham, N.C.: Duke University Press, 2012.

———. "Representing Refugees: Gender, Nation, and Diaspora in 'Vietnamese America.'" Ph.D. diss., University of California at Berkeley, 2004.

Nguyễn Ngọc Hà. *Về Người Việt Nam Định Cư ở Nước Ngoài* [On the Vietnamese Who Have Settled Abroad]. Ho Chi Minh City: Hồ Chí Minh City Publishers, 1990.

Nguyễn Ngọc Ngạn. *The Will of Heaven: A Story of One Vietnamese and the End of His World*. New York: Dutton, 1982.

Nguyen, Viet Thanh. *Nothing Ever Dies: Vietnam and the Memory of War*. Cambridge: Harvard University Press, 2016.

Nguyễn, Xuân-Lan. *Legends of the Promised Land*. Pittsburgh: Dorrance, 2011.

Nguyệt Ánh. *Em Còn Nhớ Màu Cờ* [I Still Remember the Color of Our Flag]. San Jose, Calif.: Người Việt Tự Do, 1981.

Nixon, Richard M. "Asia after Vietnam." *Foreign Affairs* 46, no. 1 (October 1967): 111–24.

———. "Nixon's 'Silent Majority' Speech," Washington, D.C., November 3, 1969. http://watergate.info/1969/11/03/nixons-silent-majority-speech.html.

Nora, Pierre. *Realms of Memory*. New York: Columbia University Press, 1998.

North, David S., Lawrence S. Lewin, and Jennifer R. Wagner. *Kaleidoscope: The Resettlement of Refugees in the U.S. by the Voluntary Agencies*. Washington, D.C.: New TransCentury, 1982.

Novick, Peter. *The Holocaust in American Life*. Boston: Houghton Mifflin, 1999.

Nugent, Nicholas. *Vietnam: The Second Revolution*. Brighton: In Print, 1996.

O'Connor, James R. *The Fiscal Crisis of the State*. New York: St. Martin's, 1973.

Ohno, Izumi. *Beyond the "East Asian Miracle": An Asian View*. New York: United Nations Development Program, 1996.

Okihiro, Gary Y. *The Columbia Guide to Asian American History*. New York: Columbia University Press, 2001.

———. *Margins and Mainstreams: Asians in American History and Culture*. Seattle: University of Washington Press, 1994.

Olsen, Dale A. *Popular Music of Vietnam: The Politics of Remembering, the Economics of Forgetting*. New York: Routledge, 2008.

Olzack, Susan, and Elizabeth West. "Ethnic Conflict and the Rise and Fall of Ethnic Newspapers." *American Sociological Review* 56, no. 4. (August 1991): 458–74.

Omi, Michael, and Howard Winant. *Racial Formation in the United States: From the 1960s to the 1990s*. 2nd ed. New York: Routledge, 1994.

Ong, Aihwa. *Flexible Citizenship: The Cultural Logics of Transnationality*. Durham, N.C.: Duke University Press, 1999.

Orange County Child Care Resource Guide. Santa Ana, Calif.: Santa Ana College, New Horizons, 1979.

Orr, Elisabeth E. "Living along the Fault Line: Community, Suburbia, and Multi-ethnicity in Garden Grove and Westminster, California, 1900–1995." Ph.D. diss., Indiana University, 2000.

Orwell, George. *Nineteen Eighty-Four: A Novel*. New York: Harcourt, Brace, 1949.

Osa, Maryjane. *Solidarity and Contention: Networks of Polish Opposition*. Minneapolis: University of Minnesota Press, 2003.

Padgett, Douglas M. "Religion, Memory, and Imagination in Vietnamese California." Ph.D. diss., Indiana University, 2007.

Park, Eul Young. "From Bilateralism to Multilateralism: Korea's Economic Relations with the United States, 1945–1980." In *Korea and the United States: A Century of Cooperation*, ed. Youngnok Koo and Dae-Xook Suh. Honolulu: University of Hawaii Press, 1984.

Park, Robert E. *The Immigrant Press and Its Control*. New York: Harper, 1922.

Parker, T. Jefferson. *Little Saigon*. New York: St. Martin's, 1988.

Patterson, Orlando. *Slavery and Social Death: A Comparative Study*. Cambridge: Harvard University Press, 2007.

Pelley, Patricia. *Postcolonial Vietnam: New Histories of the National Past*. Durham, N.C.: Duke University Press, 2002.

Penn, Shana. *Solidarity's Secret: The Women Who Defeated Communism in Poland*. Ann Arbor: University of Michigan Press, 2005.

Pérez, Louis A. *Cuba in the American Imagination: Metaphor and the Imperial Ethos*. Chapel Hill: University of North Carolina Press, 2008.

Phạm Duy. *Hồi Ký—Thời Hải Ngoại* [Memoir: The Overseas]. Vol. 4. Midway City, Calif.: Duy Cường, 2000.

Phạm Duy. *Thấm Thoắt Mười Năm* [Ten Years in Transition]. Springfield, Va.: Hội Văn Hóa Việt Nam tại Bắc Mỹ, 1985.

Phạm Ngọc Lũy. *Hồi Ký Một Đời Người* [Memoir of a Life]. Vol. 2. Tokyo: Tân Văn, 1994.

Phạm Quốc Bảo. *Cùm Đỏ* [Red Chains]. Westminster, Calif.: Người Việt, 1983.

Phạm Văn Liễu. *Trả Ta Sông Núi: Hồi Ký* [Pay Me Song Mountain: Memoir]. Vol. 3. Houston: Văn Hóa, 2004.

Pham, Vu Hong. "Beyond and before the Boat People: Vietnamese American History before 1975." Ph.D. diss., Cornell University, 2002.

Phillips, Kevin. *The Emerging Republican Majority*. New Rochelle, N.Y.: Arlington House, 1969.

Pike, Douglas. *Viet Cong: The Organization and Techniques of the National Liberation Front of South Vietnam*. Cambridge: MIT Center for International Studies, 1966.

———. "The Vietcong Secret War." In *War in the Shadows*, vol. 25 of *The Vietnam Experience*. Boston: Boston Publishing, 1988.

Piketty, Thomas. *Capital in the Twenty-First Century*. Cambridge: Belknap Press of Harvard University Press, 2014.

Plokhy, Serhii. *The Origins of Slavic Nations: Premodern Identities in Russia, Ukraine, and Belarus*. Cambridge: Cambridge University Press, 2006.

Posner, Gerald L. *Warlords of Crime: Chinese Secret Societies—The New Mafia*. New York: McGraw-Hill, 1988.

Potocky, Mariam. "The Economic Integration of Southeast Asian Refugees in California." Ph.D. diss., University of Kansas, 1993.

Powell, Colin, *My American Journey*. New York: Ballantine, 1995.

Prashad, Vijay. *Everybody Was Kung Fu Fighting: Afro-Asian Connections and the Myth of Cultural Purity*. Boston: Beacon, 2002.

Pryor, Richard. "New Niggers." From *Is It Something I Said?* (audio album), 1975.

Pulido, Laura. *Black, Brown, Yellow, and Left: Radical Activism in Los Angeles*. Berkeley: University of California Press, 2006.

Putnam, Robert D. *Bowling Alone: The Collapse and Revival of American Community*. New York: Simon and Schuster, 2000.

Rawick, George. *From Sundown to Sunup: The Making of the Black Community*. Westport, Conn.: Greenwood, 1972.

Rawnsley, Gary D. *Radio Diplomacy and Propaganda: The BBC and VOA in International Politics, 1956–1964*. New York: Macmillan, 1996.

Reeves, Thomas C. *The Life and Times of Joe McCarthy: A Biography*. New York: Stein and Day, 1982.

Resendez, Andres. *Changing National Identities at the Frontier: Texas and New Mexico, 1800–1850*. Cambridge: Cambridge University Press, 2005.

Reyes, Adelaida. *Songs of the Caged, Songs of the Free: Music and the Vietnamese Refugee Experience*. Philadelphia: Temple University Press, 1999.

Ricoeur, Paul. *Memory, History, Forgetting*. Trans. Kathleen Blamey and David Pellauer. Chicago: University of Chicago Press, 2004.

Rieff, David. *The Exile: Cuba in the Heart of Miami*. New York: Simon and Schuster, 1993.

Riis, Jacob. *How the Other Half Lives: Studies among the Tenements of New York*. New York: Scribner's, 1892.

Robinson, W. Courtland. *Terms of Refuge: The Indochinese Exodus and the International Response*. New York: Zed, 1998.

Rose, Peter I. *Dispossessed: An Anatomy of Exile*. Amherst: University of Massachusetts Press, 2005.

———. "Tempest-Tost: Exile, Ethnicity, and the Politics of Rescue." *Sociological Forum* 8, no. 1 (March 1993): 5–24.

Rostow, Walt. *The Stages of Economic Growth: A Non-Communist Manifesto*. Cambridge: Cambridge University Press, 1960.

Rowe, John Carlos. Introduction to *Post-Nationalist American Studies*, ed. John Carlos Rowe. Berkeley: University of California Press, 2000.

Rutledge, Paul James. *The Role of Religion in Ethnic Self-Identity: A Vietnamese Community*. Lanham, Md.: University Press of America, 1985.

———. *The Vietnamese Experience in America*. Bloomington: Indiana University Press, 1992.

Sachs, Dana. *The Life We Were Given: Operation Babylift, International Adoption, and the Children of War in Vietnam*. Boston: Beacon, 2010.
Said, Edward. *Orientalism*. New York: Vintage, 1979.
Saito, Leland. *Race and Politics: Asian Americans, Latinos, and Whites in a Los Angeles Suburb*. Urbana: University of Illinois Press, 1998.
Sánchez, George J. *Becoming Mexican American: Ethnicity, Culture, and Identity in Chicano Los Angeles, 1900–1945*. New York: Oxford University Press, 1993.
Schultz, Bud. *The Price of Dissent: Testimonies to Political Repression in America*. Berkeley: University of California Press, 2001.
Schulz, Nancy. *Voyagers in the Land: A Report on Unaccompanied Southeast Asian Refugee Children*. Washington, D.C.: Migration and Refugee Services, U.S. Catholic Conference, 1984.
Scott, James M. *Deciding to Intervene: The Reagan Doctrine and American Foreign Policy*. Durham, N.C.: Duke University Press, 1996.
Scott, Joanna C. *Indochina's Refugees: Oral Histories from Laos, Cambodia, and Vietnam*. Jefferson, N.C.: McFarland, 1989.
Seckler-Hudson, Catheryn. *Statelessness: With Special Reference to the United States*. Washington, D.C.: Digest Press, American University Graduate School, 1934.
Shah, Nayan. *Contagious Divides: Epidemics and Race in San Francisco's Chinatown*. Berkeley: University of California Press, 2001.
Sheehan, Neil. *A Bright Shining Lie: John Paul Vann and America in Vietnam*. New York: Vintage, 1989.
Shefter, Martin. *Political Crisis/Fiscal Crisis: The Collapse and Revival of New York City*. New York: Basic Books, 1985.
Shrecker, Ellen. *Many Are the Crimes: McCarthyism in America*. Boston: Little, Brown, 1998.
Simons, Geoff. *Vietnam Syndrome: Impact on U.S. Foreign Policy*. New York: St. Martin's, 1998.
Sinclair, Upton. *The Jungle*. New York: Grosset and Dunlap, 1906.
Smith, Anthony D. *Chosen Peoples: Sacred Sources of National Identity*. New York: Oxford University Press, 2003.
———. *The Ethnic Origins of Nations*. Oxford: Blackwell, 1986.
Smith, Daniel A. *Tax Crusaders and the Politics of Direct Democracy*. New York: Routledge, 1998.
Soja, Edward. "Inside Exopolis: Scenes from Orange County." In *Variations on a Theme Park: The New American City and the End of Public Space*, ed. Michael Sorkin. New York: Hill and Wang, 1992.
Southeast Asian Americans at a Glance. Washington, D.C.: Southeast Asia Resource Action Center, 2010.
Steinfels, Peter. *The Neoconservatives: The Men Who Are Changing America's Politics*. New York: Touchstone, 1979.

Stiglitz, Joseph E., and Shahid Yusuf, eds. *Rethinking the East Asia Miracle*. Washington, D.C.: World Bank; New York: Oxford University Press, 2001.

Stopp, G. Harry, Jr., and Mạnh Hùng Nguyễn, eds. *Proceedings of the First Annual Conference on Indochinese Refugees*. Fairfax, Va.: Citizens Applied Research Institute of George Mason University, 1979.

Strand, Paul, and Woodrow Jones Jr. *Indochinese Refugees in America: Problems of Adaptation and Assimilation*. Durham, N.C.: Duke University Press, 1985.

Sturken, Marita. *Tangled Memories: The Vietnam War, the AIDS Epidemic, and the Politics of Remembering*. Berkeley: University of California Press, 1997.

Ta, Minh-Hoa. "Twice a Minority: A Participatory Study of the Chinese-Vietnamese Adaptation Experiences in Vietnam and the United States." Ed.D. diss., University of San Francisco, 2000.

Tạ Ty. *Đáy Địa Ngục* [This Is Hell]. San Jose, Calif.: Thằng Mõ, 1985.

Tabb, William K. *The Long Default: New York City and the Urban Fiscal Crisis*. New York: Monthly Review Press, 1982.

Tachiki, Amy, Eddie Wong, Franklin Odo, and Buck Wong, eds. *Roots: An Asian American Reader*. Los Angeles: Continental Graphics, 1971.

Tai, Hue-Tam Ho, ed. *The Country of Memory: Remaking the Past in Late Socialist Vietnam*. Berkeley: University of California Press, 2001.

Takagi, Dana. *The Retreat from Race: Asian-American Admissions and Racial Politics*. New Brunswick, N.J.: Rutgers University Press, 1992.

Takaki, Ronald. *Strangers from a Different Shore: A History of Asian Americans*. New York: Penguin, 1990.

Tamura, Eileen H. *Americanization, Acculturation, and Ethnic Identity: The Nisei Generation in Hawaii*. Urbana: University of Illinois Press, 1994.

Tang, Eric. "Unsettled: On the Postcolonial Presence of Southeast Asian Refugees." Ph.D. diss., New York University, 2006.

Tanner, Marcus. *Croatia: A Nation Forged in War*. New Haven: Yale University Press, 1997.

Taylor, Philip. *Fragments of the Present: Searching for Modernity in Vietnam's South*. Honolulu: University of Hawai'i Press, 2000.

Tchen, John Kuo Wei. *New York before Chinatown: Orientalism and the Shaping of American Culture, 1776–1882*. Baltimore: Johns Hopkins University Press, 1999.

Thai, Hung Cam. *For Better or for Worse: Vietnamese International Marriages in the New Global Economy*. New Brunswick, N.J.: Rutgers University Press, 2008.

———. "Marriage across the Pacific: Family, Kinship, and Migration in Vietnam and in the Vietnamese Diaspora." Ph.D. diss., University of California at Berkeley, 2003.

Thompson, Larry Clinton. *Refugee Workers in the Indochina Exodus, 1975–1982*. Jefferson, N.C.: McFarland, 2010.

Those Who Leave: The "Problem of Vietnamese Refugees." Hanoi: Vietnam Courier, 1979.

Tran, Barbara, Monique T. D. Truong, and Luu Truong Khoi, eds. *Watermark: Vietnamese American Poetry and Prose*. New York: Asian American Writers Workshop, 1998.

Tran, De, Andrew Lam, and Hai Dai Nguyen, eds. *Once upon a Dream: The Vietnamese-American Experience*. Kansas City: Andrews and McMeel, 1995.

Trần Đình Trụ. *Việt Nam Thương Tín Con Tàu Định Mệnh: Hồi Ký* [Vietnam, the Thuong Tin, Destiny: A Memoir]. Houston, Texas: Thiên Nga, 1994.

Tran, Ham, dir. *Journey from the Fall* (film). Imaginasian, 2005.

Tran, Quan Tue. "Remembering the Boat People Exodus: A Tale of Two Memorials." *Journal of Vietnamese Studies* 7, no. 3 (Fall 2012): 80–121.

Trần Trọng Đăng Đàn. *Người Việt Nam ở Nước Ngoài* [The Overseas Vietnamese]. Hanoi: Chính Trị Quốc Gia, 1997.

———. *Người Việt Nam ở Nước Ngoài: Không Chi Có "Việt Kiều"* [The Vietnamese Abroad: Before and beyond the Post-1975 Migration]. Hanoi: Chính Trị Quốc Gia, 2005.

Truman, Harry S. *Memoirs*. Garden City, N.Y.: Doubleday, 1956.

Tsamenyi, Martin. *The Vietnamese Boat People and International Law*. Brisbane: Griffith University, School of Modern Asian Studies, Centre for the Study of Australian-Asian Relations, 1981.

Tuan, Yi-Fu. *Space and Place; The Perspective of Experience*. Rev. ed. Minneapolis: University of Minnesota Press, 2001.

Tucker, Nancy Bernkopf. *Taiwan, Hong Kong, and the United States, 1945–1992: Uncertain Friendships*. New York: Twayne, 1994.

Turley, William, and Mark Seldon. *Reinventing Vietnamese Socialism: Doi Moi in Comparative Perspective*. Boulder, Colo.: Westview, 1993.

Turner, Eugene, and James P. Allen. *An Atlas of Population Patterns in Metropolitan Los Angeles and Orange Counties, 1990*. Northridge: Center for Geographical Studies, Department of Geography, California State University at Northridge, 1991.

———. *Changing Faces, Changing Places: Mapping Southern Californians*. Northridge: Center for Geographical Studies, Department of Geography, California State University at Northridge, 2002.

———. *The Ethnic Quilt: Population Diversity in Southern California*. Northridge: Center for Geographical Studies, Department of Geography, California State University at Northridge, 1997.

Valverde, Kieu-Linh Caroline. "Making Transnational Viet Nam: Vietnamese American Community–Viet Nam Linkages through Money, Music, and Modems." Ph.D. diss., University of California at Berkeley, 2002.

———. *Transnationalizing Vietnam: Community, Culture, and Politics in the Diaspora*. Philadelphia: Temple University Press, 2013.

Verkuil, Paul R. *Outsourcing Sovereignty: Why Privatization of Government Threatens Democracy and What We Can Do about It*. Cambridge: Cambridge University Press, 2007.

Viết Về Nước Mỹ [Writing on America]. Westminster, Calif.: Việt Báo, 2000–2007.

Vietnamese Business Directory. Westminster, Calif.: Vietnamese Chamber of Commerce in Orange County, 1985–2005.

The Vietnamese Community in Orange County: An Oral History. Vol.1, *Business Development.* Santa Ana, Calif.: Newhope Library, 1991.

The Vietnamese Community in Orange County: An Oral History. Vol. 2, *Religion and Resettlement of Vietnamese Refugees in Orange County.* Santa Ana, Calif.: Newhope Library, 1991.

The Vietnamese Community in Orange County: An Oral History. Vol. 3, *Refugee Service Programs and Mutual Assistance Associations.* Santa Ana, Calif.: Newhope Public Library, 1992.

The Vietnamese Community in Orange County: An Oral History. Vol. 4, *Preservation of Cultural Heritage and the Vietnamese Media.* Santa Ana, Calif.: Newhope Public Library, 1992.

Vo, Linda Trinh, and Mary Yu Danico. "Formation of Post-Suburban Communities: Koreatown and Little Saigon, Orange County." *International Journal of Sociology and Social Policy* 24, nos. 7–8 (July 2004): 15–45.

Von Eschen, Penny M. *Satchmo Blows Up the World: Jazz Ambassadors Play the Cold War.* Cambridge: Harvard University Press, 2004.

Vu, Roy. "Rising from the Cold War Ashes: Construction of a Vietnamese American Community in Houston, 1975–2005." Ph.D. diss., University of Houston, 2006.

Wain, Barry. *The Refused: The Agony of the Indochinese Refugees.* New York: Simon and Schuster, 1981.

Waldinger, Roger, and Mehdi Bozorgmehr, eds. *Ethnic Los Angeles.* New York: Sage, 1996.

Wallerstein, Immanuel. *The Modern World-System.* Vol. 1. New York: Academic Press, 1974.

Warner, Roger. *Back Fire: The CIA's Secret War in Laos and Its Link to the Vietnam War.* New York: Simon and Schuster, 1995.

Wei, William. *The Asian American Movement.* Philadelphia: Temple University Press, 1993.

Weis, Paul. *Nationality and Statelessness in International Law.* 2nd ed. New York: Sijthoff and Noordhoff, 1979.

Whitfield, Stephen J. *The Culture of the Cold War.* Baltimore: Johns Hopkins University Press, 1996.

Wiebe, Robert. *The Search for Order, 1877–1920.* New York: Hill and Wang, 1967.

Wilentz, Sean. *The Age of Reagan: A History, 1974–2008.* New York: Harper, 2008.

Winant, Howard. *The World Is a Ghetto: Race and Democracy since World War II.* New York: Basic Books, 2001.

Winter, Jay. *Remembering War: The Great War between Memory and History in the Twentieth Century.* New Haven: Yale University Press, 2006.

Wong, Janelle. *Democracy's Promise: Immigrants and American Civic Institutions.* Ann Arbor: University of Michigan Press, 2006.

Wu, Chun-hsi. *Dollars, Dependents, and Dogma: Overseas Chinese Remittances to Communist China*. Stanford: Hoover Institution on War, Revolution, and Peace, 1967.

Yager, Joseph A. *Transforming Agriculture in Taiwan: The Experience of the Joint Commission on Rural Reconstruction*. Ithaca: Cornell University Press, 1988.

Yoo, David K. "'Read All about It': Race, Generation, and the Japanese American Press, 1925–1941." *Amerasia Journal* 19, no. 1 (1993): 69–92.

Yu, Henry. *Thinking Orientals: Migration, Contact, and Exoticism in Modern America*. New York: Oxford University Press, 2001.

Zake, Ieva, ed. *Anti-Communist Minorities in the U.S.: Political Activism of Ethnic Refugees*. New York: Palgrave Macmillan, 2009.

Zhao, Sui-sheng. *A Nation-State by Construction: Dynamics of Modern Chinese Nationalism*. Stanford: Stanford University Press, 2004.

Zhou, Min, and Carl Bankston III. *Growing Up American: How Vietnamese Children Adapt to Life in the United States*. New York: Sage, 1999.

Government Documents and Publications

Barnes, Jessica, and Claudette Bennett. *The Asian Population: 2000*. February 2002. Available at https://www.census.gov/prod/2002pubs/c2kbr01-16.pdf.

California. California Budget Project. *Proposition 13: Its Impact on California and Implications for State and Local Finance*. Sacramento: California Budget Project, 1997.

California. Health and Welfare Agency. Office of Migration and Refugee Affairs. *California State Master Plan for Refugees: Existing Programs and Policy Recommendations*. Vol. 1. Sacramento: the Office, 1982.

California. Legislature. Joint Committee on Refugee Resettlement and Immigration. *Report of Fact-Finding Mission to Refugee Camps in Southeast Asia: October 24 to November 16, 1983*. Sacramento: the Committee, 1984.

Caplan, Nathan, John Whitmore, and Quang L. Bui. *Southeast Asian Refugee Self-Sufficiency Study: Final Report*. Washington, D.C.: Office of Refugee Resettlement, U.S. Department of Health and Human Services, 1985.

Houze, Marguerite Rivera. "Remarks on Vietnamese-American Appreciation and Celebration Day on the Occasion of the 10th Anniversary of the Signing of the U.S.-Vietnamese Agreement for the Release and Resettlement of Vietnamese Political Prisoners," Houston, Texas, July 25, 1999. Available at http://www.state.gov/www/policy_remarks/1999/990725_rivera-houze.html.

JUSPAO Survey: Media Survey of Urban Vietnam—1970. Saigon: Office of Policy Plans and Research, Joint U.S. Public Affairs Office, 1972.

JUSPAO Survey: National Urban Public Opinion. Saigon: Office of Policy Plans and Research, Joint U.S. Public Affairs Office, 1966.

Nguyen Van Hien, Diana D. Bui, and Lê Xuân Khoa. *Ethnic Self-Help Organizations: Final Report*. Washington, D.C.: U.S. Department of Health and Human Services, Division of Policy and Analysis, April 1, 1983.

Bibliography

United States. Congress. House. Committee on Immigration, Refugees, and International Law. *Hearings on the Indochinese Refugee Problem, March 6, June 19, and July 31, 1979.* Washington, D.C.: U.S. Government Printing Office, 1980.

United States. Congress. House. Committee on International Relations. Subcommittee on International Organizations. *Human Rights in Vietnam: Hearings before the Subcommittee on International Organizations of the Committee on International Relations, House of Representatives, Ninety-Fifth Congress, First Session, June 16, 21, and July 26, 1977.* Washington, D.C.: U.S. Government Printing Office, 1977.

United States. Congress. Senate. Committee on Immigration and Refugee Policy. *U.S. Refugee Program in Southeast Asia: 1985.* Washington, D.C.: U.S. Government Printing Office, 1985.

United States. Congress. Senate. Committee on the Judiciary. *Review of U.S. Refugee Resettlement Programs and Policies: Report.* 96th Cong., 1st sess. Washington, D.C.: U.S. Government Printing Office, 1979.

———. *World Refugee Crisis: The International Community's Response: Report.* 96th Cong., 1st sess. Washington, D.C.: U.S. Government Printing Office, 1979.

———. *World Refugee Crisis: The International Community's Response: Report.* 96th Cong., 2nd sess. Washington, D.C.: U.S. Government Printing Office, 1980.

United States. Congress. Senate. Subcommittee on Financial Institutions of the Committee on Banking, Housing, and Urban Affairs. *Senate Hearing 98-935, "Vietnamese Currency Transfer Legislation."* 98th Cong., 2nd sess.. Washington, D.C.: U.S. Government Printing Office, 1984.

United States. Department of Health, Education, and Welfare. Interagency Task Force on Indochinese Refugees. *Report to Congress.* Washington, D.C.: Task Force, 1975.

United States. Department of Health, Education, and Welfare. Office of Refugee Resettlement. *Refugee Resettlement Program: Report to Congress.* Washington, D.C.: U.S. Government Printing Office, 1981.

United States. Department of Health, Education, and Welfare. Refugee Task Force. *Summary of Findings of Visits to Indo-Chinese Refugee Resettlement Areas and a Telephone Survey of a Selected Sample of Indo-Chinese Refugee Heads of Households.* Washington, D.C.: U.S. Government Printing Office, 1976.

———. *Task Force for Indochina Refugees: Report to Congress.* Washington, D.C.: U.S. Government Printing Office, 1977.

United States. Department of State. *Foreign Relations of the United States, 1948.* Vol. 1, pt. 2. Washington, D.C.: U.S. Government Printing Office, 1976.

———. *The Indochinese Refugee Situation: Report to the Secretary of State by the Special Refugee Advisory Panel, 12 August 1981.* Washington, D.C.: U.S. Government Printing Office, 1981.

United States. Government Accountability Office. *Refugee Program: The Orderly Departure Program from Vietnam.* 1990. http://www.gao.gov/assets/220/212436.pdf.

United States. Information Service. *VOA Program Schedule, February–April 1965.* Saigon: USIS Saigon, 1965.

United States. Library of Congress. *CRS Issue Brief for Congress: The Vietnam-U.S. Normalization Process*. Washington, D.C.: Congressional Research Service, 2005.

United States. National Security Council. "NSC 68: United States Objectives and Programs for National Security." April 14, 1950. Available at www.fas.org/irp/offdocs/nsc-hst/nsc-68.htm.

United States. President's Commission on Organized Crime. *Organized Crime of Asian Origin: Record of Hearing III, October 23–25, 1984, New York, NY*. Washington, D.C.: The Commission, 1985.

United States. Social Security Administration. Office of Refugee Affairs. *Indochinese Refugee Assistance Program: Report to Congress*. Washington, D.C.: U.S. Department of Health, Education, and Welfare, U.S. Social Security Administration, Office of Refugee Affairs, 1979.

Selected Vietnamese American Publications

Chân Trời Mới [New Horizon] (Guam),
Đất Lành [Good Land] (Fort Indiantown Gap newsletter)
Đất Mới [New Land] (Camp Eglin newsletter)
Đất Mới [New Land] (Seattle)
Hiệp Nhất [Unity] (Westminster)
Người Việt Daily News [The Vietnamese People] (Westminster)
Tân Dân [The People] (Fort Chaffee newsletter)
Thái Bình [Peace] (Santa Monica)
Thông Báo [Bulletin] (Camp Pendleton newspaper)

Index

Africa, 25
African American community, 72
Agamben, Giorgio, 31
Amerasian Homecoming Act of 1987, 5–6
"American Century" (Luce), 22
American exceptionalism, 7–9, 51
anti-Asian racism, 19
antirefugee protests, 38–40
anti-Semitism, 4
áo dài dress, 128
Armitage, Richard, 32, 90
Armstrong, William, 90
Asia: Cold War foreign policy in, 17–18; decolonization movements in, 25; dominant countries in, 20; economy of Southeast, 122; Free China model in, 23–24; scarcity in, 21; South Vietnam hope of giant in, 27–28
Asia Foundation, 25
Asian Americans, 9–10
Asian Garden Mall, *105*
assassinations, political, 94–95
assimilation: as expectation, 33, 51; politics of, 117; of Vietnamese Americans, 110; Yến on, 114
assimilationists: as model minority, 118–19; as saviors, 112
Associated Press, 66
atonement, 6, 12, 49, 103; refugee policy based on, 3
authenticity, ethnic, 6
autocrats, 24–25

Baez, Joan, 71, 72

Baldwin, Roger, 71
Barrows, David, 22
"Battle Hymn of the Republic," 39, 134
BBC radio, 55–56
Bien, Qui Le, 101
blind patriotism, 95–96
boat people. *See* Indochinese boat people
Boston Globe, 137
Bradley, Ed, 72
Brazinsky, Gregg, 18, 25
Brody, Jeffrey, 131–32
Brothers of Viet-Nam, 113
Brown, Jerry, 74
Buchoz, Kathy, 103–7
businesses, 104–5, *105*, 110–11
Bynon, Ed, 104

California State University at Fullerton, 57, 95
California State University at Long Beach, 109
Camp Eglin, 41; newsletter of, 47
Camp Pendleton, 36, 38, 79; International Rescue Committee at, 45; newsletter of, 46–47
camps, 38, 40–44; family structures in, 41; marriages at, *40*; newsletters of, 44–48; poetry in, 43–44; repatriation demand in, 155n60; sponsorship for departure from, 41–42; U.S. popular opinion of, 38. *See also* reeducation camps; South Pacific camps
capitalism, 19–20, 121–23; South Korea and, 25–26

Carle, Jon, 48–49
Carter, Jimmy, 78; on Indochinese boat people, 71–73; on Nicaragua, 83
Castro, Fidel, 30
Catholic Charities, 35, 62
Catholic Conference, U.S., 45
Catholic Welfare Bureau, 46
Centers for Disease Control, 101
Châu, Tue Phuong, 128
Chen, Roger, 107
Cherne, Leo, 71
Chiang Kai-shek, 18, 22–23
China, 17
China Lobby, 19–23
Chinatowns, 51
Christianity, 19, 22; in South Korea, 20. See also churches
Chung-in, Moon, 26
Chúng Tôi Muốn Sống (film), 27
churches: conversion hope of, 49; in ethnic community, 56–57; refugee support from, 45–46; sponsorship of, 49
city council, 117–18
Clinton, Bill, 123
Cold War, 2–3, 10; in Asia, 17–18; foreign policy agenda in, 21; gratitude in, 20; self-righteous dimension of, 18; U.S. mission of, 34
collective memory, 7–9; poetry in, 44
colleges, public, 57
Columbia University, 6
communism, 3; Indochinese boat people survival of, 54; inescapability of, for Vietnamese Americans, 115; Little Saigon protests on, 120–21; resistance movement to, 77–79, 88
conformity, 92–95
Cooper, Alice, 45
Cooperman, Edward, 57–58, 95
Cuba, 30, 151n62
Cuban Refugee Program, 50–51
Cung, Phạm, 127

Dang-Tran, Tuyet Thi, 94
Đất Mới newspaper, 86
decolonization movements, 25
deportation, 36
diaspora. See Vietnamese diaspora
Dillow, Gordon, 134
Displaced Persons Act of 1948, 6
Đỗ, Yến, 68, 73–74, 95, 102, 108; on assimilation, 114; on Hi-Tek protests, 132
domino theory, 26, 83

Dornan, Robert, 89–90, 116
Du Bois, W. E. B., 20, 27
Duong, Huu Chuong, 107
Dương, Ngọc Huê, 92
Duy, Quang, 110

Eastland, James, 71
Eastwood, Clint, 83
economy: ethnic community link with, 49–50; political, of Vietnamese Americans, 14–15; Southeast Asia boom in, 122. See also remittances
Eilberg, Joshua, 71
Eisenhower, Dwight, 6; domino theory speech of, 26
embargo. See Hanoi, U.S. embargo against
Espiritu, Yen Le, 36, 170n5
ethnic authenticity, 6
ethnic community: churches in, 56–57; economic survival link with, 49–50; foreign radio services for, 63–64; in preexisting spaces, 56; public colleges in, 57
exile: from Cuba, 30; meaning of, 53–55, 75–76; Phạm Duy on, 53–54; social work and, 75–76

Families of Vietnamese Political Prisoners Association, 125
Far Eastern Economic Review, 69–70
"Farewell, Saigon" (Nam Lộc), 62–63
Federal Indochinese Resettlement Task, U.S., 72
Feeney, Maureen, 129, 179n28
Force of Renaissance, 81
Ford, Gerald, 36, 75
Ford Foundation, 25
Foreign Affairs, 29
foreign policy: agenda in Cold War, 21; of Cold War in Asia, 17–18; realism and idealism in, 21–23
foreign radio services, 63–64. See also BBC radio; Voice of America (VOA)
Fort Chaffee, 47–48
Fort Walton Beach, Fla., 53
Frank, Marcus, 92–93
Free China model, 23–24
Fry, Frank, Jr., 122, 134; HO people and, 129–30; racial politics and, 112–14; on South Vietnam, 113; white conservatives mobilization by, 114

gang activity, 94, 169n99
Garden Grove High School, 87

Garver, John, 24
"Gift for the Motherland, A" (Một Chút Quà Cho Quê Hương) (Việt), 70
Ginsberg, Allen, 71
Government of Free Vietnam, 124
Gramscian school of cultural studies, 158n6
guilt, 1; over Holocaust, 8; in Little Saigon, 137; significance of, 9; sponsorship from, 48–49; of U.S. over South Vietnam, 29
gun control legislation, 154n34

Halbwachs, Maurice, 8
Hanoi, U.S. embargo against, 114, 117; trafficked merchandise during, 115–16
"Hat Cho Người Ở Lại" (Song for Those Who Stayed) (Phạm), 80–81
Heartbreak Ridge (film), 83
Herzstein, Robert E., 22
Hi-Tek protests, 131–35, 180n58
Hồ, Chí Minh, 120, 130
Hồ, Xuân Mai, 61, 62
Hòa Bình Market, 108
Hoàng, Cơ Minh, 86–87, *88*
Hollywood, 61–66
Hollywood Nights (video concert series), 61
Holocaust, 3, 8
Holtzman, Elizabeth, 71
HO people. *See* Humanitarian Operation program
House Immigration Subcommittee, U.S., 71
House of Representatives, U.S., 67
Hu, Shih, 19
Humanitarian Operation program (HO people), 6, 125; Fry and, 129–30; in Little Saigon, 128; in Orange County, 126–27; press and media on, 127
human rights, 67, 71
Hungarian refugees, 4, 6–7, 46

idealism, 21–23
Indochina Migration and Refugee Assistance Act of 1975, 5
Indochinese boat people, 124, 158n2; African American community on, 72; Carter administration on, 71–73, and communism, 54; crisis of, 66–71; in Little Saigon, 73–74; noncommunist world's recognition of, 76; press and media on, 55; refugee status for, 69–70; refugee wave of, 54; rescue of, 55; U.S. advocates for, 71–72; U.S. on, 67–68, 71–73; Vietnamese Americans for, 68; VOA on, 70–71
Interagency Task Force, 37–38, 45

International Rescue Committee, 45, 71
interracial marriages, 19

Jacobson, Matthew Frye, 10
Jang, Lindsey, 131
Jao, Frank, 107
Japanese War Bride (film), 19
Jeffords, Susan, 78–79
John Birch Society, 38
Johnson, Chalmers, 21
Johnson, Lyndon B., 18
Jordan, Vernon, 38–39
Judd, Walter, 21–22

Kaplan, Robert, 17
Karnow, Stanley, 9, 13
Kelly, Gail Paradise, 13
Kennan, George, 21
Kennedy, Joe, *40*
Kennedy, Rory, 1
Kennedy, Ted, 71
Kerry, John, 177n13
Khúc, Minh Thơ, 125
Kibria, Nazli, 41, 88, 167n59
Kiều Chinh, 87
Kiều Nguyên Tá, 93
Kim, Lester, 45
Knowland, William, 21–22
Korean War, 18, 25–26, 82, 149n9

Lâm, Tony, 97, 110, 117–18, 129; on Hi-Tek protests, 131; on spending, 143–44
Last Days of Saigon (documentary), 1
Le, Phuong, 128
Lê, Quang Anh, 134–35
Le, Triết, 94
Lê, Văn, 70
Liberation Daily, 80
Life magazine, 23, 26–27
Lin, Maya, 84
Little Saigon (Parker), 98
Little Saigon, Orange County, Calif.: Asian Garden Mall in, *105*; centrality of local politics in, 135–38; communism protests in, 120–21; end of refugee community in, 124–29; establishment of, 10–11; evolution of, 144–45; fear and violence promotion in, 94; guilt in, 137; Hi-Tek protests in, 131–35; HO people in, 128; Indochinese boat people in, 73–74; memorial in, 133–35; name of, 111; nostalgia of, 99; political assassinations in, 94–95; press and media in, 93;

Little Saigon, Orange County, Calif. (*continued*): refugee nationalism in, 1–2, 11–13; resistance movement in, 85; statehood claim of, 2; support in, 74–75; as tourist attraction, 129; violence in, 98; white backlash of 1989 and, 109–12
Lloyd, David, 121
Los Angeles Shrine Auditorium, 87
Los Angeles Times, 66–67, 80, 100, 113, 132
Luce, Henry Robinson, 22
luxuries, 35–36

MacArthur, Douglas, 21–22
Magnum, P.I. (TV show), 98
Mai, Quốc Linh, 126
Manning, Clarence, 6
Marcell, Jo, 110
marriages: at camps, 40; interracial, 19
masculinity: in resistance movement, 90–91; of Vietnamese Americans, 79; in Vietnam War, 59
Matthews, Ben, 48
Matthews, Ellen, 48, 50, 58
McCain, John, 144–45
McCarran, Pat, 4
media. *See* press and media
Medi-Cal crisis, 101–2, 108, 171n16
Metzger, Tom, 109
militarism, 22
"militarized refuge," 36–37
Mineta, Norm, 39
model minority, 11, 97; assimilationists as, 118–19; restoration of, 34; Vietnamese Americans' image as, 98–99, 102, 107
modernization theory, 19–20
Mondale, Walter, 73
money. *See* remittances
"Một Chút Quà Cho Quê Hương" (A Gift for the Motherland) (Việt), 70
Mutual Defense Treaty, 150n25

National Conservative Political Action Committee, U.S., 83
National Day of Founding, 91
nationalism, of *Trắng Đen*, 77–78. *See also* refugee nationalism
National United Front for the Liberation of Vietnam, 86–88; beauty pageants from, 92; Dornan with, 89–90; fall of, 95–96; newsletter of, 91; phở restaurant investment of, 93
National Urban League, 38–39

neoconservatism, 82
Neuharth, Al, 123
New Deal, 177n8
New Life (band), 61
newsletters: of Camp Eglin, 47; of Camp Pendleton, 46–47; of camps, 44–48; early articles in, 45; of National United Front for the Liberation of Vietnam, 91
Newsweek, 67
New World Order, 123
New York Times, 8, 23
Ngô, Đình Diệm, 26–27, 91
Ngọc, Minh, 69
Người Việt Daily News, 68, 74, 87, 128–29
Nguyễn, Cao Kỳ: economic status of, 41, 94; and government in exile, 80, 86, 124; on leaving South Vietnam, 35; Phạm and, 141–42; on U.S. approach to Vietnam 26, 28
Nguyễn, Công Hoan, 67
Nguyen, Dam Phong, 94
Nguyễn, Derek, 136
Nguyễn, Đông Sơn, 96
Nguyễn, Jimmy Tong, 117–18
Nguyễn, Nam Lộc, 61–63, 109, 133
Nguyễn, Ngọc Ngạn, 59
Nguyen, The Hung, 40
Nguyen, Thi Kieu, 40
Nguyen, Thi Tuyet, 40
Nguyễn, Thomas, 49
Nguyễn, Tuấn, 130
Nguyen, Tuyet Ngan, 43–44
Nguyễn, Văn Linh, 122
Nguyễn, Xuân Bảo, 127
Nhan, Vu, 130
Nicaragua, 83
Nineteen Eighty-Four (Orwell), 6
Nixon, Richard, 29, 75
Northern Virginia Community College, 57
North Vietnamese, in South Vietnam, 30. *See also* Vietnam War
nostalgia, 2, 99

Operation Frequent Wind, 29
Operation New Life, 33
Orange County, Calif.: as Government of Free Vietnam headquarters, 124; HO people in, 126–27; tuberculosis rates in, 101; Vietnamese American Chamber of Commerce in, 97, 104, 128. *See also* Little Saigon, Orange County, Calif.
Orange County Human Relations Commission, 113

Orange County League of Cities, 101
Orange County Register, 113, 115
Orderly Departure Program, 5, 126
Orientalism, 21
Orwell, George, 6

Panetta, Leon, 39
paternalism: of Republicans, 100–108; sponsorship as, 48–49
patriotism, blind, 95–96
Patterson, Jerry, 101
perfection, as price of rescue, 34–35
Phạm, Duy, 31, 33, 41, 181n1; continued career of, 75; on exile meaning, 53–54; musical accomplishments of, 139–40; Nguyễn Cao Kỳ and, 141; on postcamp life, 48; refugee community renunciation of, 141–42; resistance movement song by, 80–81; in Vietnam, 141
Phạm, Nga, 128
Phạm, Văn Liễu, 93, 96
phở restaurants, 93
Phuong, Van Hai, *40*
"Plight of the Refugees" (Nguyen Tuyet Ngan), 43–44
poetry: in camps, 43–44; for collective memory, 44
political assassinations, 94–95
political economy, 14–15
political prisoners, 125. *See also* reeducation camps
politics: of assimilation, 117; centrality of local, 135–38; of race, 112–14; of rescue, 34, 78–79, 148n27
popular opinion: "Americans first" theme as, 38; on resistance movement, 92–93; on Vietnamese refugees, 38
pragmatism, 17
press and media, 8, 161n56; on antirefugee protests, 39–40; on Hi-Tek protests, 132; on HO people, 127; on Indochinese boat people, 55; in Little Saigon, 93; on Ngô, 26–27; on resistance movement, 80; on Vietnamese high government officials, 35; for Vietnamese refugees, 63–66
Prisoner, The (play), 90
prisoners, political, 125. *See also* reeducation camps
propaganda, 6, 137; from foreign radio services, 63; at Fort Chaffee, 47–48; of resistance movement, 90–91; of Vietnamese refugees, 100

protests, 177n2; antirefugee, 38–40; of communism, 120–21; over Hi-Tek, 131–35, 180n58
Pryor, David, 39
Pryor, Richard, 39
public colleges, 57

Quê Hương newspaper, 93
Quirino, Elpidio, 18

racial politics, 112–14
racism, 98, 101; anti-Asian, 19
radio services, foreign, 63–64. *See also* BBC radio; Voice of America (VOA)
Reagan, Ronald, 78, 81; influence of, 82–84; neoconservatism of, 82; secret army of, 83; on Vietnam Syndrome, 82–83
Reagan Doctrine, 83; responses to, 84–85
realism, 21–23
reeducation camps, 59, 69; as amnesty, 80; and beliefs about remittances, 115; and HO program, 126; memoirs about, 73; scholarship on, 159n27; wives and widows of inmates of, 60, 125, 128, 143
Refugee Act of 1980, 5, 36–37, 74
refugee admissions, U.S.: historical resistance to, 4; increase in, 124; majority opposition to, 4–5. *See also* antirefugee protests
Refugee Americans, 6; becoming, 13–14, 77; identity accomplishments of, 138; identity learning of, 34, 51–52; as minorities in multiple locations, 10; requirement of, 44–45; resettlement of, 35
refugee nationalism, 135–36, 171n24; American exceptionalism and, 7–9; collective memory and, 7–9; development of, 11–13; diplomatic tensions for, 75; history of, 3–7; of Hungarians, 6–7; in Little Saigon, 1–2, 11–13; U.S. identity in, 2
remittances, 60, 100, 114–16, 119; centers for, 94; and Vietnamese economy, 76
Republicans: paternalism of, 100–108; Vietnamese Americans with, 11, 102–4
rescue: of Indochinese boat people, 55; and militarized refuge, 36–37; perfection as price for, 34–35; politics of, 34, 78–79, 148n27; racial and class biases with, 35
resettlement: obstacles to success of, 37–40; of Refugee Americans, 35; by social class, 36
resistance movement: to communism, 77–79, 88; economic concerns of, 88–89;

resistance movement (*continued*): extremists in, 79; in Little Saigon, 85; Los Angeles Shrine Auditorium event for, 87–88; masculinity in, 90–91; murders associated with, 93–94; Phạm Duy song for, 80–81; pop culture of, 90–92; popular opinion on, 92–93; press and media on, 80; propaganda of, 90–91; as taking flight, 84–89; U.S. sympathizers with, 89–90; Vietnamese refugees on, 81. *See also* National United Front for the Liberation of Vietnam
Rhee, Syngman, 18
Riles, Wilson, 39
Roosevelt, Franklin, 8, 177n8
Roosevelt Hotel, 61
Rose, Peter, 10, 42
Roybal, Edward, 39
Royce, Ed, 103, 111

Saigon, Vietnam, evacuation of, 29–32. *See also* Little Saigon, Orange County, Calif.
Saigon Market, 108
Saigon USA (documentary), 131
Sánchez, Loretta, 128–29, 136
Santa Ana College, 57
savior: assimilationists as, 112; Cold War narrative of Western, 34; U.S. identity as, 1, 3. *See also* rescue
Sayonara (film), 19
scarcity, 21
Shevchenko, Taras, 6
60 Minutes, 102
Smith, Chuck, 103
Snyder, Art, 68
social class: in Refugee Act of 1980, 36–37; resettlement by, 36
social work: exile meaning and, 75–76; of *Trắng Đen*, 67
"Song for Those Who Stayed" (Hat Cho Người Ở Lại) (Phạm), 80–81
Southeast Asia economy, 122
Southern California community, 160n38. *See also* Orange County, Calif.
South Korea: Christianity in, 20; geopolitical position of, 25; relationship with U.S., 20
South Korean Ministry of Patriots and Veterans Affairs, 20
South Pacific camps, 37
South Vietnam: Fry on, 113; North Vietnamese soldiers in, 30; as potential giant, 27–28; rise and fall of, 26–32; U.S. guilt with, 29. *See also* Vietnam War
Soviet Union, 4, 123
sponsorship: bubble of, 48–52; for camp departure, 41–42; as Christianized, 38; of churches, 49; from guilt, 48–49; from Interagency Task Force, 45; as paternalism, 48–49; success stories of, 44–48
Stalin, Josef, 24
"Star Spangled Banner," 39
stereotypes: anti-Asian racism and, 19; of dirty Asians, 101; of Western savior, 34. *See also* model minority
Sumner, Bruce, 117
Sun, Yat-sen, 22

Takaki, Ronald, 2, 9
Talcott, Burt, 39
Talented Tenth, 27
Taylor, George E., 25
Tết holiday, 97–98
Tết Offensive, 109, 112
Thái Bình tabloid, 91
Three Soldiers, The (statue), 84
Time magazine, 22
totalitarianism, 18
tourism, 129
Tran, Ly Le, 42
Trần, Minh Công, 92–93, 96, 170n6
Trần, Quốc Sỹ, 41
Trần, Thị Nam, 36
Trần, Văn Trường, 131
Trang, Sĩ Tấn, 35
Trắng Đen newspaper, 64–66, 65, 74; on Force of Renaissance, 81; nationalism of, 77–78; social work of, 67
Triêu, Anh Tuấn, 47
Trịnh, Công Sơn, 58
Trinh, Phil, 110
Truman, Harry S., 18
Trump, Donald, 147n8
tuberculosis, 101

Uchida, M. B., 48
United Nations, 3
United States, 38; atonement of, 3; Cold War mission of, 34; embargo against Hanoi, 114–17; global savior identity of, 1, 3; guilt over South Vietnam, 29; on Indochinese boat people, 67–68, 71–73; in New World Order, 123; refugee admissions to, 4–5, 124; resistance movement

sympathizers of, 89–90; South Korea relationship with, 20; supremacy myth of, 7; Vietnamese population in, 5–6. *See also* American exceptionalism; refugee admissions, U.S.; Vietnam War
University of California system, 74
University of Massachusetts at Boston, 137
University of Southern California, 92
USA Today, 123
U.S. House of Representatives, 67; Immigration Subcommittee, 71

Van, Tran, 111
Van de Kamp, John, 101–2
Veterans of Foreign Wars, 82
Viết Báo Daily News, 142
Việt-Cộng, 14, 78, 150n51
Việt Dzũng, 55, 58, 70, 71
Vietnam: human rights in, 67; Phạm Duy in, 141; political prisoners of, 125; resistance movement in, 79–81; and Southeast Asia's economy, 122; trafficked merchandise to, 115; Vietnam War of, 79–81; VOA in, 129
Vietnamese American Chamber of Commerce, 97, 104, 128
Vietnamese American Mutual Association, 101, 172n44
Vietnamese American Republican National Federation, 85
Vietnamese Americans, 5–6; assimilation of, 110; Buchoz with, 103–7; businesses of, 104–5, *105*, 110–11; for city council, 117–18; communism inescapability of, 115; conformity of, 92–95; criminal treatment of, lack of, 116; Cuban exiles and, 30; early civil society for, 56–57; early crises of, 100–108; for Indochinese boat people, 68; masculinity of, 79; in medicine, 164n110; model minority image of, 98–99, 102, 107; negative associations of, 109; political economy of, 14–15; political priorities of, 129–30; racism toward, 101; as refugee majority, 120; with Republican Party, 11, 102–4; songs by, 68–69; support for, 74–75; on welfare, 108. *See also* Little Saigon, Orange County, Calif.
Vietnamese diaspora, 10–11; impact of, 33; radio stories on, 64
Vietnamese Former Detainees Mutual Association, 130

Vietnamese language, 14–15; English and, 41, 155n72
Vietnamese music, 159n24; genres of, 58–59; of refugees, 57–60. *See also* Phạm, Duy
Vietnamese refugees: assimilation expectation of, 33, 51; Chinatown access of, 51; Christianized sponsorship for, 38; correspondence of, 60–61; English-speaking abilities of, 41, 155n72; in Hollywood, 61–66; music of, 57–60; Operation New Life for, 33; popular opinion of, 38; press and media for, 63–66; propaganda of, 100; proponents for, 39; racial and class biases for, 35; on resistance movement, 81; welcoming of, 39–40. *See also specific topics*
Vietnam in the Year of the Cat (documentary), 57
Vietnamization, 29
Vietnam Syndrome, 77; Reagan on, 82–83
Vietnam Veterans Memorial, 84
Vietnam War, 1, 10; literature on, 147n1, 148n17; masculinity in, 59; Nixon on, 29; outcomes of, 7–8; reasoning for, 17; second winning of, 122–23; victors of, 99–100; of Vietnam, 79–81
Vietnam War Memorial, 133
Việt-Tân (Reform Party), 87
Võ, Đại Tôn, 78, 85, 86
Voice of America (VOA), 29, 55–56, 63; on Indochinese boat people, 70–71; in Vietnam, 129
Vũ, Tuấn Tú, 56
Vũ, Việt Dương, 47

Washington Post, 97–98
Watanabe, Teresa, 123
welfare, 101–2, 108
Westminster, *13*; Vietnamese-American Memorial in, *133*; Vietnamese businesses in, 110
Westminster Chamber of Commerce, 106
Westminster Journal, 104
Westmoreland, William, 48, 83
Wiesel, Elie, 73
William Joiner Center, 137
Wilson, Pete, 45
Winn, Robert, 131
World War II, 1, 112; Hollywood films on, 19

Yung, Wing, 19

PHUONG TRAN NGUYEN was born in Vietnam and migrated to the United States a few years after the Vietnam War. He is an assistant professor of history at California State University, Monterey Bay.

The Asian American Experience

The Hood River Issei: An Oral History of Japanese Settlers in Oregon's
 Hood River Valley   *Linda Tamura*
Americanization, Acculturation, and Ethnic Identity: The Nisei Generation
 in Hawaii   *Eileen H. Tamura*
Sui Sin Far/Edith Maude Eaton: A Literary Biography   *Annette White-Parks*
Mrs. Spring Fragrance and Other Writings   *Sui Sin Far; edited by Amy Ling
 and Annette White-Parks*
The Golden Mountain: The Autobiography of a Korean Immigrant,
 1895–1960   *Easurk Emsen Charr; edited and with an introduction
 by Wayne Patterson*
Race and Politics: Asian Americans, Latinos, and Whites in a
 Los Angeles Suburb   *Leland T. Saito*
Achieving the Impossible Dream: How Japanese Americans
 Obtained Redress   *Mitchell T. Maki, Harry H. L. Kitano,
 and S. Megan Berthold*
If They Don't Bring Their Women Here: Chinese Female Immigration
 before Exclusion   *George Anthony Peffer*
Growing Up Nisei: Race, Generation, and Culture among Japanese Americans
 of California, 1924–49   *David K. Yoo*
Chinese American Literature since the 1850s   *Xiao-huang Yin*
Pacific Pioneers: Japanese Journeys to America and Hawaii, 1850–80
 John E. Van Sant
Holding Up More Than Half the Sky: Chinese Women Garment Workers
 in New York City, 1948–92   *Xiaolan Bao*
Onoto Watanna: The Story of Winnifred Eaton   *Diana Birchall*
Edith and Winnifred Eaton: Chinatown Missions and Japanese
 Romances   *Dominika Ferens*
Being Chinese, Becoming Chinese American   *Shehong Chen*
"A Half Caste" and Other Writings   *Onoto Watanna;
 edited by Linda Trinh Moser and Elizabeth Rooney*
Chinese Immigrants, African Americans, and Racial Anxiety
 in the United States, 1848–82   *Najia Aarim-Heriot*
Not Just Victims: Conversations with Cambodian Community Leaders
 in the United States   *Edited and with an introduction by Sucheng Chan;
 interviews conducted by Audrey U. Kim*
The Japanese in Latin America   *Daniel M. Masterson
 with Sayaka Funada-Classen*
Survivors: Cambodian Refugees in the United States   *Sucheng Chan*
From Concentration Camp to Campus: Japanese American Students
 and World War II   *Allan W. Austin*

Japanese American Midwives: Culture, Community, and Health Politics
   Susan L. Smith
In Defense of Asian American Studies: The Politics of Teaching and
   Program Building   *Sucheng Chan*
Lost and Found: Reclaiming the Japanese American Incarceration
   Karen L. Ishizuka
Religion and Spirituality in Korean America   *Edited by David K. Yoo
   and Ruth H. Chung*
Moving Images: Photography and the Japanese American Incarceration
   Jasmine Alinder
Camp Harmony: Seattle's Japanese Americans and the Puyallup
   Assembly Center   *Louis Fiset*
Chinese American Transnational Politics   *Him Mark Lai;
   edited and with an introduction by Madeline Y. Hsu*
Issei Buddhism in the Americas   *Edited by Duncan Ryûken Williams
   and Tomoe Moriya*
Hmong America: Reconstructing Community in Diaspora   *Chia Youyee Vang*
In Pursuit of Gold: Chinese American Miners and Merchants
   in the American West   *Sue Fawn Chung*
Pacific Citizens: Larry and Guyo Tajiri and Japanese American Journalism
   in the World War II Era   *Edited by Greg Robinson*
Indian Accents: Brown Voice and Racial Performance in American Television
   and Film   *Shilpa S. Davé*
Yellow Power, Yellow Soul: The Radical Art of Fred Ho
   Edited by Roger N. Buckley and Tamara Roberts
Fighting from a Distance: How Filipino Exiles Helped Topple a Dictator
   Jose V. Fuentecilla
In Defense of Justice: Joseph Kurihara and the Japanese American Struggle
   for Equality   *Eileen H. Tamura*
Asian Americans in Dixie: Race and Migration in the South
   Edited by Jigna Desai and Khyati Y. Joshi
Undercover Asian: Multiracial Asian Americans in Visual Culture
   Leilani Nishime
Islanders in the Empire: Filipino and Puerto Rican Laborers
   in Hawai'i   *JoAnna Poblete*
Virtual Homelands: Indian Immigrants and Online Cultures in the
   United States   *Madhavi Mallapragada*
Building Filipino Hawai'i   *Roderick N. Labrador*
Legitimizing Empire: Filipino American and U.S. Puerto Rican
   Cultural Critique   *Faye Caronan*
Chinese in the Woods: Logging and Lumbering in the American West
   Sue Fawn Chung

The Minor Intimacies of Race: Asian Publics in North America   *Christine Kim*
Reading Together, Reading Apart: Identity, Belonging, and South Asian
    American Community   *Tamara Bhalla*
Chino: Anti-Chinese Racism in Mexico, 1880–1940   *Jason Oliver Chang*
Asianfail: Narratives of Disenchantment and the Model Minority   *Eleanor Ty*
Becoming Refugee American: The Politics of Rescue in Little Saigon
    Phuong Tran Nguyen